Ideal homes

MANCHESTER
1824

Manchester University Press

Ideal homes

Uncovering the history and design
of the interwar house

Deborah Sugg Ryan

Manchester University Press

The right of Deborah Sugg Ryan to be identified as the author of this work has been asserted by her in accordance with the Copyright, Designs and Patents Act 1988.

Published by Manchester University Press
Altrincham Street, Manchester M1 7JA
www.manchesteruniversitypress.co.uk

British Library Cataloguing-in-Publication Data
A catalogue record for this book is available from the British Library

ISBN   978 1 5261 5067 7   paperback

First published 2020

This paperback edition first published 2020

The publisher has no responsibility for the persistence or accuracy of URLs for any external or third-party internet websites referred to in this book, and does not guarantee that any content on such websites is, or will remain, accurate or appropriate.

Typeset in 10/14 Minion by
Servis Filmsetting Ltd, Stockport, Cheshire
Printed in Great Britain by Bell & Bain Ltd, Glasgow

For James, Mark and Gwendaline Ryan,
with whom I have made my ideal home

Contents

Plates

Figures

Every effort has been made to obtain permission to reproduce copyright material, and the publisher will be pleased to be informed of any errors and omissions for correction in future editions.

Acknowledgements

I conceived this book in 2003 when my children were infants, but it has taken much longer to reach maturity than them. I have worked on it through sleepless nights in the highs and lows of parenthood, intense periods of house renovation and DIY, and the pressures of academic jobs at the universities of Ulster, Loughborough, Falmouth and Portsmouth. Progress was interrupted further by cancer and its treatment and complications, from which I feel extremely lucky to have survived. I would like to thank particularly my consultant Professor Phil Drew, my oncologist Mr Duncan Wheatley and all the nurses at the Mermaid Centre in Truro and St Michael's Hospital in Hayle for helping me get to the position where I had the strength to finish the book.

My research was funded by a British Academy for Humanities and Social Sciences' Mid-Career Research Fellowship in 2012–13, which gave me the luxury of revisiting my sources, time to think and write, and support for research trips and illustrations. A Design History Society 25th Anniversary Award and a grant from the Faculty of Creative and Cultural Industries at the University of Portsmouth also funded the book's illustrations.

Librarians and archivists at the following institutions have been immensely helpful: Brighton University's Design Archives, the British Library in St Pancras and Colindale Newspaper Library, the Daily

Mail Picture Library, Earls Court and Olympia Ltd's archives, Geffrye Museum, Mass Observation Archives, Middlesex University's Museum of Domestic Design and Architecture, Royal Institute of British Architects' Library, the V&A's National Art Library, Archive of Art & Design and RIBA Reading Room. I am grateful to Simon Willey for giving me access to his family's Easiwork Ltd collection.

I give my heartfelt thanks to Christopher Breward, the series editor, for his faith in me. I have benefited from his encouragement and discussion over the years and from his friendship. I am also grateful to Manchester University Press for letting the contract roll over for more time than I thought possible. I would particularly like to thank Sally Alexander, Zoe Hendon, Alison Rowley and Damon Taylor for many discussions about the wider class and gender politics of this project.

I have had lots of conversations about my research, both formally when I presented it at conferences, symposia and research seminars, as well as in lectures to my students, and informally with my academic colleagues and PhD students at the universities where I have worked and further afield. I have benefited hugely from the insights and support of the following: Pennie Alfrey, Paul Atkinson, the late Judy Attfield, Caterina Benincasa-Sharman, Tracy Bhamra, Lis Bogdan, Sian Bonnell, Fan Carter, Claire Catterall, Alison Clarke, Elizabeth Darling, Stuart Evans, Kjetil Fallan, Joan Farrer, Paul Greenhalgh, Fiona Hackney, Catherine Harper, Ben Highmore, Julian Holder, Greta Jones, Trevor Keeble, Alison Light, Lesley Hoskins, Moya Lloyd, Helen Marton, Anne Massey, Ruth Morrow, Sean O'Connell, Saskia Partington, Rebecca Preston, Caroline Pullee, Tim Putnam, Julia Reeve, Timo de Rijk, Julie Ripley, Mike Saler, the late Raphael Samuel, Bill Schwarz, Peter Scott, Lorna Sheppard, Penny Sparke, Phil Stenton, Kate Strasdin, Meg Sweet, Andrew Thacker, Amanda Vickery, Elizabeth Wilson and Jonathan Woodham.

Chapter 5 extends a journal article, 'Living in a "half-baked pageant": the Tudorbethan semi and suburban modernity in Britain, 1918–39', that was published in *Home Cultures*, 8.3 (2011), 217–44. I am grateful to the editors of the journal for allowing me to reuse parts of it here.

Many of those I have already mentioned are also close friends and have provided much-needed personal support and light relief. I would like to thank the following friends and family as well in this respect: Jemma Bagley, John Brodribb, James Brook, Vicki Clark, Bill Cramer, Cherry Cramer, Viv Minton, Wendy Roberts and Caroline Scobie. The book owes a particular debt to my maternal grandparents, Rob and Nora Roberts, who provoked my interest in home ownership, class and taste through their life histories which took them from working-class backgrounds in North Wales and south-east London respectively to the purchase of their corporation house in Stevenage New Town, which they kitted out with the most modern Ercol furniture.

My children, Mark and Gwendaline, have grown up as they have endured my absorption in the research and writing of this book. As a family, we have moved house four times in this period and on each occasion I have been immersed in complex renovations along with my husband, James R. Ryan. He has patiently put up with my desire to curate my domestic space, my collecting and acquisitions from auctions, junk shops, car boot fairs and eBay and my general mess. James has also read and discussed every single word I have written with enormous patience and insight.

Finally, I spent a great deal of time 'at home' over the gestation of this book: on maternity leave, enduring and convalescing from illness, preparing lectures, marking assignments and writing. At the same time, I have been immersed in homemaking, as an expression of love for my family and also simply as a source of deep and real pleasure and creativity. I'm not somebody who enjoys tidying and cleaning but I love to decorate – to choose paint colours and wallpaper, to get furniture, furnishings, pictures and ornaments 'just so', to arrange flowers – as well as to sew, bake, cook and entertain. I hope this gives me some real empathy with the interwar homeowners and homemakers who are the subject of this book.

Introduction:
Doing interwar house histories

The first edition of this book was published just as the first series of BBC Two's *A House Through Time* was broadcast in the UK.[1] Each series tells the story of a single house and its occupants from when it was built to the present. I appear in all three series as a historical consultant, and my particular role focuses on the design, layout and decoration of the house and how it changes through time. I tell these stories through the experiences of the house's residents, and in this book you will find some of the research I have drawn on for the programme. For example, in series one, I talked about the 1930s kitchen cabinet (see chapter 4, on Efficiency).

In this book, you will meet four families who were the first occupants of newly built, modest interwar houses. I chose these as typical examples of interwar homeowners, with particular attention paid to their social mobility and aspirations, and also women's experiences. In chapter one, I introduce working-class, first-time homeowners Vernon and Cecilia Collett and their sons Basil and Roy. In 1934, the Colletts purchased a small semi-detached house with a parlour, kitchen-living room, two bedrooms, a box room and a downstairs bathroom in Wolvercote, near Oxford. In chapter two, I tell the story of Ronald Kingham, a linoleum layer, and his wife Miriam, who purchased their house with three bedrooms, two receptions, a small kitchenette and an upstairs bedroom in Edmonton, Middlesex in 1932. In chapter three, I discuss the intense desire of engineer Marks Freedman and his wife Tillie to make a modern home in Tottenham in 1943. Purchased for £1020, it was the largest house of my examples and as the first house in the road had a generous corner plot. In chapter four, I tell the story of Mass Observation's Respondent 082, a housewife living in Marlow, Buckinghamshire with her husband and daughter, who gave an account in 1937-8 of living in a house with five rooms and a bathroom and a kitchen-living room arrangement. I constructed all four of these fascinating case studies by using a variety of sources. For each of them, I found that creating a family tree proved invaluable, and I did that by using the tools and resources available from a digital genealogy provider.

Title deeds

If you are researching a particular house then one of the best sources available to you is the title deeds. If you do not have them yourself then they may be with your solicitor or mortgage company. If you are lucky, you will hold deeds recording all the owners of your house since it was built, including details of purchase price and mortgages. Occupations and incomes may also be included.

Local archives

The best place to start researching the history of a house, its occupants and the surrounding area is in a local archive. This might be a local studies centre or a local county archive, where you may find local maps, title deeds, electoral registers and family and estate papers, all of which can be useful when tracing the history of a house. You will need to know the relevant county and registration district of your house (bearing in mind any boundary changes over time). You may be able to find building plans, which would have been submitted to the local urban or rural district council for buildings regulation approval before construction.

Local record offices may hold copies and they may be available online via council's planning departments. For example, a search of Oxford City Council's planning website told me that permission was granted in 1949 for a scullery extension to the Colletts' house at 17 Rosamund Road, and also that in 2001 another application was approved for that same extension to be demolished and replaced.

The National Archives' catalogue contains collections and contact details of local archives around the UK and beyond (http://www.nationalarchives.gov.uk). Many local archives publish their own guides to doing house history and may even organise training events. There are some useful guides by national organisations:

- Historic England
  https://historicengland.org.uk/advice/your-home/
  your-homes-history/how-to-find-out/history-of-house/
- National Archives
  https://www.nationalarchives.gov.uk/help-with-your-research/
  research-guides/houses/

Census Records

Census records are very useful for finding out about the residents of houses in the past.[2] At the time of writing, the most recent census available is 1911. I found it an invaluable resource for this book in tracing the family histories of my four case studies. It allowed me to pin down class backgrounds by looking at their parents' occupations, and this in turn helped me to tell the story of mobility and aspirations. For example, Ronald Kingham's occupation of linoleum layer was a step up from his father who was a bricklayer. It also allowed me to tease out the nuances of class differences between married couples, and to understand more about their cultural heritage. In the case of Marks and Tillie Freedman, I found that their parents had been born in Russia and Poland, respectively.

The digitised 1921 census is expected to be released in January 2022. It was taken on 19th June 1921 at a time when the population of England and Wales was over 37 million, and gives greater detail than any previous census, so this will be very exciting for anyone interested in the history of how British people lived their lives. In addition to the questions asked in the 1911 census, the 1921 census included more information about occupations: the materials people worked in, their places of work, and their employers' names. For those over the age of 15, they collected information about marital status, including whether the person was divorced. For those under 15, the census recorded whether either or both parents were alive or had died. It also had detailed questions on education including whether individuals were in full-time or part-time education. The census taken in 1931 was destroyed during the Second World War and no census was carried out in 1941 due to the on-going conflict.

The 1939 Register

Since I published the first edition of the book, the 1939 Register held in the UK's National Archives has become available in digital form.[3] It contains data only for England and Wales and does not include records from households in Scotland, Northern Ireland, the Channel Islands or the Isle of Man, but it is a fascinating and rich resource, nevertheless. It catalogues 41 million lives recorded at the outbreak of the Second World War on 29th September 1939. You can see who lived in any house, town or street in England and Wales before the draft. It is possible to search by address, and you can find details of individuals in the register: name; gender; address; date of birth; marital status; occupation; whether they were a visitor, officer, servant, patient or inmate; details of family members, and other members of the same household. Care needs to be taken with the 1939 Register as it does not always clearly record who was resident at the address and who was visiting.

Sometimes you may see extra information on the right-hand side of the image, such as details of voluntary war work. You may see names crossed out with another name written in an annotation above or at the side, such as women's married names and other name changes. This is because the register was used to track the civilian population over the following decades and from 1948 as the basis of the National Health Service Register. Names have been redacted to protect the privacy of those still alive. Records are added annually for those with birth dates of over 100 years ago, and those whose record of death has been reported to the National Archives.

In researching my case studies, I found that Marks Freedman (described as a heating and ventilating technical engineer) was visiting his parents in Bethnal Green and Tillie was visiting 64-year-old widow Mary Cree (described as 'living on her own means') in Letchworth, Hertfordshire. In the case of the Colletts, Vernon was working as a printer's warehouseman and Roy as a printer's warehouse boy. Basil does not appear at the same address and I have been unable to find him elsewhere. Ronald Kingham was working part-time as a member of the Auxiliary Fire Service. Miriam was staying with her mother in Hemel Hempstead.

The 1939 Register sheds the most light on Mass Observation's Respondent 082 and her family.[4] All I had to work on previously was her married name (which I have been unable to disclose in this book due to the restrictions placed on the use of Mass Observation) and an address. The 1939 Register reveals that her husband was no longer employed as a bus driver but was doing war work erecting metal aircraft frames. Working backwards from this information has allowed me to dig into the family backgrounds of the couple. In her Mass Observation day reports, Respondent 082 complained about the snobbery of her husband's family, which she was acutely aware of because of her own more humble origins. More investigation led me to discover that her father was a bricklayer, while her father-in-law was as an accountant. I also uncovered the distinguished war record of her husband and the fact that she was active in the WAAFs in the First World War.

Other sources

Electoral registers are another key resource for interwar house history, and many more have been digitised since I wrote the first edition of the book. They are available in digitised form via genealogy websites and in public libraries, including the British Library website.[5] They allow you to trace where people lived during single years, and it is possible to search by address, so you can use them to ascertain the exact year somebody moved to a particular house and for how long they lived there.

I found estate agents' websites to be a very useful source of information about my case study houses. They allowed me to see photographs and plans of my case study houses and their interiors over time and often had relevant written information such as the dimensions of rooms. You can also track changing prices. At the time of writing, Your Move and Zoopla are the most useful sites for that information.[6]

Street and trade directories are a good source of information about addresses and occupations. The National Archives website lets you access various sources, including historical directories for England and Wales for the period 1750 to 1919.[7] They recommend that you start with the person's name, the geographical area where they worked and a date range to focus your search.

Visual clues

If you are researching the house that you live in (or a house to which you have access) then one of the best things you can do is to examine the house thoroughly for visual clues about its original architecture and design and how it has changed through time. The first thing to do is to look at the outside of your house and compare it with that of its neighbours. Does it have its original footprint or has it been altered with an extension or a porch? Are its original materials visible or has it had a later rendering such as pebbledash? Does it still have its original windows and doors? If they have been replaced, do they follow the original design? For example, if it is like 17 Rosamund Road, it may originally have had metal Crittall windows divided into small rectangular panes.

On the inside, does the house have its original floor plan or have rooms been knocked through or extended? Are there any original fireplaces and decorative mouldings such as picture rails? Are the interior doors and their fittings original? Your kitchen and bathroom are very unlikely to be original and may well have been relocated and/or extended, unless you live in a 'time capsule' house, unaltered since it was built, like the one that this book begins with in chapter one. If you do some decorating, look out for traces of original paint and wallpaper. If you remove floor coverings you may well find evidence of dark stained floorboards around the edge of the room; there would have originally been unfitted carpet or linoleum.

In this book, I describe what interwar houses would have looked like at the time they were built. In chapter one, I go into detail about my visual sources, which include junk shops, charity shops, car boot fairs and online auction sites, as well as museums, archives and libraries. One of the most useful was Middlesex University's Museum of Domestic Design and Architecture, from which many of the book's illustrations are taken.[8] It has wonderful collections of wallpaper samples, builders', estate agents' and building society marketing materials and furniture trade catalogues, as well as domestic advice manuals and homemaking magazines. Many of these have been digitised and can be freely accessed on their website. If you want to delve deeper, you can make an appointment to visit in person. Other places you might want to access online or in person are:

- Design Museum (https://designmuseum.org)
- Modernist Britain (http://www.modernistbritain.co.uk)
- Modernism in Metro-Land
  (http://www.modernism-in-metroland.co.uk)

- Museum of the Home (formerly Geffrye Museum)
  (https://www.museumofthehome.org.uk)
- V&A (including its National Art Library and Archive of Art and
  Design) (https://www.vam.ac.uk)
- Royal Institute of British Architects (library and study rooms)
  (https://www.architecture.com/about/riba-library-and-collections)
- Warner Textile Archive
  (https://www.warnertextilearchive.co.uk)
- Whitworth Art Gallery
  (https://www.whitworth.manchester.ac.uk)

Places to visit

I hope that this book will inspire readers to do their own interwar house histories of either their own family or the house that they live in. One of the best things that you can do is to pay a visit to an example of an interwar house open to the public. The Twentieth Century Society and its regional branches sometimes organise special visits and tours.[9] Please note that opening hours and displays are subject to change and some are only accessible via pre-booked tours so do check before you visit. Here are some that I especially recommend, many of which have been featured in my segments on *A House Through Time*.

For 'ordinary' lived in exteriors and interiors:

- Avoncroft Museum of Historic Buildings (Arcon Mk V Prefab,
  c.1945), Worcestershire
  https://avoncroft.org.uk
- Beamish (1900s town, 1940s farm and new 1950s town under development), County Durham
  http://www.beamish.org.uk
- Black Country Living Museum (1930s high street and 1930s domestic
  rooms)
  https://www.bclm.co.uk

- Forties House and Police Box, Cupar, Fife
  https://www.fortieshouse.co.uk/forties-house
- Old Forge Wartime House, Sittingbourne, Kent
  https://oldforgewartimehouse.co.uk
- Piermaster's, House Liverpool (1850s house staged as wartime house)
  https://www.liverpoolmuseums.org.uk/mol/visit/galleries/
  piermasters-house.aspx
- Mr Straw's House, Blythe Grove, Worksop (National Trust) 1920s
  time capsule interior belonging to a grocer's family in a semi-detached
  house, Nottinghamshire
  https://www.nationaltrust.org.uk/mr-straws-house
- Portsmouth Museum (1930s kitchen and 1930s dining room by Betty
  Joel)
  http://portsmouthcitymuseums.co.uk
- St Fagan's National Museum of History (Llwyn-yr-eos Farmhouse
  staged as 1930s), Cardiff
  https://museum.wales/stfagans/

For examples of Modernism and the Moderne:

- 2 Willow Rd, Hampstead, London (National Trust). Designed by
  architect Erno Goldfinger for his family in 1939
  https://www.nationaltrust.org.uk/2-willow-road
- Bata Heritage Centre, Bata Estate, East Tilsbury, Essex. Model estate
  designed by Czech architects František Lydie Gahura and Vladimír
  Karfík for workers at Bata Shoe Company.
  https://www.bataheritagecentre.org.uk
- Coleton Fishacre, Devon (National Trust). Designed in the 1920s
  for Rupert D'Oyly Carte, combines Moderne and Arts and Crafts
  interiors
  https://www.nationaltrust.org.uk/coleton-fishacre
- Eltham Palace, London (English Heritage). A former medieval and

Tudor royal residence transformed into a striking Moderne mansion by architects Seely Paget Stephen and Virginia Courtauld in the 1930s.
https://www.english-heritage.org.uk/visit/places/
eltham-palace-and-gardens/

- Isokon Gallery tells the story of the Isokon building, a pioneering modern apartment block opened in 1934 as an experiment in new ways of urban living, London
http://www.isokongallery.co.uk

- Silver End, Witham, Essex. Model housing by Thomas S. Tait for workers at the Crittall Windows Company.
http://www.silverendheritagesociety.co.uk/pages/
history-of-silver-end

- The Homewood, Esher, Surrey (National Trust) Designed by architect Patrick Gwynne for his family in 1937
https://www.nationaltrust.org.uk/the-homewood

- Upton House, Warwickshire (National Trust), large country house redmodelled in 1927-9. Highlights include the red, black and silver Moderne bathroom
https://www.nationaltrust.org.uk/upton-house-and-gardens

For interwar Arts and Crafts:

- Goddards Arts and Crafts House, Dringhouses, York (National Trust) Designed by Walter Brierley for the Terry family (of chocolate fame) in 1926 in a fusion of different styles including Jacobean, Queen Anne, Vernacular, neo-Georgian but predominantly Arts and Crafts
https://www.nationaltrust.org.uk/goddards-house-and-garden/
features/the-house-at-goddards
- See also Coleton Fishacre above

Further reading

Backe-Hansen, M. *House Histories: The Secrets Behind Your Front Door* (Cheltenham, The History Press, 2019)

Blanchard, G. *Tracing Your House History: A Guide for Family Historians* (Barnsley, Pen and Sword Books, 2013)

All website addresses are correct at the time of writing.

1

The interwar house:
ideal homes and domestic design

Number 17 Rosamund Road, Wolvercote, Oxford

A 1930's three bedroom semi detached home in need of modernisation on the western side of this popular road.
* Entrance Hall * Sitting Room * Dining Room * Kitchen * Bathroom
* Three Bedrooms * Gardens *[1]

We arrived at number 17 Rosamund Road, Lower Wolvercote, a village on the edge of Oxford's Port Meadow, on our bicycles on a sunny day in May 1995 (Figure 1.1). We were surprised to be there as we had previously ruled the area out as too expensive. We were newly married and house-sitting in Oxford, having moved there from London where we knew we had no chance of buying a house. My husband James had a junior lecturer post at the University of Oxford, and I was a Postdoctoral Research Fellow at Royal Holloway University of London. We may have had middle-class professional jobs but we were on modest salaries and still recovering from the financial effects of years of full-time postgraduate study. The house was just within our budget and ticked the box of 'needing modernisation'.

James clutched the estate agent's details. 'What do you think?', he said to me. The house had a pitched roof with a central chimney stack. The

Chancellors

Established 1807

E S T A T E   A G E N T S

17 ROSAMUND ROAD
WOLVERCOTE
OXFORD

A 1930'S THREE BEDROOMED SEMI DETACHED HOME IN NEED OF
MODERNISATION ON THE WESTERN SIDE OF THIS POPULAR ROAD.

PRICE £62,500   FREEHOLD

---

* Entrance Hall * Sitting Room * Dining Room * Kitchen * Bathroom * Three
Bedrooms * Gardens *

VIEWING: By prior appointment through Chancellors
255 Banbury Road Summertown Oxford OX2 7HN Tel. 01865 516161

ESTATE AGENTS * RESIDENTIAL LETTINGS & PROPERTY MANAGEMENT * SURVEYORS & VALUERS

1.1 Leaflet by Chancellors Estate Agents advertising 17 Rosamund Rd,
Wolvercote, Oxfordshire, 1995

façade was rendered and the only decoration was a moulded diamond above the front door. The front door itself was the original wooden one with six panes of glass occupying its top third. There was a large double bay with the original metal Crittall windows with their distinctive small rectangular panes, which appeared slightly at odds with the tall narrow window to the left of the front door, which had a more 'modernistic' look. The windows and door had not been replaced with uPVC I noted with relief. 'Well, the unpainted render makes it look a bit gloomy and I would have preferred it to look a bit more "modernistic" like the houses in Botley, but I like the diamond above the front door and it's got its original Crittall windows. I guess it's sort of cottagey Arts and Crafts. I like the double bay', I said. The garden gate was rusting and lopsided and the surprisingly big front garden (a depth of twenty-six feet (7.9 m), according to the estate agent's details) consisted of a tangle of bindweed and brambles. We made our way up the path, James opened the front door and I gasped.

Entrance Hall: with stairs off, two understairs [sic] cupboards, gas fire. I felt like a time traveller. The first thing we saw, directly opposite the front door, was the staircase, fitted with a faded and heavily worn stair runner patterned with geometrics and florals, held in place by dirty, copper-coloured stair clips. To the right, the floor of the narrow hallway was covered in grubby linoleum in more geometrics and florals in a palette of turquoise, orange and brown. The hall was lit by a mottled orange and white alabaster bowl suspended from the ceiling on three chains, filled with the customary dead flies. Immediately to the right in the hall was a door, original I noted (rectangular panel at the top, with a horizontal band underneath and then vertical panels), that opened into the front room.

Sitting Room: 12' × 11' [3.6 × 3.3 m] into alcoves and bay window to front, picture rail, central tiled fireplace. The front room was pale green below the picture rail, with yellowing white paintwork above (Plate 1). The ceiling was thick with cobwebs. Each wall was edged with narrow cream and brown textured border paper to give a half-frame effect. On the party wall sat a stepped 'Devon' tiled fireplace in mottled beige tiles with powder blue tiles in the top corners forming a diamond shape.[2] A compact, brown, leatherette three-piece suite in a style that combined 'modernistic' curves with 'Jacobethan' studs took up most of the available floor space, even though its proportions were very small.[3] It consisted of a two-seater sofa and 'his' (with a winged back) and 'hers' armchairs. The little area of floor we could see was covered with unfitted linoleum and the foot or so of floorboards that showed around the edges were stained dark brown. Another alabaster bowl hung in the centre of the room. The room was tiny but it was lovely and bright because of its bay window.

Heading back into the hall, there was a door to the left under the stairs. I opened it and found a rudimentary larder with a small, high, square window, through which the sun streamed, with a stone slab underneath. Straight ahead at the end of the hall was another door, which I assumed led into the kitchen. Opening it we found the bathroom.

Bathroom: With bath and wc [sic]. Immediately to the left was a toilet with a high cistern. Straight ahead was a stained and alarmingly short rolltop bath with peculiar 'globe' taps with spouts directly under the handles rather than in the customary 'h'-shaped bend. There was more lino on the floor. Only later did we realise that there was no washbasin in the bathroom.

Dining Room: 12' × 9'6 [3.6 × 2.8 m] into alcoves, central tiled fireplace, picture rail, television aerial point. At the bottom of the hall to the right was another door, leading into the dining room. Crammed into this room on the right was a sideboard that combined bulbous 'Jacobethan' legs and carved 'modernistic' details; opposite it was a small, green, leatherette two-seater sofa. On the left-hand wall there was a folding gate-leg table and chairs. The right-hand wall featured another tiled fireplace in beige, plainer than the one in the front room. Behind the sofa on the far wall a window overlooked the long rear garden. To the left of it was another door. To get to it, we had to walk around the table and squeeze through the gap between it and the sofa.

Kitchen: 8′8 × 8′ [2.6 × 2.4 m]. With sink unit, gas point, side door outside. We entered through the door into a tiny square kitchen (Plate 2). The walls were covered in dirty, cream, peeling eggshell paint and thick with grease. Underneath the window on the centre of the far wall that looked out on to the garden was a large, deep, porcelain 'Belfast' sink. Either side of it was a narrow, enamelled, metal-topped table. There were some rudimentary shelves mounted on the dividing wall. On the right-hand wall was an old gas cooker. Perhaps the left-hand wall had once had a dresser or a kitchen cabinet against it?

A rotting back door on the left opened out to the side path and there was a 'side store' built into the external wall of the house, originally intended for storing coal. At the end of the path a gate opened into a long, narrow garden 'with a depth of approximately 70 [feet] [21 m]', which, the estate agent's details noted, 'is currently overgrown'.[4] It was choked with weeds and vicious brambles that pushed at the back wall of the house. On the left was what looked like the original waist-height wire fence dividing the garden from the house next door, and on the right a decrepit wooden fence that separated the garden from the one belonging to the adjoining semi. We retraced our steps through the garden and the ground floor of the house and headed upstairs.

Landing: With access to roof space. Off the landing, we found three bedrooms. Like downstairs, all the rooms had unfitted lino. The two larger bedrooms still had their original furniture.

Bedroom 1: 14′10 × 9′ [4.5 × 2.7 m] into alcoves plus bay window to front, central tiled fireplace, picture rail. We went first into the master bedroom, the largest room in the house, situated at the front. There was a small, pretty double bed with a wooden headboard decorated with carved stylised flowers. A Queen Anne style dressing table with bowed cabriole legs sat in the front bay. The right-hand side of the bedroom extended over the staircase, giving room for a wardrobe. There was more space for furniture in the alcoves on either side of the fireplace. The fireplace consisted of a cast iron insert in an Art Nouveau style with elongated stylised flowers, more typical of the design of twenty years before the house was built. I wondered if this was leftover builders' stock, or did fireplaces keep being produced in this style because they were popular?

Bedroom 2: 10'11 × 10'2 [3.3 × 3.1 m] into alcoves, central fireplace, picture rail. Moving into the second bedroom at the rear of the house, we found a smaller, metal fireplace insert with geometric chequered decoration. It had a portcullis-patterned, solid grid designed for a gas supply rather than an opening.

Bedroom 3: 7'2 × 6'7 [2.2 × 2m]. With cupboard housing hot water cylinder in one corner. Also at the rear of the house was a tiny box room. Suitable for a baby, I noted with great longing. The airing cupboard dominated the space. There and then I decided that it would have to go.

I was totally smitten with the house. As a former curator at the Victoria and Albert Museum, I pictured it as a series of period rooms that I could restore. Plus, over the last five years I had been immersed in the archives of the 1920s and 1930s Ideal Home exhibitions, along with trade catalogues, household advice manuals, memoirs, novels and films of the period for my recently completed PhD research.[5] Like the heroines of the 'middlebrow' domestic novels that I had read, I was newly married, seriously broody and keen to set up home.[6]

I knew from the estate agent's details that the house was built in 1934, which seemed an especially good omen as it was my favourite year of the Ideal Home Exhibition. My subsequent research revealed that it was built by the local builder Hinkins and Frewin.[7] The house was in one of three streets of speculatively built houses in Lower Wolvercote aimed at the better-paid workers of the Oxford University Press paper mill situated nearby. In its layout and compact dimensions, it was quite typical of the modest houses built in the interwar years. The downstairs bathroom saved money on plumbing. I later found out that the lean-to kitchen was a later addition. The third bedroom was very small. Such modest

houses, which sprang up in increasing numbers when mortgage conditions became more favourable after 1932, were intended to appeal to the
better-off working classes and lower middle classes.[8] In the 1930s houses
on Oxford's speculatively built estates typically sold for less than £525.
Because of the demand from motor workers, they were priced higher
than in most other parts of the country outside London, where prices
averaged between £400 and £500.[9] For paper mill workers who could not
stretch to home ownership but could afford the rent, the alternative was
the red-brick, cottage-style, local authority houses in short terraces built
in the 1930s in Upper Wolvercote, separated from Lower Wolvercote by
the canal and railway line.

The estate agent told us that the house was a 'deceased estate'.
Leaving the house, we stopped to chat to the next-door-but-one neighbours, who introduced themselves as Eddie and Nicky Clarke and their
two sons James and Adam. Nicky told us that number 17 had been
owned by her recently deceased grandmother, Cecilia Collett, who had
lived into her nineties. Nicky's grandfather, a worker at the Wolvercote
paper mill on a modest wage, had purchased the house when it was
newly built. He died in the 1960s, which explained why the house had
remained largely unmodernised.

It turned out that the newly built number 17 Rosamund Road was
purchased around 1934–35 by Vernon Victor Collett (1900–60) and his
wife Cecilia (née Wells, 1897–1995). They moved into the house with
their sons Basil, aged about 13, and Roy, aged about 10.[10] Between 1840
and 1918 Colletts made up 483 out of the 1,074 surnames found in the
parish registers.[11] Both Vernon and Cecilia were from solid working-
class backgrounds. Vernon was the third of six children of Percy
Thomas Collett (1877–1948) and Gertrude Hall (1877–1967). The Colletts
were a well-known family of stonemasons (an occupation carried out
by Percy's father) but Percy had broken with the family tradition and
worked as a dairyman. Gertrude had worked in domestic service before
her marriage and was the daughter of an innkeeper. Cecilia was the

fourth of five children of Harry Wells (1860–1910), a house builder (formerly a tallow boiler and labourer), and Sarah Ellen Cox (1859–1951), daughter of a journeyman plasterer. After Sarah was widowed in 1910 she worked as a charwoman to support her family.[12] Nicky told me that in purchasing number 17, Vernon Collett became the first person in his family to own his own home. The Colletts had only two children, in contrast to their own families of six and seven children. The small family of two or three children was typical of the respectable working and aspiring lower middle classes in the interwar years who sought to improve their standard of living, and was also dictated by the size and number of bedrooms in the typical interwar semi.[13]

That first visit to 17 Rosamund Road in 1995 was a catalyst to the research and thinking that would eventually become this book, which has been influenced profoundly by my personal experience of living in and renovating the house. I have also tried to keep my eyes open to the primary sources I have found, rather than trying to fit examples to predetermined theories of Modernism and modernity. It has also been motivated by the desire to tell the story of families like the Colletts, and indeed my own family, whose experience of first-time home ownership and its accompanying design and decoration affected their social standing and domestic practices and tastes.

A note on sources

When I started to think about this book at the turn of the twenty-first century, three indispensable books on the English interwar suburban home were already in existence: first, the social historian Alan Jackson's *Semi-Detached London: Suburban Development, Life and Transport, 1900–39* (1991); secondly, architectural historians Paul Oliver, Ian Davis and Ian Bentley's defensive polemic *Dunroamin: The Suburban Semi and Its Enemies* (1981); and thirdly, a book that accompanied the exhibition of the same name by the former Middlesex Polytechnic's Silver Studio

Collection (now incorporated into Middlesex University's Museum of Domestic Design and Architecture, also known as MoDA), *Little Palaces: The Suburban House in North London 1919–1939* (1987).[14] All three books were ground-breaking in their own ways and others have since been published, some of which are aimed at the owners of interwar houses who are planning to restore period details.[15] I am also particularly indebted to the careful work done by the economic historian Peter Scott on interwar home ownership in his book *The Making of the Modern British Home: The Suburban Semi and Family Life between the Wars* (2013).[16] However, I set out to redress the insufficient attention paid to gendered roles in the design and decoration of the home in all four books. In addition, I have also tried to give a more nuanced, complex and fluid reading of the role of design and taste in the formation of class identities.

This book draws on and extends my extensive doctoral research on the interwar Daily Mail Ideal Home exhibitions, which included unprecedented access to the *Daily Mail*'s archives, and my earlier book *The Ideal Home through the Twentieth Century* (1997) and related articles and conference papers.[17] From the outset, I intended this book to take an interdisciplinary approach, reflecting and drawing upon recent debates in design history, visual culture, material culture studies, cultural history, cultural and historical geography and gender studies.

Although this book takes an interdisciplinary approach, it is grounded in the discipline of design history. As the design historian Judy Attfield argued, with the exception of Oliver et al.'s *Dunroamin*, the interwar semi has tended to be regarded as an object lesson in 'bad design', 'all the better to demonstrate the virtues of modern mass production exemplified by bent plywood and tubular steel furniture'.[18] In this book I challenge the dominance of Modernist aesthetics and values on writing on design, architecture and consumption by exploring popular conceptions of the 'modern' that accommodated past and present, nostalgia and modernity within their social and historical contexts. I also stress suburbanites' own agency as consumers, especially where they resisted and contested official notions of 'good' taste and design. Thus, this book reveals the shifting constituencies of taste and the social aspirations of interwar consumers as a commercial culture of homemaking became established.

A belief in the Modernist project in design has impacted on the discipline of design history.[19] The design historian Kjetil Fallan has gone so far as to suggest that 'the vast masses of modern material culture not conforming to the modernist ethos ... [are] excluded from our histories of design'.[20] There are some exceptions to this, such as Attfield's pioneering work on the traditional High Wycombe furniture manufacturer J. Clarke and Jonathan Woodham's recent essay on twentieth-century Tudor revivals, as well as Fallan's own work on traditionalesque Scandinavian china.[21] I very much hope that this book will act as a further corrective.

I have also questioned my encounters with 'period' rooms in museums, nearly always seen through the lens of the invented retrospective term 'Art Deco'. As Mark Turner, the former curator of Middlesex University's Silver Studio Collection, said,

> In all the years I have spent looking at untouched interwar houses, I have never once seen an interior that was the riot of Art Deco Moderne which museums and television would have us believe was typical. Very few suburban residents could buy all their furniture new and immediately. Pieces were acquired as money allowed, and Modernism was thought to be more appropriate for easily replaceable wallpaper and mats.[22]

What we now call Art Deco was referred to at the time by terms such as 'Jazz Modern', 'Modernistic' or 'Moderne'. I have adopted the term 'Modernistic' in this book, for reasons I will discuss more fully in Chapter 3.

This book will contribute to recent literature by art and design historians on 'other' Modernisms. For example, Christopher Reed argues that what he terms the 'amusing style' was a specific form of modernity formulated by the Bloomsbury set in their homes.[23] Michael Saler suggests that the Arts and Crafts movement inspired 'Medieval Modernism' in the design of the London Underground.[24] Paul Greenhalgh describes an 'English compromise' as a response to Modernism.[25] Alan Powers identifies a 'modern George VI style'.[26] Katherine Wilson describes 'liveable modernism' as a phenomenon related to the conditions of post-war America.[27]

However, these studies are few and far between, and design historians have lagged behind literary critics such as Nicola Humble, Alison Light, Melissa Sullivan and Sophie Blanch, who have exhaustively studied multiple Modernisms, particularly focusing on what they term 'middlebrow' writers, outside of the canon of literary Modernism.[28] I want to take up especially Bridget Elliott's interdisciplinary work which calls for a more careful reading of 'definitional dissonances … looking at the slippery nature of words like *modern*, *moderne*, *modernistic* and *modernist* which have been routinely evoked to make value judgments that have shaped the early twentieth-century architectural canon'.[29] Therefore this book calls for an understanding of multiple, nuanced and even conflicting forms of Modernism in architecture and design.

My approach stresses that the meaning of objects is not just formed at the site of production by designers but also throughout their lives by users. This is especially useful for understanding objects for which there is no known designer or readily identifiable style. Design historians, particularly those writing from a feminist viewpoint on women as consumers of design, have been influenced by a 'material culture' turn in design history, which has more recently also influenced art history.[30] Both disciplines have been influenced by social anthropologists who investigate how objects embody sets of social relations and acquire values and symbolism through use, and help form personal identities.[31] They have been especially informed by the work of social anthropologist Daniel Miller and sociologist Pierre Bourdieu, both of whom consider the social meanings that goods acquire, as well as their role in constructing social identities.[32]

This book is the result of a great deal of time spent poring over the surviving representations and actual material culture of the home in repositories such as Middlesex University's Museum of Domestic Design and Architecture, Getty Images (which incorporates the Hulton Picture Library, which supplied publications such as *Picture Post*), newspapers (especially the *Daily Mail*) and the publications and records of the Daily Mail Ideal Home exhibitions. But I have also scoured the unofficial spaces of antique shops and fairs, auctions, car boot fairs, charity shops and eBay. Thus, this book draws on exhibitions, advice manuals, trade literature, advertisements, magazines, novels, memoirs, photographs and films as well as actual examples of suburban architecture, interiors and material culture.

I am mindful of my non-textual visual and material sources as representations that acquire layered, multiple and, sometimes, contradictory meanings as they are constructed, circulated, mediated and consumed. I have tried to take into account the biographies of my sources as they travel through time and also their roles as what the anthropologist Janet Hoskins has called 'biographical objects'.[33] Furthermore, as Bourdieu describes in his theory of 'habitus', individuals form their relationship to social groups through shared sets of attitudes and tastes.[34] So this book asks, how did the domestic design of the interwar suburban home in England both dictate and express the identities and sense of belonging of homeowners to wider communities and networks, including their hopes, desires and aspirations?

In writing this book I have been influenced by novels and memoirs, both interwar and contemporary, in which stories of houses and home-making activities feature prominently.[35] Several books present biographies of houses fused with personal memoir, notably Julie Myerson's *Home: The Story of Everyone Who Ever Lived in Our House* (2005), Rosa Ainley's *2 Ennerdale Drive: An Unauthorised Biography* (2011) and Margaret Forster's *My Life in Houses* (2014). Akiko Busch's *Geography of Home: Writings on Where We Live* (1999) and Ben Highmore's *The*

Great Indoors: At Home in the Modern British House (2014) also deserve particular mention for their fusion of historical and sociological observations on the design and use of the twentieth-century home with the authors' own experiences.[36]

Encountering the material culture of the interwar home in more or less its original state at 17 Rosamund Road has proved a useful counterpoint to the ideals of advertisements, trade catalogues, promotional literature, consumer journalism and advice manuals, room sets from shops and exhibitions and show homes. My personal experience of this interwar home also stands in for a more systematic trawl of diaries and memoirs to reconstruct the experience of living in the interwar home. This has been outside the remit of this project, which is first and foremost concentrated on the meanings of domestic design in terms of style.

Snapshots

One of the biggest challenges in writing this book has been to try and capture the domestic design of the interwar home as it was inhabited and lived in. I looked hard for photographs of lived interiors in modest semi-detached homes that had not been tidied up for the camera. Rare before the accessibility, availability and popularity of flash photography, the interwar amateur domestic interior snapshot has proved elusive. However, photographs of working-class rented homes from the interwar period, particularly slum dwellings, are more readily available. These continued a tradition of photography as a tool of social exploration that started with John Thomson in the 1870s and continued in the twentieth century with the post-First World War concern with slum clearance and the ethnography of Humphrey Spender's Mass Observation photographs.[37] A rich vein of interwar photographs reveal slum interiors located in older nineteenth- and eighteenth-century buildings.

One case in point is a photograph of a working-class home showing a family eating a meal in their kitchen/living room (Figure 1.2). Washing is

1.2 Alfred Smith and family photographed by Kurt Hutton for *Picture Post*, 11 March 1939

strung over the table and there is a traditional range. Yet on the wall there is startling Modernistic wallpaper (see also Plate 14). I found many other examples where the modernity of some of the interior decoration is in striking contrast with items from an older period. Most often this takes the form of wallpaper in a riot of 'Jazz Modern' patterns, which could be purchased cheaply and was frequently papered over previous layers. Or sometimes it is a small item of ceramics, as in the example here of a vase depicting a camel, no doubt influenced by the Egyptomania craze that followed the discovery of the tomb of Tutankhamen.[38] These elements sit alongside traditional Windsor chairs and a piece of lace covering the mantelshelf over the range. A photograph like this suggests the evolution of an interior and a sense of 'making do'. It points to a very real human need for colour, pattern and modernity. It also goes some way to explaining why such wallpaper might have been seen in its time by designers and cultural critics as cheap, nasty and vulgar – in 'bad taste' and as an example of 'bad design'.

Relatively few people decorated their homes, or went out and bought brand new furniture and furnishings, all in one go. Moreover, few subscribed to one particular style, and fewer still to the tenets of Modernist 'good design' advocated by the design reformers of the interwar years. New homeowners who had struggled to scrape together the deposit for their houses and strained to make the monthly repayments often had to make do with borrowed things. There was a thriving market in second-hand furniture, with some big furniture shops selling used furniture alongside brand new.[39] However, if they were given a choice and had the means, many opted for new furniture but in a reassuring traditional form. They did not value antique furniture for its patina, which for them was too associated with dirt and making do. Moreover, it was common for people to hang on to their furniture for years, whether for sentimental or purely pragmatic reasons.

Consequently, when I have been lucky enough to stumble upon unstaged amateur photographs, which are nearly always undated, they are also nearly always impossible to place within a design history chronology of style, progress and fashion. A photograph found in the Hulton Collection in the online Getty Images collection is a case in point (Figure 1.3). It appeals to me because of its seemingly casual quality: the informal pose of the child sitting on her mother's knee; the mother's sideways glance; the discarded toys on the floor; the clutter of ornaments on top of the display cabinet and the screen propped against its side. This is reinforced by the photo's skewed horizontal. However, this is a photo that resists further research. Simply captioned 'Mother and daughter in armchair 1922', I have been unable to find out the identity of the sitters or its original purpose.

For many like the Colletts at 17 Rosamund Road, the home they made in the interwar years stayed very much the same for subsequent years once it was 'done'. The modernity – or otherwise – of the interwar years

1.3 Mother and daughter in armchair, 1922

stalled because of the Second World War. Years of rationing and auster-ity compelled people simply to 'make do and mend', as a government campaign advised. After the war, exhibitions such as 'Britain Can Make It' (1946) and the Festival of Britain (1951) promised the modernity of the 'Contemporary Style'.[40] In the dream palace of the cinema, British audiences swooned over the new consumer world of goods depicted in American films. However, even if such luxuries as a fitted kitchen made of Formica were available, for the majority they remained firmly out of reach, prohibited by cost, lack of credit and the legacies of the 'make do and mend' of two world wars.

A photograph of a 'sub-standard' kitchen in London County Council's archives is a case in point (Figure 1.4). At first glance it is a typical interwar kitchen, very reminiscent of the one at number 17, with its gas cooker, Belfast sink and enamelled table top. However, its date is 1962, not 1932 as it first appears. This serves as a reminder of the slippery

1.4 'Sub-standard kitchen', 43 Rigault Rd, London, 1962

nature of visual sources, particularly photographs. It is also a reminder of the changing nature of ideals: the dream kitchen of 1932 is the substandard kitchen of thirty years later.

A black-and-white snapshot of a sitting room that I found on eBay has

1.5 Anonymous photograph of *c.* 1930s sitting room, purchased by the author on eBay

especially intrigued me (Figure 1.5). The seller could tell me nothing about its provenance. The furniture and furnishings appear to date from the interwar period but the photo may have been taken much later. A 'Devon' tiled fireplace, most likely coloured in a mottled orange-brown and beige, is slightly off centre. Its geometric form and stylised diamond central decorative feature nod to the Modernistic. The compact three-piece suite – remember the small dimensions of 17 Rosamund Road – is quite traditional but a little bit Modernistic. The cushions, especially the patchwork one, look homemade, a reminder of the popularity of home crafts as part of the domestic repertoire of the 'professional' housewife advocated by women's and homemaking magazines.[41] There is a hint of the Modernistic in the design of the china cabinet and a glimpse of a Queen Anne leg on a side table (reproduction rather than original surely?). The mantelpiece holds family photographs of men in military uniform, recording proud moments and perhaps loved ones lost. The mounted horns that sit on top of the display cabinet are perhaps part of the detritus of Empire, washed

1.6 The Beaver family listening to the wireless, 1937

up in the British home through military service, family networks and trade connections. But these are all speculations.

If only the armchairs in the photo were not empty then perhaps I could read something more about the interior from the appearance of its inhabitants, particularly their clothes. So, I will turn to another found photograph of a family listening to the wireless in England in the 1930s (Figure 1.6). Like many of the digitised images found in online picture libraries, there is no record of its provenance and original use. However, this example seems to be one of a sequence of photos showing a day in the life of the lady of the house, Mrs Beaver, as she goes about her business feeding her family and cleaning. The family here may be dressed for the camera: the father is in his suit, the son is in a jacket, the mother and the two daughters are in pretty dresses. All look smart and the epitome of middle-class respectability.

What I like so much about this photo is the fact that the furniture has been rearranged – there is another photo in the sequence of the same room with the furniture in different positions – to allow the family to listen to the radio. The photograph reveals a variety of different styles of furniture and furnishings. There is a 'Devon' tiled fireplace on which sits a barley twist candlestick. The furniture includes a heavy, dark brown cabinet under the window, a monolithic radiogram, a vaguely Jacobean armchair upholstered in geometric fabric and a curved armchair covered in different geometric fabric. There are different but similar patterns in the fabrics on the piano stool and *pouffé*. Mottled wallpaper, likely to be beige, is decorated with borders of country cottage flowers. The carpet has a stylised geometric floral pattern. Mother's dress is covered in a Jacobean floral pattern, strikingly similar to the fabric that covers the loose cushion that she leans against on her chair. This is a lived interior, albeit one staged for the camera.

There is one photo that has intrigued me above all others. Systematically working my way through files of photographs in the *Daily Mail* picture library over twenty years ago, I found an image that stopped me in my tracks (Figure 1.7). A battered photograph depicted a lamp 'designed' in an 'antique' style. Its base appears to be made of a dark wood, in vaguely Regency style, topped with a fringed, chintz-patterned shade. The circular base of the lamp contains doors that open to reveal a gramophone player. A caption on the reverse revealed that it is a 'phono-lamp' exhibited at the 1923 Ideal Home Exhibition, describing it as a 'novelty light: artistic lamp, provider of music and decorative item'. The phono-lamp has obsessed me ever since. It is an object that appears to exist outside of existing histories of design. Perhaps the only place in the discourses of design that it might have been found is on one of the lantern slides produced by the Design and Industries Association to helpfully instruct the public through comparisons of 'good design' and 'bad design'.[42] It would not have been out of place at 17 Rosamund Road but its exemplary status as 'bad design' has made it invisible to subsequent historians of design. How then might I make sense of it?

1.7 The Phono-lamp, 1923

In his *Homes Sweet Homes* (1939), which satirised the interwar English obsession with homemaking, the cartoonist Osbert Lancaster commented on a noted tendency to produce multi-purpose objects:

> It is significant that the Old English fondness for disguising everything as something else now attained the dimensions of a serious pathological affliction. Gramophones masquerade as cocktail cabinets; cocktail cabinets as book-cases; radios lurk in tea-caddies and bronze nudes burst asunder at the waist-line to reveal cigarette lighters; and nothing is what it seems.[43]

Lancaster's description seems to hint at what would have been called at the time a Modernistic style. The term Art Deco, which we would now use, does not adequately describe let alone explain the phono-lamp or its currency in interwar popular taste.

Perhaps the best way to understand the phono-lamp is through the networks of people and things in which it acted. The French sociologist Bruno Latour's notion of the dynamic networks of relationships between people and things – as 'actants' – is useful in understanding this.[44] As this book goes on to show, there was an active relationship between the small suburban semi, its decoration and furnishings, and its inhabitants. The phono-lamp was an object intended to make the most of the space of the tiny interwar home, built just at or even below the government's minimum standards for space to make it affordable for the emerging lower middle classes. The phono-lamp's multi-functionalism was an absolute essential in such very limited interiors, where every inch of space had to be made to act efficiently. Furthermore, the gramophone lamp implies an action of sitting in a comfy chair with a nice cup of tea, listening to music. Placed within networks of class aspirations, speculative housebuilding and commercial cultures of homemaking, such an object can be understood as a non-Modernist and even non-Modernistic but 'modern' thing, acting as part of a distinctly modern way of life. It is an exemplar of the material culture of suburban Modernism.

The ideal home?

The focus of this book is on the meanings of the domestic design – architecture, interiors, decoration, furniture and furnishings – of the modest, semi-detached, privately owned, 'modern' suburban house in the interwar years.[45] These meanings were not solely made at the point of production but were formulated by homeowners, changing over time. Home ownership became established as an ideal in the interwar period and almost three million houses were built for private sale. This was the period during which the idea of Britain as a nation of homeowners became established. There was also a substantial local authority building campaign of over one million 'homes fit for heroes' that brought improved housing and a new way of suburban living to the 'respectable' working classes.[46] While some areas of the country, particularly those with traditional manufacturing industries, suffered badly from economic depression, those that hosted new industries in the south of England and better-off towns and cities in the Midlands and the north boomed.[47]

In the interwar period the idea of 'home' became increasingly important to the huge numbers of people like the Colletts, skilled manual workers and non-professional, non-manual workers. Seeking to better themselves, many such people moved up the social scale by entering white-collar professions and moving into houses in the new local authority and speculatively built suburbs. Together they constituted the aspirational lower middle classes. While many in this category earned little more, or sometimes even less, than their contemporaries in lower-status manual work, they had aspirations towards a modern way of living, one that was markedly different to that of their parents, and home ownership was part and parcel of this. The First World War and its aftermath threw traditional class boundaries into disarray and presented new opportunities for social advancement. While many of the established middle classes – dubbed the 'New Poor' – were hit hard in the economic climate following the war, the respectable working classes and lower middle class remade themselves as the 'New Rich' through their consumer aspirations, gleaned from their betters and from the new media such as the *Daily Mail* (launched in 1896) and its Ideal Home Exhibition (launched in 1908), magazines such as *Good Housekeeping* and *Modern Home* (launched in 1922 and 1928 respectively), advertising and cinema.

Women took on the new identity of professional housewife, promulgated in the new women's and homemaking magazines and household advice manuals, often having to make do without servants.[48] In this book I have made particular use of *Modern Home* magazine because of its direct address to the new, modern ways of life that emerged in the suburbs.[49] Its front covers depict couples engaged in homemaking activities such as choosing paint colours, shopping for furniture and doing the dishes. For example, November 1931's cover depicts a woman seated in front of a scale model of an 'ideal home' (Plate 3). Beside it are scissors and paint, implying that she has made it herself. A man crouches with one arm around her shoulders, his hand clutching her arm. His other hand holds blueprint plans for the house, which she also holds. This is an image that may be read as the man exerting control over the design of the house, or it may be read as a joint act of homemaking and a vision of a new form of 'companionate' marriage.[50] This points to the slippery nature of evidence, particularly when it depicts 'ideals'.

Women's identities as mothers also changed in the interwar years. The desire for an increased standard of living, together with advice on birth control, meant that smaller families like that of the Colletts became more common.[51] The small, three-bedroom semi like 17 Rosamund Road was both a response to the 'ideal' family of four and their consumer aspirations, but also went on to shape both family size and the scaled-down, multi-purpose and 'metamorphic' furniture and other objects that occupied it.

A sense of 'home' was essential as a place of shelter for individual family units and the making of new communities. The meaning of home, after all, is not solely confined to shelter and well-being, but to emotional, spiritual and moral values, as well as nourishment.[52] Home is and was, as Davidoff and Hall have said, 'as much a social construct and a state of mind as a reality of bricks and mortar'.[53] In the first half of the twentieth century 'home' was also the nation at the heart of the British Empire. The words of the King – 'The foundations of the nation's greatness are laid in the homes of the people' – were used on the frontispiece of the Ideal Home Exhibition catalogue in 1928, accompanied by a graphic illustration of a cat sitting in front of a fireplace, where a man relaxed in slippers and a woman knitted, conjuring up an image of cosy, harmonious domesticity (Figure 1.8). The quotation was taken from a speech that King George V had made to the Convocation of York on 8 July 1910.[54] Questions of nationhood, patriotism and race were important in the early twentieth century, when Britain was struggling to maintain its economic and military position in the world. 'Home' was the site of production of the citizens of the future, as well as of morality.[55] The King's speech fused home and Church in a conservative response to the uncertainties of modernity.

It is also worth noting that 'home' in an imperial context embraces the microscopic, in the form of the individual dwelling, and the macroscopic, as the 'mother country', looking outwards to the wider shores of the Empire. Thus, this book also looks at the impact of the further flung colonies and dominions on the British 'ideal home', as sources for raw materials and exotic objects as well as places from which the home is imagined and on which the home is mapped.

I first became fascinated with what was 'modern' in the discourses of the Ideal Home Exhibition and its catalogues and publications, its sponsor the *Daily Mail* and the trade catalogues and other ephemera produced by exhibitors. I argued that a specifically 'suburban modernity' emerged in the interwar years that combined new technologies with new forms of the past.[56] This could not be explained by a notion of art and design history, where Modernism and in particular the Modern Movement in design is defined by a very particular set of

Daily Mail

IDEAL HOME
EXHIBITION

OLYMPIA·LONDON·W
FEBRUARY 28 ···
MARCH 24 · 1928

" The foundations of the National Glory are set in the Homes of the People."

—KING GEORGE V.

1.8 Frontispiece, *Daily Mail Ideal Home Exhibition Catalogue 1928*

Bauhaus-derived dictums that are encapsulated in the phrase 'form follows function'. Even the practice of the discipline of design history itself is sometimes framed as a Modernist one of progress. In developing my research in this book, I focus particularly on the tensions between the longings for the past and the aspirations for the future displayed in interwar suburbia. Many of the objects and decorative schemes of the interwar home that I encountered could not be accounted for within the existing framework of design history. Suburban Modernism, I argue here, was dependent upon a mixture of symbols of progress, such as labour-saving appliances, and peculiarly English invented traditions, such as the Tudorbethan semi. The interwar home was both a retreat from the outside world and a site of change and experimentation.

In the next chapter I discuss the growth of suburbia in the interwar years and the constituents of the 'suburban'. This is contextualised by a discussion of the emerging class identities of the 'New Poor', the established middle classes whose fortunes had been affected by the First World War, and the 'New Rich', comprised of those who had moved up the social scale to form the new lower middle classes. I also discuss the representation of the new home-centred identities of the professional housewife and suburban husband. I consider how these issues impacted the rise of home ownership, which the increased availability of cheap mortgages brought within the reach of new working- and lower-middle-class households. I end by discussing the use of the term 'suburban' as an insult, through the material culture of the parlour, the mantelpiece and the napkin ring.

The constituents of what it was to be 'modern' in the home through the idea of suburban Modernism are the focus of Chapter 3. I relate the condition of modernity and the practice of Modernism to the culture of suburbia. I examine the ways in which the architecture and design of the Modern Movement was interpreted by speculative builders, manufacturers and retailers in the form of what was termed 'Modernistic' by design critics and reformers. I show how critics in England damned popular suburban Modernistic taste as 'bad design', in opposition to Modernism's 'good design'. I discuss how homeowners engaged with and responded to modernisation through the choices they made in the decoration and furnishing of their homes. Finally, I discuss the emergence of 'metamorphic Modernism': multi-functional furniture and objects, like the phono-lamp discussed above, that responded to the compact interwar home.

The development of the 'Efficiency' style, which drew on debates about labour-saving in the home and the emergence of the middle-class professional housewife who had to do without servants, is the focus of Chapter 4. I also examine the points of view of architects, housing reformers, manufacturers and retailers and how they influenced or otherwise 'ordinary' housewives. The post-war 'servant problem' and the constraints of lower-middle-class incomes meant that the role of the housewife became professionalised. The discourses of exhibitions, magazines and advice manuals appealed to lower-middle-class housewives by presenting a vision of domestic progress that addressed housework as both work and leisure, and posited specifically modern gender identities. I focus on the design and equipment of the kitchen and examine the ways in which it appealed to suburbanites' aspirations for modern identities. The 'ideal home' was constructed as a site of change and experimentation, with the term 'labour-saving' signifying a suburban Modernism far removed from the dictums of the Modern Movement in architecture and design.

The role of nostalgia and tradition in the home is explored in Chapter 5. This was manifest in the fondness for an imagined Old England and the detritus of the British Empire, which I argue was an intrinsic component of the suburban vision of Modernism that interwar suburbia offered. The Tudor period held a particular appeal in interwar Britain. Speculative builders' Tudorbethan was the architectural style that most characterised interwar suburbia. There was also a fashion for antique, reproduction, cottage-style and 'Jacobethan' furniture and interiors. Cultural critics denigrated the popular taste for 'Old England' as 'sham' Tudor, 'Jerrybethan' or 'Stockbroker's Tudor'. Contrary to these critics, who dismissed the Tudorbethan as ersatz and backward looking, the Tudorbethan signified a coming together of nostalgia and a particularly suburban form of Modernism that allowed suburbanites to dwell in the past, while looking forward to the future. The chapter also considers the relationship between 'home' and Empire through the notion of imperial suburbs. Crafts produced by so-called 'peasant workers' were highly prized in Britain, as, for example, the rows of ebony elephants and the like that can still be found in many homes testify.

The interwar suburban home has not only influenced the architecture and design of subsequent housing but has also become an 'ideal'. Just why is it that the compact, three-bedroom, semi-detached suburban house with a pitched roof and bay windows still holds such popular appeal? Despite the fact that there are now several books available on the restoration of the interwar home, there is little sense, beyond a few vintage enthusiasts who live a vintage lifestyle, that interwar houses, beyond a few Art Deco or Modernist examples, are valued as period properties to be conserved and restored. Indeed, greater regard seems to be given to 'Mid-Century Modern' and Brutalist styles. The book ends by considering the modernisation of the interwar home. I look briefly at subsequent housebuilding and the expansion of suburbia, the rise of home ownership and the adoption and adaptation of interwar houses by their contemporary residents.

Suburbia and suburbanites have continued to be denigrated by sections of the intelligentsia and the architectural and design press. Home ownership is now out of reach for many who earn the present-day equivalent of the individuals I discuss in the chapters that follow, in which I investigate the period during which Britain became a nation of homeowners. Nevertheless, there are some parallels in our current age of austerity in the search for the authentic and the resurgence of craft or an interwar 'making do' spirit. To some extent, as I go on to show, the interwar suburban semi still epitomises the 'ideal home' and occupies a significant space in the popular imagination.

2

Suburban: class, gender and home ownership

In 1932 Ronald Kingham, a linoleum layer, and his wife of four years, Miriam, became homeowners for the first time. The couple were in their mid-twenties and had no children. They purchased 23 Bromley Road, Edmonton, Middlesex, a newly built house with three bedrooms, two reception rooms, a small 'kitchenette' and an upstairs bathroom (Figure 2.1). As a skilled manual worker, Ronald's income probably matched or even exceeded some of those in lower-paid clerical occupations. The Kinghams purchased the house directly from the builders, H. Smith Bros, for £699 (freehold) with a deposit of £49 and a mortgage for the balance from the National Building Society.[1] Assuming that as a skilled manual worker Ronald earned somewhere between £4 and £5 a week (between £208 and £260 per annum), the mortgage payments of 21 shillings a week represented between approximately 21 per cent and 26 per cent of his weekly income; the total purchase price represented between 2.7 and 3.4 times his annual income.[2]

In the 1930s such smaller, speculatively built suburban houses, the increased supply of which reduced house prices, were affordable for the better-off working classes and lower middle classes. House prices peaked in 1931 and started to fall in 1932, continuing to do so for the rest of the decade, representing a proportionately lower multiple of annual income than at any time before or since. Mortgages became cheaper and

1932

SMITH'S Famous for Value HOUSES

HUXLEY GARDEN ESTATE
Cambridge Arterial Road, N.9

Ideal Houses in a Premier Position at the Right Price
WITH CLEAN CONCRETE ROADS

Large Rooms, Two Reception, Three Bed., Tiled Kitchenette, Ideal Type Boiler, Hygena Kitchen Cabinet, Larder, Gas Copper, Deep Butler's Sink, Draining Board, Marble Bathroom, Modern Enclosed Bath, Hand Basin, Chromium Fittings, Two W.Cs. Brick Coal Shed. White Atlas Cement Finish to Exterior. Electric Light Fittings, complete to Pendants. Decorations to Choice.

FREEHOLD PRICE £699
END HOUSES WITH ROOM FOR GARAGE From £725
Total Deposit : £50

£5 Secures, Balance by Arrangement
No Road Charges. No Stamp Duties. No Legal Costs. No Survey Fees
NO EXTRAS WHATSOEVER

Repayments to Building Society 21/- PER WEEK, for 20 years

Rates: 6/5 in the £ for half-year, March, 1932.   Electricity : 4d. per unit, lighting.
Gas: 8.6d. per therm.   Water : Supplied by the Metropolitan Water Board.

These well-designed houses represent the last word in Modern Planning. The pleasing Mediaeval Elevation lends striking contrast to the exceptionally Light, Spacious and Convenient Interior.

HOW TO GET THERE.—From Liverpool Street to SILVER STREET Station, EDMONTON, in about 20 minutes—trains every few minutes, bus or walk to Cambridge Arterial Road, one mile ; or Tube to Finsbury Park and tram or bus to North Circular Rd., by Cambridge Arterial Road. Nearer TUBE Stations under construction : Bowes Road and Wood Green. Frequent bus services within five minutes : No. 201, Stroud Green to EDMONTON ; No. 551, Whetstone to EDMONTON ; No. 602, Muswell Hill to Chingford ; No. 299, Victoria to LOWER EDMONTON. PASSES ESTATE.

H. SMITH BROS., Builders & Contractors

Huxley Garden Estate Office, Cambridge Arterial Rd., EDMONTON

Phone: PALMERS GREEN 5922 & 5923.   OPEN WEEK-ENDS.

Estates at GOLDERS GREEN, KENTON, KINGSBURY, LOUGHTON, WALTHAMSTOW, WESTCLIFF-ON-SEA

2.1 Promotional leaflet by H. Smith Bros advertising Huxley Garden Estate, 1932

more readily available, making the 1930s the most favourable period for house purchase in England in the twentieth century. This brought home ownership increasingly within reach of those like Ronald Kingham on modest incomes from skilled, blue-collar manual trades and white-collar work.

Recent work by economic historians has carefully unpicked the statistics that lie behind these facts. They have discovered that working-class owner-occupation was much more common than previously thought, especially after 1932.[3] As they have argued, the majority of houses built were much smaller and consequently much cheaper than previously claimed, with many breaking the minimum specifications of the Tudor Walters Report that set the standards for public housing in 1918.[4]

This is vividly illustrated by a close examination of H. Smith Bros' advertising flyer for their houses in Bromley Road, which has a photograph of what appears at first glance to be a pair of semi-detached houses (Figure 2.1). In fact, what it depicts is the 'end house' 'with room for garage' on the left (also distinguished by its swept gable) and its neighbour on the right, which were the first two of a row of houses that were built in a terrace. This terrace formation reduced the plot size and frontages for the individual houses and kept the purchase price down. However, the advertising image played to prospective homeowners' aspirations for semi-detachment and car ownership. It was common for builders to feature the biggest houses on the best plots in their developments on their promotional literature. And, indeed, the Kinghams did not buy the house illustrated in the flyer; number 23 was located in the middle of the terrace, not on the generous end plot, and had no garage. Thus, in this chapter I consider how a young couple such as the Kinghams went about becoming suburban homeowners. As I show, home ownership brought with it anxieties about status and respectability. Critics, designers and architects despaired of popular taste, and for them the term 'suburban' became an insult. Yet for the Kinghams, suburban home ownership and homemaking offered both daunting and exciting social opportunities.

The 'New Rich' and the 'New Poor'

Ronald Frederick Kingham (1905–61) and his wife Miriam (née Hughes, 1904–96) were examples of what were known as the 'New Rich' in the 1920s. Born in Edmonton, Ronald was the eldest son of William James Kingham (1876–1961), a bricklayer from Kilburn in north London, and Sarah Mead (1877–1963), the daughter of a bricklayer. Ronald's father had been sent to the Marylebone Workhouse along with his three siblings some time after 1881, staying there until 1885 when their father reclaimed them. At the age of 15 William was sent to work in harsh conditions on the training ship *Exmouth* on the River Thames off Grays, Essex, along with other boys from destitute families. By 1887 William's father, James, was listed as a lunatic and he appears to have died in Hanwell asylum before 1901. William's mother, Hannah, appears to have remarried and the family were resident in Edmonton by 1901. Ronald's wife, Miriam, was born in Hackney, the eldest daughter of George Edward Hughes (1882–1937), a shop and office fitter, and Harriet Larbey (1881–1969), who was the daughter of a wood carver and had worked as a mailing room attendant before her marriage. By 1911 the family had also relocated to Edmonton.[5]

Given his family background, Ronald's purchase of 24 Bromley Road meant that he had really come up in the world. He moved up the social scale, occupying a position somewhere between skilled working class and lower middle class. In his case, his occupation of linoleum layer was perhaps more respectable white-collar rather than manual blue-collar. An illustration of a linoleum layer in a brochure for Catesbys linoleum depicts him in trousers, shirt and waistcoat, presumably with a tie out of sight and having removed his jacket, rather than in blue-collar overalls (Figure 2.2). The occupation may have brought with it similar pressures to those felt by clerks to be presentable and respectable not only in terms of dress but in lifestyle as well.[6] This occupation was intrinsically bound up with broader shifts in English life as increasing numbers

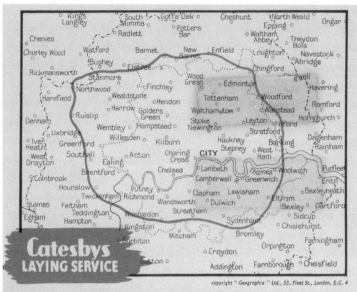

IF YOU LIVE within the red circle area shown on the map, Catesbys trained Planners lay your lino FREE OF CHARGE on lino orders of £2 and over.

Beyond this area a nominal charge is made for time and expenses.

Catesbys Planners are experts in laying lino, the majority having had over 20 years' experience.

These men are acknowledged the most highly skilled in the trade, having worked on some of the largest lino contracts in the country.

You are invited to take advantage of this specialist laying service. Advice on floor treatments is gladly given without obligation.

Note : For specialized laying, i.e., Planned Floors, Border work, Bathrooms, etc., please ask for estimate.

2.2 Illustration of linoleum layer, from *Catesbys Colourful Cork Lino*, 1938

of people moved out to new suburbs and became the owners of new houses, which needed decorating and furnishing from top to bottom. Manufactured in Scottish towns such as Kirkcaldy and Dundee, linoleum was a popular choice of floor covering, sold by companies such as Catesbys (Plates 6 and 7). The journalist and broadcaster Paul Vaughan's father was 'something in linoleum' in the interwar years, rising to be secretary of the Linoleum (and Floorcloth) Manufacturers Association. Vaughan described the appeal of the material thus: 'Linoleum was the thing, a cheap, durable covering for the floors of the new houses going up all round the outskirts of London and other big cities – lino that looked like marble, like parquet, like tiles or possibly a carpet, inlaid with a pattern of flowers or scenery or something "abstract".'[7] Ronald Kingham's occupation would have meant that he frequently visited new houses, which perhaps impressed upon him the desirability of home ownership and gave him ideas about taste, style and decoration.

In the first half of the twentieth century, the middle classes both expanded and changed. At the beginning of the century there had been a real improvement, albeit small, in the living standards of most people, who now had a surplus to spend on needs other than basic subsistence. Perhaps as a result of aspirations towards a better standard of living and the purchase of new consumer goods, smaller families were common. People exercised choice over how and where to spend their money. Desires were furnished by increasingly sophisticated retailers of products that were the fruits of newly mechanised factories, aided by the 'easy payment' or hire purchase system.[8]

New work opportunities in government departments and clerical and managerial work, notably with the emergence of big business, led many people who might have hitherto been employed in manual, waged occupations to become salaried. In 1911 there were 2.4 million workers in such occupations; in 1931 there were 3.4 million, an increase of 41 per cent. Moreover, 69 per cent of this increase was in relatively humble clerical jobs.[9] Although clerks' pay was often the same as or little more than that of skilled manual workers, their social standing and expectations were higher, which often meant a struggle to keep up appearances.[10]

Recent research suggests that when building costs and interest rates fell in the early 1930s, 'house purchase came within the reach for the first time of large numbers of manual and lower-paid non-manual workers', among the wages of whom there was a large overlap.[11] It is a mistake simply to categorise this group as 'working-class'. As non-salaried non-professionals, they may not fit the economist's definition of 'middle-class'. However, it could be argued that in their aspirations, particularly the ownership and decoration of their homes, they became the 'New Rich' lower middle classes. As the economic historian George Speight argues, 'Contemporaries drew an important distinction between lower-paid non-manual and better-paid manual workers on the one hand, and less well-paid manual workers on the other; and they often applied the term "working class" only to the latter.'[12] In other words, as the assistant editor of *The Economist* put it in 1936, the families who purchased new homes were from 'the lower middle class, the clerk and artisan class, numerically very much smaller than the unskilled labouring class'. The contemporary definition of 'working-class' was 'manual and less-skilled non-manual workers', which meant that 77 per cent of employed adult males were 'working-class' in 1931. Thus, the quarter of working-class households who were 'better off' and became homeowners constituted a group almost as big as the whole of the middle class.[13]

There were particular shifts in the position of working-class women during the First World War that continued to resonate afterwards. Many working-class women were drafted into war work in factories, enabling them to give up much-loathed domestic service.[14] Women thus entered into a more active form of citizenship by their deeds during the war. The opportunities that women had taken to work outside the home during the First World War – both paid and unpaid – affected their position within the home.[15] Women like Miriam Kingham, who might have been employed as domestic servants before the First World War, also had new opportunities to work in factories producing consumer goods, as well as offices and shops after the war.[16] The civilian army of working-class women in new industries had more freedom and money than employment in domestic service had given them.[17] Many women entered the ranks of the lower middle classes due to the new employment opportunities provided by the expansion in clerical and administrative work. Despite paying little more than skilled manual work, such occupations brought with them increased expectations and aspirations. Cinema, the expansion of shops selling cheaper manufactured goods and new women's magazines – such as *Women's Weekly*, *Home Chat*, *Modern Woman* and *Woman* – also gave women aspirations and opportunities to purchase consumer goods that contributed to the formation of the new identity of the professional housewife.[18] Women took on this new role when they moved into newly built municipal houses as tenants or became owner-occupiers, running their homes without paid domestic help, as will be discussed in more detail in Chapter 4. The identity of professional housewife brought with it expectations about respectability, often expressed through dress codes and home décor. For example, interwar Coventry homeowners, interviewed by Lesley Whitworth in 1997, furnished their hall first so that the house appeared respectable when the front door was opened.[19] There was an emphasis on cleanliness, privacy and 'keeping ourselves to ourselves'.[20]

The home – and particularly owner-occupation – was also linked to citizenship and social status, especially for women.[21] The granting of suffrage in 1918 to all men over 21 and women over 30, as well as women over 21 who were householders or married to householders, gave legal and political rights to those who owned their own homes (in 1928 the vote was extended to all women over 21). Home ownership was thus intrinsically linked to political enfranchisement.

There were huge regional variations in the fortunes of the 'New Rich' in the interwar years. They tended to be concentrated in the southeast and the better-off industrial towns in the Midlands. For many working-class people, the years immediately after the First World War were very difficult, with high inflation and poor housing. The established middle classes whose comfortable lives were threatened by economic recession and inflation after the First World War, and who were now in reduced circumstances, became known as the 'New Poor'. In 1919, the *Daily Mail* described them:

> Trying to keep up the appearance of living in middle-class comfort and actually living in penury, scraping and saving to make both ends meet, fearful lest the next knock at the door may mean the unforeseen expense, in utter dejection over a doctor's or a dentist's bill – such is the chronic state of many who are, perforce, the New Poor. The New Poor is a vast, silent and increasing section of the community.[22]

Salaries had failed to keep up with the rise in prices, and the increases in taxation introduced during the war remained in force. The *Daily Mail* claimed that the 'New Poor' was a growing group: 'Economic pressure has ruthlessly forced new recruits into its ranks. Every day shows how rates, taxes and other financial burdens are widening the circle.'[23] The 'New Poor' were said to include male clerical workers in the private sector, the retired, the widowed and middle-class women who stayed at home and employed servants. The latter, especially, found life increasingly difficult and many complained about the difficulties of securing reliable domestic help due to the 'servant problem', although this might well have been used as a way of disguising the fact that they could no longer afford to employ servants.

The concept of the 'New Poor' was a brilliant strategy of the *Daily Mail* to appeal to the aspirations of its readers. It was a category that was to some extent self-defining; it allowed readers to construct themselves as people who had once had money but could no longer afford to partake in a more genteel lifestyle because of economic circumstances quite beyond their control. Thus, membership of the 'New Poor' allowed readers to reinvent grander histories for themselves. However, some of the 'New Poor' might never have been able to afford the lifestyle evoked by that most resonant of phrases, 'before the war', which conjured up a picture of a golden age of luxury. At the end of the First World War, Lord Northcliffe, proprietor of the *Daily Mail*, appointed Constance Peel, who as 'Mrs Peel' wrote household advice for middle-class people on moderate incomes, as 'Editress' of the women's page.[24] The *Daily Mail* and its Ideal Home Exhibition greatly benefited from Peel's expertise on household management and new ways of labour-saving. In February 1918 she set up a Food Bureau to provide recipes and information regarding food and cookery to help the paper's impoverished readers. Peel served as Editress of the women's page until 1920 when she resigned due to ill-health.[25]

Evidence of the straitened circumstances that many faced after the First World War can be gleaned from Peel's book on the history of the social and domestic lives of the middle classes. Post-war inflation, she claimed, was such that where once it was possible to keep a nurse, cook and house-parlourmaid on an income of £1,000, this was now only sufficient for one servant.[26] Working-class wages, Peel noted, had risen in the hundred years between the end of the Napoleonic Wars and the end of the First World War to such an extent that many skilled artisans were better off than many clerical workers of whom a higher standard of living was expected. That clerical work was thought to be worth more than manual work was, claimed Mrs Peel, due to a survival of the values that were attached to reading and writing when they were rare skills. She said that in homes of limited means, 'what I should like to have must give way to what I can have'.[27] Moreover, she claimed that the lives of many of the lower middle classes had not changed drastically since 1820. They still cooked and ate in much the same way and still did not have bathrooms or electric lighting. The housewife of small means did her washing at home in order to save money; domestic arrangements were simplified to save expense and to make it possible to achieve all that was needed with only one servant.[28]

Life was certainly increasingly difficult for many families in Britain in the years after the First World War. The government did attempt to help: in July 1919 the Chancellor of the Exchequer made a concession that married men with no children would pay no income tax on an income of £250.[29] This benefited many of those in clerical occupations and the poorer paid professions, such as the clergy. There was even some anxiety expressed in the *Daily Mail* and elsewhere that young men would no longer be prepared to enter into marriage because of the effect of wartime inflation on prices.[30] The newspaper whipped up hysteria about the two million so-called 'surplus' unmarried women in the British Isles, even suggesting that they should be sent off to the colonies to marry.[31]

Many middle-class families indeed had to live on incomes that would usually be associated with those much lower down the social scale. The protagonist of George Orwell's novel *Coming Up for Air* (1939) described his wife Hilda's 'New Poor' family upbringing:

> It was through Hilda that I first got a notion of what these decayed middle-class families are really like. The essential fact about them is that all their vitality has been drained away by lack of money. In families like that, which live on tiny pensions and annuities – that's to say on incomes which never get bigger and generally get smaller – there's more sense of poverty, more crust-wiping, and looking twice at sixpence, than you'd find in any farm-labourer's family, let alone a family like mine. Hilda's often told me that almost the first thing she can remember is a ghastly feeling that there was never enough money for anything.[32]

A man using the pseudonym 'Shabby' wrote about 'family life on £124 a year' (approximately £2 8s a week) in 1919 to the letters column of the *Daily Mail*: 'It seems to have become a settled belief that no one, from the road sweeper upwards, can live on less than £4 a week, plus a bonus. This is fallacious, for how do any of that long-suffering stratum of society, the middle class, manage – men of fair education and some refinement?' The writer said that his own case was 'public school, university scholar and exhibitioner, wife and two boys'. There were, he said, many similar cases;

but 'it is not living, but merely carrying on a desperately grim battle for existence, but it can be done'.[33] Magazines such as *Homes and Gardens* and *Ideal Home* advised their readers to supplement their dwindling incomes with chicken farming and dog breeding.

By the mid-1920s the fortunes of the 'New Poor' had begun to look up. There was a rise in their living standards as prices fell, but life would never be the same. Many of the middle classes were hit again, just as their fortunes recovered, by the General Strike of 1926 and the ensuing economic 'slump' and mass unemployment that lasted from 1929–32, which especially affected the heavy industry regions of northern and western Britain. There began to be a convergence between the living standards of the 'New Poor' and the 'New Rich'. The new municipal and speculatively built houses of the 1920s and 1930s reflected a change in the lifestyle of the upwardly mobile working classes, who were recruited into the ranks of the lower middle classes, towards a more private, home-centred way of life. More people enjoyed middle-class lifestyles, in both a real and an aspirational sense. After 1932 things took a turn for the better for all who were working. The world economic depression meant that for many of the middle classes, more could be bought with less money as prices fell faster than salaries.

Did the act of house purchase mean that homeowners such as the Kinghams made the transition from working to lower middle class? The term 'middle-class' was an amorphous category; class identities were temporal and under constant renegotiation.[34] Class identities were also subject to aspirations and fantasies. For example, magazines and advertisements may have addressed their readers as solidly middle-class employers of servants when many of them were in fact the new lower middle class reading 'up', and trying to negotiate the nuances of their new identities.

The professional housewife and the suburban husband

Ronald and Miriam Kingham moved into their new house at a time when a new commercial culture of homemaking with distinct gender and class identities was emerging. As historian Judy Giles points out, 'the suburban council house and the small semi-detached house became cultural and spatial sites where official discourses of gender and class intersected, as well as providing icons around which women's dreams for a better life circulated and a focus for the articulation and assertion of aspirations'.[35] The suburban husband's counterpart was the professional housewife. The hard work of housework, it was claimed, could be eased only if the home was a labour-saving one, something I consider in more detail in Chapter 4. Miriam would have probably worn an apron (a 'pinny', often decorated with flowers or trimmed with a coloured frill to distinguish her from a servant) or an overall or housedress to conduct her housework, but she would have been expected to hide her labour when the doorbell rang by whipping it off before answering callers (Plates 10 and 11).[36] She would also have been likely to hide her hard work from Ronald when he returned home by removing her work garments and freshening her hair and make-up (which was becoming increasingly acceptable). She could shut the door on the mess left from the preparations of the evening meal, serving it either via a hatch to the dining room or wheeled in on a hostess trolley. The professional housewife was both a fiction and an economic reality.[37]

Life in the new suburbs was liberating for many women who left poor-quality housing and overcrowding behind. Many had only previously dreamed of proper bathrooms and WCs, running hot water, electricity and other modern conveniences. However, some found being uprooted from their community difficult and struggled to make new friends, which led to feelings of isolation and loneliness. Added to this were money worries, as for many it was a constant struggle to make ends meet as the family extended their finances to the hilt to afford a mortgage and hire purchase payments for new furniture. Some lived under the very real threat of having their new house repossessed.[38] Consequently, Dr Stephen Taylor identified 'suburban neurosis' as a problem in lower-middle-class women who moved to the suburbs in a 1938 article published in *The Lancet*, which received widespread attention.[39] Suburban domesticity was represented as stultifying and emasculating by George Bowling, the insurance salesman hero of Orwell's *Coming Up for Air*, who felt trapped by his wife and their two young children in a semi-detached house in the London suburb of West Bletchley.

It is likely, given the family income, that Miriam Kingham was solely responsible for the running of the house without the assistance of domestic service. For both the 'New Poor' and the 'New Rich', the 'servant problem' changed their relation to the home. For women like Miriam, professional housewives who did not undertake paid work outside the home, there are particular problems in defining their class positions. Was Miriam's class defined by her husband's occupation or her father's? Was her father, a shop and office fitter, more respectable than Ronald's father, who was a bricklayer (skilled manual)? Did Ronald's occupation of linoleum layer have more status than his father's or father-in-law's? In 1947 when the Kinghams remortgaged their house, Ronald listed his occupation as 'metal products inspector'.[40] This was an industry that expanded hugely between 1929 and 1938, employing rapidly increasing numbers of salaried staff, and representing a definite rise in Ronald's occupational status and presumably his wages.[41]

The tenants of new municipal estates and new owner-occupiers like the Kinghams contributed to a transition in English culture and national life between the wars where, as Alison Light argues, inward-looking, domestic and private values took on a new national significance.[42] This was symbolised by images of 'pipe smoking "little men" with their quietly competent partners' who became a powerful symbol for a new private, 'feminised' and home-centred Englishness – 'a nation of gardeners and housewives'.[43] This image provided a model for a 'companionate' marriage where couples worked in partnership as homemakers. Such an image was regularly invoked in advertisements by building societies such as the Halifax (Figure 2.3). The National Building Society, from which the Kinghams obtained their mortgage, declared on one of its posters: 'Their happiness can be yours' (Plate 4). It depicted a dreamy painting of a couple in a hollyhock-filled back garden set against a house's rear patio doors. The pretty housewife stands in service to her pipe-smoking husband who is seated in a deckchair, while a little girl and a Scottie dog play at his feet.

The stereotyped, home-loving, suburban husband of the interwar years was also frequently represented sitting in an armchair with his pipe and slippers (Figure 1.8), reading the paper, or pottering around in the garden (Figure 2.3). The shift towards a greater domestication and a more home-centred life were most apparent for lower-middle-class men where there were no domestic servants and children were not away at boarding school.[44] However, women were more likely to be assisted in domestic tasks by their daughters, mothers and sisters, rather than by their husbands. Husbands participated in homemaking through distinctly gendered activities. There were a few magazines such as *The Woodworker* that catered to husbands, but unlike women's magazines they constructed activities as a matter of choice, rather than duty. Indeed, it has been suggested that home improvements did not become a hobby until much later because new houses needed very little maintenance and there was a 'vast pool of willing and cheap labour'.[45]

The building of suburbia

The suburbia to which the Kinghams moved expanded massively in the interwar years when most of the 3,998,000 new houses that were built were located in the suburbs (Plate 9). 2,886,000 of these houses were built by speculative builders, with the remainder built by local authorities for rental.[46] Many of the occupants of these new houses relocated

2.3 Advertisement for Halifax Building Society, from *Daily Mail Ideal Home Exhibition Catalogue 1932*

2.4 A typical 1930s suburban street in Ilford, London, 1936

from inner cities to suburbia. Every major city had housebuilding activity around its perimeter and along its arterial roads (Figure 2.4).

The Edmonton-based builders H. Smith Bros who built the Kinghams' house at 23 Bromley Road also had developments in Golders Green, Kenton, Kingsbury, Loughton, Walthamstow and Westcliff-on-Sea. Their advertising leaflet (Figure 2.1) described their development as 'Huxley Garden Estate', no doubt as a conscious echo of the Garden City movement. They also stressed that the estate was near the Cambridge Arterial Road (now the A10 Great Cambridge Road), to which it ran parallel, presumably in an acknowledgement that many of their purchasers might need to commute to work. The brochure detailed various public transport connections by foot, bus, tram, train and London Underground.

As the transition to home ownership was made in England and Wales in the interwar years, people moved to very different types of houses. From the eighteenth century until the early twentieth century the vast majority of houses were built in rows – terraces – in all sizes and price ranges. Consequently in 1911 only about 3 per cent of all dwellings in England and Wales were flats, and only around 10 per cent were detached or semi-detached. In contrast, in Scotland and the rest of Europe, there were widely spaced detached houses in the outer suburbs and country-side and dense blocks of flats in the inner suburban and urban areas. However, in England and Wales there was widespread distaste for, and distrust of, high block dwellings. In addition, the middle classes refused to live in close proximity to the poorer classes. The latter tended to multi-occupancy dwellings that other classes had left behind, leading to overcrowding.

The legacy of the First World War greatly fuelled the expansion of suburbia. The rise of the munitions industry and the concentration of military personnel produced a dramatic increase in demand for accom-modation. These wants were not met by new housing, which was very limited. A notable exception were the 1300 houses built on Garden City lines for Woolwich Arsenal munitions workers in 1915, renamed the Progress Estate in 1925, which acted as a model for local authority hous-ing after the war.

The desire to improve housing came in part from the government's fear of the prospect of a homegrown version of the 1917 Russian Revolution if the four million demobbed soldiers found their housing condition worse than ever and their rents vastly increased. There were also official concerns about the detrimental effect of poor housing on the health of young men. Wartime recruitment campaigns had found that many men who lived in inner-city slum dwellings were not fit for service. There was also a feeling that the sacrifices made in the war by ordinary men and women should be rewarded by improved housing. Consequently, there was a demand for 'homes fit for heroes'.[47] At the suggestion of the industrialist and social reformer Seebohm Rowntree, Richard L. Reiss was seconded to the Ministry of Reconstruction to work on the problems of post-war reconstruction. Reiss had served in the war but prior to that

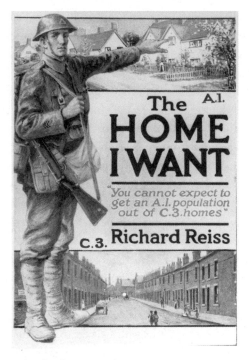

2.5 Front cover of Richard L. Reiss, *The Home I Want*, 1918

had developed an interest in housing conditions from his experiences of social work among the poor in Bermondsey, research on the standards of rural homes for the National Land and Home League, and as chairman of the Housing Committee from 1911.[48] The cover of Reiss's 1918 book *The Home I Want* shows an ordinary soldier pointing to an idyllic suburban vista of Arts and Crafts, cottage-style houses in short rows with leafy, lawned front gardens (Figure 2.5). At his feet lie monotonous rows of city terraces, built directly on to the pavement, without a blade of grass or a leaf in sight. Alongside these contrasting images of housing was a quote from Reiss: 'You cannot expect to get an A.1. population out of C.3. homes.' Reiss became an activist in the New Towns movement from the end of the First World War and was made chairman of the Garden Cities and Town Planning Association in 1918. He went on to work for Ebenezer Howard's Garden City Company and was one of the founders of Welwyn Garden City.[49]

Garden City principles influenced the development of speculatively built developments such as the Huxley Garden Estate where the Kinghams lived. They also became enshrined in the legislation that defined post-war social housing. The government in 1917 commissioned the Tudor Walters Report into municipal housing. The report set standards for local authority housing, the provision of which was prescribed by the Addison (1919), Chamberlain (1923) and Wheatley (1924) Housing Acts. The Tudor Walters Report was the first comprehensive treatise on public housing design that stressed quality as well as quantity. The report demanded low densities on Garden City lines of no more than twelve 'cottage'-style houses an acre, built in short terraced or semi-detached formations with wide frontages to maximise daylight, and enhanced by front and rear gardens. The Liberal government was returned to power in the election of December 1918 with a pledge to construct 500,000 new houses in three years, which were to be let by local authority landlords at subsidised rents.

Some of those who could not afford home ownership benefited from the housebuilding programme that local authorities embarked on in the 1920s. The Addison Act allowed London County Council to build outside the county of London, and between 1921 and 1935 it constructed the Becontree Estate, covering four square miles in the parishes of Barking, Dagenham and Ilford in Essex (Figure 2.6). The architects employed by local authorities interpreted the principle of 'fitness for purpose' through a simplified neo-Georgian style that fulfilled the quest for a 'justified' architecture with order and consistency, and signified public collectivity and community. Influenced by the ideals of the Garden City movement, which in turn drew on the Arts and Crafts movement, they built 'cottage' estates, often arranged in cul-de-sacs and closes around open spaces that

2.6 New houses being built in Becontree, London Borough of Barking and Dagenham, 1924

imitated traditional, rural village, non-planned forms of layout around green spaces. By the outbreak of the Second World War, local authorities had built 1,112,000 houses for rent, meaning that they owned 10 per cent of Britain's housing stock.[50]

Local authority houses were only affordable to the better-paid working classes with regular wages. Many people continued to live in extremely poor slum conditions throughout the interwar period, in both urban and rural areas that were not much different to those described by the feminist and socialist Maud Pember Reeves in her 1913 study *Round About a Pound a Week*. For example, families in Dupont Street in Limehouse in London in 1925 lived in houses with their roofs temporarily covered to keep out rain and with unglazed windows (Figure 2.7). In 1939 Margery Spring Rice published *Working Class Wives: Their Health and Conditions*, an account of interwar poverty and poor housing, which showed that for many very little had changed.[51]

Housing problems were exacerbated by massive inflation when the war ended in November 1918. Retail prices were 225 per cent higher

2.7 Slum houses, Dupont Street, Limehouse, London, 1925

than they had been in 1914. With acute housing shortages, some took matters into their own hands and created temporary makeshift dwellings. The entrepreneur Charles Neville established Peacehaven in East Sussex, originally known as Anzac-on-Sea, for First World War veterans in 1916 as a Garden City by the sea.[52] The 'plotlands' movement went a step further.[53] Residents mainly consisted of working-class city dwellers who built makeshift homes for themselves out of whatever was available to them, such as railways carriages and former army huts, on small plots of land. Their plots were sold to them by railway companies and developers, often created out of former farmland, purchased from farmers who had gone bankrupt because of cheap imports. For example, Jaywick Sands in Essex was created by Frank Stedman, a surveyor, who bought several hundred acres of reclaimed marshlands in 1928. Unable to put in proper drains, he sold off the site for holiday chalets and beach huts, with plots twenty feet wide by thirty feet deep going for £30 in the 1930s. Originally intended for weekends and holidays and usually lacking electricity or running water and accessed via unmade roads, many dwellings gradually became permanent, with residents expanding them as their families grew. Many plotlands developed a strong sense of community. Some were even envisaged as more radical utopian experiments with communal living.[54] Eventually councils put in services such as water and electricity and dwellings were constructed out of more permanent materials. Most took the form of bungalows, and their unplanned structure and siting contributed to the antipathy towards this housing type on the part of architects and reformers, such as Clough Williams-Ellis. In his *England and the Octopus* (1928) he condemned 'greedy little sneak-builders', along with speculative builders.[55]

For homeowners like the Kinghams, the interwar years witnessed an important shift in the tenure of property away from renting. Most houses, both those for rent and those for sale, were, and still are, built by speculative builders without a particular purchaser in mind. Under this system, the builder bought (freehold) or leased (leasehold) plots of land from landowners. The Tudor Walters Report forced speculative builders to raise their standards and differentiate their houses from those built by local authorities. This meant that the 'ideal home' of the interwar years was partially defined by government legislation that had been intended for working-class rented housing. This set the agenda for housing in general and filtered *upwards*. The layout and the semi-detached form of Tudor Walters architecture, if not its style, was adapted to the needs of both the established middle classes who had smaller families and no longer employed live-in servants, and also the better-off working classes and new lower middle classes like the Kinghams, who needed more affordable, smaller houses.

The small to medium-sized, speculatively built, owner-occupied, single-family house like that the Kinghams purchased in Edmonton evolved in the interwar years as a distinctive type. Such houses tended to be planned around the central core of hall and staircase and were lighter and airier than their Edwardian predecessors. Most had a reasonably sized back garden, accessible from the house, with more room for sheds, garages and greenhouses. The exterior, which could be terraced like the Kinghams' (often in short rows), semi-detached or narrowly detached, tried to mark out individual houses and there was scope for individuality in its decoration. Modern building techniques were used to create a diversity of styles and adornments. Newly built, owner-occupied, interwar suburban houses had piped water, most were wired for mains electricity, and many had gas.[56]

Like many new interwar houses, the exterior of the Kinghams' new house in Edmonton was designed in the Tudorbethan style, a popular suburban style that I discuss in more detail in Chapter 5. The interior had all modern conveniences, including electricity to power lighting and small appliances such as irons and toasters, gas and hot water. The 'kitchenette' came complete with a kitchen cabinet and the bathroom had a 'modern enclosed bath'. The house followed the common interwar plan of two reception rooms and a kitchenette downstairs, with a bathroom upstairs (with separate WC and an additional WC downstairs) and three upstairs bedrooms, the third of which was only big enough to accommodate a single bed. It had 'electric light fittings. Complete to pendants' and a brick coal shed. The purchase price also included 'decorations to choice'.[57]

The layout of the Kinghams' house, preferably built in semi-detached pairs, became standard. Speculative builders built at lower densities of eight to ten houses per acre, aided by cheap land beyond urban boundaries and taking advantage of new transport links. As with the Kinghams' house, many speculative builders differentiated their private housing from that provided by local authorities through decorative details to the façades. Most adopted a Tudorbethan or other historic style in contrast to the neo-Georgian Arts and Crafts 'cottage' style of municipal houses. Occasionally they built in Modernistic 'Suntrap' styles, with curved façades, Crittall metal windows divided into small rectangular panes and

2.8 Promotional leaflet for Wates, '15 lovely estates', c. 1930s

roofs with green pantiles or, very rarely, flat roofs. It was common for builders such as Wates to flit between a variety of styles, as can be seen in their brochure advertising '15 lovely estates' (Figure 2.8).

Some developers even tried the spatial segregation of private estates from municipal ones by the use of walls. For example, in 1934 Clive

2.9 Cutteslowe walls photographed from an adjacent house, Oxford, 1934

Saxton of the Urban Housing Company built what became known as the 'Cutteslowe walls' (Figure 2.9) to divide his new private estate in Oxford intended for owner-occupation from the city council's Cutteslowe estate of rented housing, fearing that prospective purchasers would be put off by the proximity of what he termed 'slum dwellers'. The walls he built were over two metres high and topped with lethal spikes. The city council demolished the walls in 1938 but was forced to rebuild them, only finally demolishing them in 1959.[58]

The six years from 1933 to 1938 account for well over half of all privately built houses in the interwar period, when more than 350,000 houses were completed each year.[59] In this building boom most builders concentrated on the lower end of the market. Builders produced very small houses like the Colletts' 17 Rosamund Road and the Kinghams' 23

Bromley Road, well below minimum Tudor Walters space standards, to bring home ownership within the reach of working-class purchasers. Many were built in monotonous strip layouts beside trunk roads (Figure 2.4), abandoning Garden City ideals of short rows and cul-de-sacs arranged in landscaped green space. Some builders built terraces rather than semi-detached houses to reduce frontages, omitted the front parlour and put the bathroom downstairs or even omitted it altogether, requiring the use of a portable bath in the kitchen, to cut costs. A few builders cut standards to make houses more affordable and there was widespread concern about 'jerrybuilding' or poor building techniques, which left many new homeowners with bills for repairs. This resulted in a much-reported case when Elsy Borders, the wife of a London taxi driver, took legal action against the developers Morrells and the Bradford Third Equitable Building Society regarding her house on the Coney Hall Estate, West Wickham, Kent, which had developed serious faults.[60]

Home ownership

Before they bought the house in Bromley Road, the Kinghams were resident at 22 South Road, a small, Victorian, terraced house in Lower Edmonton, which they almost certainly rented.[61] The house was part of the older Huxley Estate, developed between the late 1800s and early 1900s. Ronald's parents lived next door at number 24 and he had lived with them there before his marriage. This was quite a step up in respectability for Ronald's father from the Marylebone workhouse.

In 1914, 90 per cent of the housing stock was rented out by private landlords and less than 1 per cent of Britain's housing stock was municipally owned.[62] By 1932, 21 per cent of the population owned their own homes, more than double the number who were owner-occupiers before the First World War. For the vast majority of people, the largest single fixed charge in their weekly budget was rent. The majority of housing was rented out by private landlords who might own one or two houses or several hundred. Houses were owned by builders and speculators, as well as small shopkeepers and traders. Conditions of letting varied: the middle classes tended to pay their rent quarterly or half-yearly; the working classes every week. Many of the latter had little security; some were subject to eviction at only a week's notice. Lots of them lived in poor, overcrowded conditions.[63]

A great strain was placed on the private rented sector during the First World War. Rents soared and there were widespread evictions and growing unrest. The government passed the Increase of Rent and Mortgage (War Restrictions) Act in 1915, which forced landlords to freeze their rents, and building societies their interest rates, at the figures current at the outbreak of the war. This important piece of legislation ultimately created the owner-occupier housing market. The rents of millions of existing dwellings remained frozen at 1914 rates and landlords began to see their assets as liabilities. An estimated 1.1 million privately rented houses were sold to owner-occupiers in the interwar period, most of them during the 1920s. Most of these were older terraced properties without modern amenities such as bathrooms and other utilities, and many were in a poor state of repair. This brought them within the reach of those who could not have afforded a new, modern house.[64] For the middle classes who lived outside cities, tasteful conversions of dilapidated cottages became popular in the 1920s (Figure 2.10). *Ideal Home* and *Homes and Gardens* magazines often featured photographs of those owned by 'real', often famous, people.[65]

Property values changed sharply in line with general movements in costs and prices. Immediately after the First World War property was expensive due to pent-up demand combined with scarcities of materials and general inflation. Prices fell from the summer of 1920, reducing the average cost of a small, three-bedroom, non-parlour house from £930 to £436 by 1922. The rate of building climbed steadily from 1923 onwards, apart from temporary setbacks in 1927–28, and prices continued their downward drift. This was aided by general deflation and a decrease in

2.10 Mill Cottage, Mill Corner, Northiam, East Sussex, 1921

building costs, aided by the standardisation of building parts, labour-saving techniques and the use of cheap, unskilled, non-apprenticed labour on piecework. Prices usually depended upon the social status of the suburb, the plot size, especially the frontage, and the number and size of rooms. By the late 1920s a 'standard' two-reception, three-bedroom semi in Greater London cost between £600 and £850. House prices peaked in 1931 and then fell for the rest of the decade. By 1932, three-bedroom, two-reception semis could be found in the Home Counties for as little as £395 freehold and £295 leasehold. Bungalows were often even more affordable, which led to concerns about unplanned 'bungaloid growth', a term coined by the clergyman and journalist Dean W.R. Inge in 1927.[66]

In the late 1930s semi-detached houses in Greater London were available from £400 – about twice the annual salary of an average professional

man – and were concentrated between £550 and about £750.[67] At the
top end, £1,500 would buy a large, semi-detached home in a fashionable
London suburb. It is more difficult to arrive at an estimate for 'provin-
cial' towns because the term encompasses such a wide area. Analysis in
The Economist put the 'datum value' at £400 to £500 for new houses.[68]
In the Midlands a small, semi-detached bungalow could cost as little as
£250. As John Burnett said, 'Low interest rates, low material costs and
low wages [in the building industry] were combining to bring about a
housing revolution which profoundly affected the lives of millions of
people.'[69]

As well as benefiting from the lower cost of houses, couples like the
Kinghams were able to choose from a growing range of mortgages and
lending institutions. In the first two decades of the twentieth century
mortgages generally required a 25 per cent deposit, which generally
restricted home ownership to managers and the professional classes,
although there were regional variations. In the first decade of the twentieth century in the Midlands and the north of England, some of the
better-paid artisans were homeowners and secured mortgages from
Permanent Building Societies. Owner-occupation in England and Wales
rose to 21 per cent in 1929 and 32 per cent in 1939, a more than threefold
increase since the outbreak of the First World War.[70]

Such levels of home ownership would not have become so widespread
without building societies, which in the second half of the 1930s made
mortgages available on 'easy' terms with an average interest rate of 4.5
per cent. Thus, repayments came within reach of most of the middle
classes and a significant proportion of the better-off working classes.
Indeed, the creation of a mass market for home ownership in the twentieth century depended upon the expansion of building societies which,
although well known since their origins in the 1830s, had generally been
small-scale, local and little developed.

Modern building societies have their origins in the late eighteenth
century when groups of relatively well-paid building artisans got together

and built houses for themselves. These informal groups evolved into the organised building clubs of the Victorian era, which consisted of groups of working men who pooled their capital and labour to build themselves houses. Each man's turn was allocated by a ballot. These early building societies were technically 'terminating' societies, wound up when every member was satisfied. They could be found in towns where there was a strong history of Friendly Societies and other mutual associations, such as Birmingham, Wolverhampton, Leeds and the Potteries. Such building clubs enabled a small group of working men the opportunity to become homeowners, bringing with it respectability, independence and even the vote.

By the 1840s, Permanent Building Societies had developed in towns throughout Britain. They did not usually actually build any houses, but instead paid a dividend on shareholders' investments and made loans available to those wishing to buy a house on a mortgage, although only artisans with secure jobs could afford repayments. These permanent societies became an important route to home ownership for a minority of working people in manufacturing and mining districts in the north and the Midlands in the late nineteenth century. By 1910 there were 1,723 societies, which advanced £9,292,000 on mortgages at interest rates of about 4.5 per cent. The total balance due on all mortgages was £59,696,000. This figure grew rapidly in the interwar years: £137,000,000 was advanced in 1938 alone, nearly a 15-fold increase. Cheaper house prices and lower interest rates in the 1930s extended the possibility of a mortgage from white-collar salaried occupations to at least some higher-paid manual workers. For example, 37 per cent of the members of the Abbey Road Society were wage earners.

The critical questions for borrowers like the Kinghams were, as now, the amount of the deposit and the monthly payments required, which varied with the cost of the house and the state of the credit market. Societies worked on the general principle that outgoings, including local rates, should not exceed a quarter of net income, which meant, in the

1920s, that a minimum salary of £4 a week would allow repayments of 15s a week upwards on a modest house. Average repayments were £1 to £1 10s a week. Societies did, of course, need to be assured of a regular income in a period of mass unemployment. In 1923 legislation allowed local authorities to lend up to 90 per cent for the purchase of houses valued up to £1,500.[71]

The major difficulty for lower-income house buyers like the Kinghams was often the deposit rather than the repayments. They were helped by the Builders' Pool system whereby the builder advanced cash to the society to make up the difference between the mortgage and the valuation, which limited the purchasers' deposit to 5 per cent or even less. Reducing deposits to as little as £30 or even £25 opened up the possibilities of home ownership to working-class buyers. Sometimes the deposit could be omitted altogether by using life assurance policies or occupational pension schemes as security. Legal charges were often covered by slightly increased repayments. Building societies also extended mortgage periods from twenty to twenty-five or even thirty years, which bought repayments down.

The Kinghams paid a purchase price of £699 freehold for 23 Bromley Road. They had a deposit of £50, which it may be assumed they had saved up during their four years of marriage. The builder's advertisement was keen to stress that there were no extras such as road duties, stamp duties, legal costs or survey fees. It also helpfully set out the repayment fees of 21 shillings a week over twenty years and the rates of 6s 5d for the half-year; electricity at 4d a week for lighting, gas at 8s 6d per therm and water supplied by the Metropolitan Water Board at an unspecified price.[72] Ronald obtained a mortgage for £649 from the National Building Society and made monthly repayments of £4 10s.[73] Building societies, which had previously required a 24 per cent deposit, offered 95 per cent mortgages at rates as low as 4.5 per cent by 1934. On 27 November 1935 Ronald was informed that the interest rate would be reduced to a rate varying from time to time, always 0.5 per cent above the Bank Rate but not falling below £550 per annum, and that his monthly instalments would be reduced to £4 8s 10d.[74]

New houses have never been so cheap or so widely available as in the mid-1930s when the length of time that a man earning the average industrial wage would have to work to buy one was two and a half years. A regular salary or wage of £200 a year was enough to secure a mortgage which might involve repayments of as little as 9s a week, well within the reach of engineers, fitters, printers, engine-drivers and other paid workers. Generally, in the 1930s, earnings of £1 a week bought the standard, three-bedroom £650 house, while earnings of £300 to £500 a year (teachers, bank officials, executive-class civil servants and lower-paid professionals) would comfortably buy substantial semis or even detached houses of £1,000 or more. Deposits became as low as £25 towards the end of the 1930s. For example, one London company offered houses for £800 on a payment of 25 per cent deposit with all legal expenses paid by the builder.

The Kinghams' move to home ownership was encouraged not only as a financial opportunity but as an emotional and social advance. The advertising and promotional literature for building societies, speculative builders and estate agents all presented images of 'ideal homes' (Plate 9). They advertised heavily in national and local newspapers, sometimes in special property pull-out supplements, and on billboards. It was common for them to depict large detached houses in advertisements that were aimed at audiences that could only have afforded a modest semi. Building societies went to great lengths to persuade the British to become a nation of homeowners in the interwar years.[75] A series of advertisements placed in the catalogues of the Ideal Home Exhibition by the Halifax Building Society exemplify this. In 1926 its advertisement was headlined 'The Ideal Home is not rented' and declared: 'Rent is wasteful. Home ownership is the true solution for the person who looks to secure an Ideal Home that will be a refuge of strength – come what may … The borrower is his own landlord from the very outset; enjoying the full and unrestricted benefits of ownership.'[76] As renting was previously widespread among all social classes, building societies had to make a case for the desirability of home ownership. The copy in this advertisement played on people's insecurities, particularly those of the aspirational lower middle classes, in the year which saw the General Strike. It offered the allure of independence, with a free booklet entitled *How to become your own Landlord*.

Within a space of only four years, the same building society was able to place an advertisement that reflected a growing confidence in home ownership, declaring 'We loan – You own'.[77] The Halifax offered 75–95 per cent mortgages and stated that in the previous year alone it had lent over £12 million 'to assist Borrowers to purchase Homes of their own'. This phrase was important, as it implied that a rented house could not be a home of your own. This also sought to reassure new working-class mortgage applicants who had been traditionally fearful of debt.

Home ownership was rapidly humanised in the advertisements of the 1930s which used documentary-style, though heavily posed, photographs of happy and fulfilled suburbanites in front of their dream homes. For example, in 1932, the year the Kinghams moved into their new home, a couple were captured with their lawnmower in front of their detached, Georgian, cottage-style home, declaring 'We bought our house through the Halifax Building Society' (Figure 2.3). This was an aspirational image, given the size and grandeur of the house. Building societies also sought to reassure those who might not have encountered middle-class professionals before. For example, an advertisement in 1933 sought to reassure those nervously entering the home-buying process for the first time by depicting a young couple accompanied by an authoritative-looking man with a clipboard pointing out a detail of a house in a street of suburban semis. Significantly, the male half of the couple accompanied the professional man outside the house, while the woman is shown in the interior looking out. More reassurance was provided by the slogan 'Homebuying is cheaper through the Halifax'.[78]

Prospective purchasers were able to visit builders' own fully furnished show homes, which allowed them to project themselves into the space. Mindful that many did not own cars and that public transport links were sometimes still under construction, builders often provided a complimentary chauffeur-driven car for a first visit. Some builders even built show homes at central locations near workplaces. For example, in 1934 Davis Estates had a show house at Charing Cross station and Laings had one at Kings Cross station.[79] Builders also displayed show houses at exhibitions, the best known of which was the annual Daily Mail Ideal Home Exhibition, which was founded in 1908, and had a number of regional offshoots in cities such as Birmingham. Other exhibitions included the North London Exhibition and the New Homes Exhibition in Oxford Street, which displayed four show houses.[80] Visiting hours for show houses in all these different locations often encompassed evenings and Sundays, which gave them the feeling of a leisure activity.

Given this aspirational marketing, it is not surprising that the families of lower-paid professionals and better-paid manual workers, now able to qualify for a mortgage, wished to move from their small, rented, terraced house, or in cities two or three rented rooms, to a suburban house all of their own. These inhabitants of the new suburbia became 'suburban', a term that was very loaded, especially when applied to questions of architecture, design, style and taste.

The parlour, the mantelpiece and the napkin ring

One space within the home that became a popular touchstone for new suburban identities was the parlour (Figure 1.5). The Kinghams were likely to have used their front reception room as a parlour. In contrast to their rear living room where meals were taken and day-to-day living was done, the parlour was where 'good' furniture and furnishings and precious ornaments were displayed. Visitors could be received here; births and marriages celebrated and deaths could be mourned. A piano, a gramophone or a wireless set (Figure 1.6) could provide entertainment. It was also a quiet space where Miriam could escape her domestic duties, for example by reading a book. For many families, the parlour was a quiet space where children could do homework.

Parlours were not just desired by homeowners. A report by the Women's Housing Sub-Committee of the Ministry of Reconstruction in 1919 demanded that houses should include a parlour.[81] This came out of their consultation with 'ordinary' women who demanded a parlour for 'best' as the respectable public face of their homes and as a status symbol. This proved controversial, as many politicians, architects and reformers thought the parlour was snobbish and pretentious, and a waste of space.[82]

Some householders prioritised the furnishing of the parlour as the public face of the house that denoted respectability. The display of appropriate material goods was used to symbolise status. The piano had long been a prized possession; this was joined or superseded by the gramophone and the wireless. The cocktail cabinet became popular, which as Judy Attfield argues, was not so much for its actual use but for the symbolic possibilities it represented of a glamorous lifestyle. Indeed, the cocktail cabinet became a substitute for the parlour; a microcosm in furniture form.[83]

These concerns with display and respectability might explain the reason why the occupants of new houses, both as tenants and owners, hung on to the concept of the parlour as a room kept for 'best' in which visitors were entertained. Builders responded to this desire by squeezing two reception rooms into the smallest of houses, even if it meant locating the kitchenette in a minute, lean-to extension at the rear of the house. This infuriated feminist and design reformers who rationalised that the parlour was a waste of space.

The parlour was, first and foremost, a space for display, where things saved 'for best' were kept in cabinets, on sideboards and on mantelpieces. An insight into the latter is given in Mass Observation's 1937 directive on mantelpieces, which asked participants to '[w]rite down in order from left to right, all the objects on your mantelpiece, mentioning what is in the middle'. They also asked people to make lists for mantelpieces in other people's houses, noting details such as age, 'whether they are old middle-aged or young, whether they are well-off or otherwise' and 'what class (roughly) they belong to'.[84] In total, the directive elicited 158 individual reports about mantelpieces in people's own houses and, in most cases, those of other people as well. Some reports were accompanied by drawings but, despite an explicit request, only one by a photograph, which will be discussed in Chapter 4.

The mantelpieces in Mass Observation's 1937 survey commonly displayed ornaments, family photographs and a mantel clock, with a mirror hanging above it. Ornaments comprised examples such as 'Old English' Toby and character jugs, shepherdesses and crinoline ladies, objects associated with fire lighting and the accoutrements of smoking such as pipes (Plate 20). Objects such as ebony elephants brought memories of the British Empire, which will be discussed in Chapter 5. Mantelpieces not only had consciously placed displays of paired objects such as vases and a central clock, but also the clutter of everyday life. It was an important site for the display of objects pertaining to people's identities and memories.[85] The Mass Observation survey revealed that some mantelpiece displays may have been consciously curated, but others acted as an informal and rather messy filing cabinet of lives lived.

One object that cropped up frequently in the Mass Observation mantelpiece survey was the napkin ring. Available in a variety of materials and forms including ivory (real or imitation), silver (solid to electroplated) engraved with initials, wood, coloured Bakelite animals and Carltonware in the form of crinoline ladies, the napkin ring was as much a decorative and symbolic item as a functional object. The writer Roy Lewis and the journalist Angus Maude threw light on the meaning of the napkin ring in their 1949 book on the English middle classes:

Before the war, when textile supplies and laundry facilities were more ample, it might perhaps have been held that the middle classes were composed of all those who used napkin rings (on the grounds that the working class did not use table napkins at all, while members of the upper class used a clean napkin at every meal) and that the dividing line between the upper-middle and lower-middle classes was at the point at which a napkin became a serviette.[86]

Their point may be intentionally satirical, but it neatly throws a spotlight on the minutiae of design and material culture as signifiers of class and taste.

The difference between the serviette and the napkin was also explained by Nancy Mitford, who in 1954, inspired by the linguist Alan S.C. Ross who had coined the terms 'U' and 'Non-U' to describe differences in the usage of language by the upper classes, published a glossary of terms. Mitford's pairings of 'Non-U' and 'U' included toilet/lavatory or loo; lounge or drawing room; settee or couch/sofa; mirror or looking glass; mantelpiece or chimneypiece; and serviette or napkin. It is especially notable that many of Mitford's pairings concern words associated with the home, which reinforces my argument that many people became middle class via owner-occupation between the wars. I do not know what the Kinghams' household interior actually looked like; however, they almost certainly would have had a mantelpiece on which they displayed their new suburban identities, including – perhaps – napkin rings.

'Suburban'

Cultural critics and novelists in the interwar years despised the world of 'The Suburbs and the Clerks', labelling their aspirational values as trivial and gendering them feminine.[87] Suburbia was associated with a particular kind of feminised modernity that embraced the trappings of mass culture, such as magazines, cosmetics and cinema.[88] According to D.H. Lawrence, women's consumer desires trapped men in suburbia's 'horrid red rat-traps'.[89] Women in particular were identified with mass culture, as 'modernism's other'.[90] Moreover, many intellectuals saw suburbia as emasculated; to them, 'suburban' was a derogatory and disparaging term, albeit with a shifting meaning.

For the architectural historian and critic Harry Joseph Birnstingl, the lower middle classes and their homes were inherently vulgar. His short book entitled *Lares et Penates* (loosely translated as 'household gods') *or The Home of the Future* was published in Kegan Paul's To-day and To-morrow series in 1928.[91] In it Birnstingl said:

> Between the upper and nether millstone lies the vast and variegated range of lower-middle class houses and they have, for the most part, one characteristic in common. It is their vulgarity; utterly devoid of taste in their outward appearance and their inward furnishings, and in the very names that are inscribed in distorted letters upon their gate rails, they reflect from ridge to foundation this besetting characteristic of the present age.[92]

His description invokes suburbia as well as the masses. As the literary critic John Carey has pointed out:

> Like 'masses', the word 'suburban' is a sign for the unknowable. But 'suburban' is distinctive in combining topographical with intellectual disdain. It relates human worth to habitat. The history of the word shows how a development in human geography that caused widespread dismay came to dictate the intellectuals' reading of twentieth-century culture.[93]

Indeed, as Carey, together with the architectural historian Julian Holder[94] and others have shown, designers, architects and writers of the Modern Movement, together with the English intelligentsia on both the left and right, shared a contempt for what was, in the historian Alison Light's words, 'the only truly modern form of life in the 1930s [...] the suburban semi and the bungalow'.[95]

Defences of suburban architecture were rare in the twentieth century. The champion of architectural Modernism and editor of *The Architectural Review*, J.M. Richards, shocked his contemporaries with his 1946 book, *The Castles on the Ground*. With its affectionate account of suburbia and its inhabitants, this book seems to go against all of Richards' previous principles. It is significant that he wrote the book while abroad, mainly in Cairo, which made him nostalgic for the English suburbs.[96] Richards' account of suburbia was more tolerant than John Betjeman's account of Metroland, which defended Victorian villadom and its residents against the horrors of interwar spec-builders and migrating clerks.[97]

Despite, or indeed because of, its undoubted popular appeal, cultural commentators then and now have denigrated and mocked interwar suburbia. Many have felt uncomfortable with its reflection of consumer aspirations for goods and lifestyles that they have thought of as frivolous and empty; by the display of what the historian Carolyn Steedman calls a 'proper envy'.[98] Yet the history of suburbia is the history of the hopes, dreams and aspirations of the respectable working classes and lower middle classes, of what Valerie Walkerdine calls 'conservative, and respectable ordinariness'.[99] Cultural critics, particularly those on the left, have felt uncomfortable with such desires, seeing them as a betrayal of working-class communities and cultures.[100] The term 'suburban' became an insult, and when applied as an adjective to architecture and design it was very negative indeed.

Conclusion

Interwar, speculatively built suburban housing reflected a change in lifestyle of the upwardly mobile working classes like the Kinghams who entered the ranks of the lower middle classes and began to experience a more private, home-centred way of life. The idea and experience of the 'servant problem' substantially changed the relationship of the established middle classes to the home.

The 1930s were the most favourable period for house purchase in the twentieth century. Builders and building societies, aided by deflation and other favourable economic conditions, not only brought home ownership within the reach of new lower-middle-class and working-class households but also persuaded them of its desirability as an indicator of respectability and status. It is perhaps paradoxical, given that this was also a time of high unemployment, hunger marches and strikes, that for many of the middle classes in the interwar years, life was better than it had ever been, with higher real wages, a lower cost of living (which decreased the price of food and manufactured goods) and increased leisure time to enjoy cinema and radio. This enabled new levels of consumption of goods, upon the production of which Britain's industrial growth was based. Furthermore, the economic climate varied geographically: while depression was concentrated in the old industrial areas, the new suburbs boomed in the south. It became possible for the average salaried person to buy a house on a mortgage and afford consumer durables that would have been quite unthinkable twenty years before.[101]

This chapter has considered how the shifting consumer acquisitions and aspirations of home ownership, design, decoration and taste marked out social identity. 'Suburban' was a loaded term in interwar England. While the majority of critics denigrated and deplored it, for men and women like the Kinghams it offered a new opportunity to make a modern 'ideal home'. Was entering into home ownership enough for the Kinghams to become middle class? It is perhaps not surprising that Nancy Mitford distinguished between 'home' and 'house' in her essay on aristocratic speech which defined upper-class and non-upper-class terms. 'Home' in the example 'They have [got] a very nice home' was 'Non-U', as opposed to 'U': 'They've a very nice house.'

3

Modernisms: 'good design' and 'bad design'

Osbert Lancaster, cartoonist and satirist of the suburbs, provided rich examples of two very different 'modern' tendencies in the design of the interwar home: the 'Functional' and the 'Modernistic'. These images appeared in his *Homes Sweet Homes* (1939), a satirical look into the history of the interior of the British house.[1]

In 'Functional' (Figure 3.1) a weedy, pipe-smoking, intellectual man in a scratchy tweed jacket, book in hand, is depicted all alone, perched uncomfortably on a stool by Finnish Modernist designer Alvar Aalto. The room is furnished with angular bookcases, a bent ply chair and table, and a geometric wireless. It is lit by industrial lighting and heated by a flush, wall-mounted gas or electric fire, which does not appear to be lit. Lancaster commented:

> the cactus sprouts where once flourished the aspidistra and the rubber-plant, the little bronze from Benin grimaces where smiled the shepherdess from Dresden, and in the place of honour formerly occupied by the kindly Labradors of Sir Edwin Landseer there now prance the tireless horses of Monsieur Chirico.[2]

The view through the large picture window reveals a sun terrace with tubular metal Bauhaus-style furniture drowning in pouring rain – a comment on the inappropriateness of the Modern Movement to the

3.1 Illustration of 'Functional' by Osbert Lancaster, from *Homes Sweet Homes*, 1939

British climate. Lancaster dubbed this type of householder one of the 'new Puritans' and explained that they were influenced by the doctrines of Walter Gropius, Le Corbusier and Louis Mumford. He said, 'The open plan, the mass-produced steel and plywood furniture, the uncompromising display of all the structural elements, are all in theory perfectly logical, but in the home logic has always been at a discount.'[3]

By contrast, in 'Modernistic' (Figure 3.2) Lancaster depicted a voluptuous woman sitting in a comfortable lounge. There are many obvious points of comparison with the 'Functional' room; every angular detail has a sensuous curved equivalent in the 'Modernistic' room. Thus the woman sits on a generously upholstered sofa with jazz modern cushions, facing a blazing log fire with a rounded surround, facing another chair,

3.2 Illustration of 'Modernistic' by Osbert Lancaster, from *Homes Sweet Homes*, 1939

accompanied by a fashionable Pekinese dog and a cat adorned with a bow. At her side on a low, round table is a novelty cigarette lighter and ashtray and an open box of chocolates, and the gramophone, styled with a sunburst, appears to be playing. There are no books. The room is decorated with a jazzy border and at the window, shutting out the outside world, are heavy draped curtains, reminiscent of an Odeon cinema. Modernistic knick-knacks adorn the room, including a begging dog, a reclining nude female and a square mantel clock. The room is softly lit by a standard lamp and decorative wall lights. Lancaster described the Modernistic as 'a nightmare amalgam of a variety of elements derived from several sources'.[4] This included the 'Jazz style' that was the fruit of a fearful union between the flashier side of the Ballet Russes and a hopelessly vulgarized version of Cubism. To this were added elements derived from the *style colonial* popularized by the Paris Exhibition of 1927, such as an all too generous use of the obscure and most hideous woods and a half-hearted simplicity that derived from a complete misunderstanding of the ideals of the Corbusier-Gropius school of architects and found uneasy expression in unvarnished wood and chromium plate, relentlessly misapplied.[5]

According to critics like Lancaster, Functionalism and the Modern Movement were watered down, or 'bastardised', and combined with elements from the 'Moderne' to make the 'Modernistic'.

Lancaster satirised the fact that the influence of Modernism in architecture and design was limited in the average interwar English semi, much to the chagrin of designers, architects and design reformers, who despaired of its 'bad design'. The ideas of the Modern Movement in architecture and design were promulgated by design reform organisations such as the Design and Industries Association (DIA) and an influx of European émigré architects and designers in Britain. However, Lancaster's cartoons suggested that the influence and appeal of Modernism was limited due to what he and other critics perceived as the conservatism of the builders who catered to suburbia and those who lived there.

Yet despite the apparent rejection of the 'good design' of Modernism, the residents of interwar suburbia were intensely interested in creating a 'modern' home. They were influenced by a plethora of advice in women's and homemaking magazines, displays in furniture stores and events such as the Ideal Home Exhibition. What did first-time homeowners think of as 'modern' design in their homes? Just what lengths did they go to be modern? In this chapter I seek to answer such questions by revealing interwar owner-occupiers as discriminating consumers actively engaged in the formation of suburban Modernism in the decoration and furnishing of their homes.

Suburban modernity and Modernism

'Modernity' is a very difficult word to define and periodise satisfactorily, particularly when it is used imprecisely and interchangeably with 'Modernism'.[6] However, in this book I want to retain definite distinctions between the two. I consider modernity as a condition or experience, while I consider Modernism – with a capital 'M' – as an aesthetic practice in 'design' in its broadest sense.

Modernity is a useful concept that encapsulates the social, cultural and material changes that occurred in the late nineteenth and early twentieth centuries in the Western world. Indeed, the idea of constant and accelerated change is central to its definition. Art historians and others have tended to draw on Baudelaire's description of modernity in his 1863 essay 'The Painter of Modern Life', where he used the term *modernité* to mean not just the present, but a particular attitude towards the present and its difference from the past.[7]

Certainly, at the turn of the twentieth century there was a real sense of living in a new epoch, in a peculiarly modern time that, as the historian Jose Harris has pointed out, was 'essentially a mental construct rather than an objective, external measuring rod'.[8] Marshall Berman has described the way in which modernity is a condition where everything is in a constant state of flux; when, in Marx's words, 'all that is solid melts into air'.[9] The processes of modernisation brought about conditions and experiences of modernity that gave the sense, in material ways, of living in a new world that had broken with the past as never before. Among the numerous social, political and cultural changes that illustrate this point are the explosion of scientific knowledge and the development of new technologies, enabling new modes of production and consumption that resulted in new forms of work. In pursuit of new work, populations moved from rural to urban centres and consequently cities and their suburbs grew enormously. Massive imperial expansion resulted in European values and organisational structures being imposed on other cultures. Developments in transport and communications made possible movement within cities and the wider shores of Empire. The enfranchisement of the wider population created not only new definitions of citizenship, but also gender and class conflicts. Increased education and literacy also enabled more active citizenship (and provided a market for the newspaper of the British suburban middle classes, the *Daily Mail*, which was launched in 1896) and expanded the horizons of work for many.

Consequently, in the interwar years the general public in England were exposed to modernity and modern design in their homes, workplaces and their leisure activities, including shopping and the cinema. The novelist, playwright, critic and broadcaster J.B. Priestley neatly evoked the landscape of interwar modernity:

> The England of arterial and by-pass roads, of filling stations and factories that look like exhibition buildings, of giant cinemas and dance-halls and cafes, bungalows with tiny garages, cocktail bars, Woolworths, motorcoaches, wireless, hiking, factory girls looking like actresses, greyhound racing and dirt tracks, swimming pools, and everything given away for cigarette coupons.[10]

Thomas Wallis's 1932 Hoover Factory, with its gleaming white ziggurat façade on which were applied Egyptian motifs, was a vivid illustration of this modernity.[11] What is missing, surprisingly, from Priestley's description is the suburban semi.

Of particular importance to this book are those changes that had an impact on the home. The growth of the lower middle classes and the occupations open to them, together with rises in their standard of living and increased leisure time and activities, formed the new homeowners of interwar suburbia. As I argued in the previous chapter, the availability of cheap mortgages and the rise of speculatively built suburban and state housing meant that more families were in sole occupancy of their homes. Builders employed new techniques and materials and ways of organising production, for example through the standardisation of building parts,

in the construction of such housing. The establishment and standardisation of the gas, water and electricity public utilities revolutionised the
home and enabled improved standards of hygiene and comfort.[12] As I go
on to discuss in Chapter 4, changes in patterns of work for women led to
a perceived 'servant problem' to which the notion of the modern 'professional' housewife was a response.

The new commercial culture of homemaking that emerged between
the wars could, as Alison Light argues, 'accommodate the past in new
forms of the present; it was a deferral of modernity and yet it also
demanded a different sort of conservatism from that which had gone
before'.[13] Light identifies what she calls a 'conservative modernity' that
was 'felt and lived in the most interior and private of places'.[14] Other
literary critics such as Nicola Humble, Melissa Sullivan and Sophie
Blanch have argued that there was a 'middlebrow' Modernism in popular women's fiction that was a very real response to modernity in the
home.[15]

Much of the literature on modernity has focused on the city and on
Walter Benjamin's figure of the *flâneur* 'botanizing on the asphalt'.[16]
There has been some debate about whether a female equivalent to
Benjamin's bohemian – a *flâneuse* – is possible.[17] What is interesting here
is not whether such women actually existed, but the implicit assumption in these accounts that the suburbs are somehow outside modernity,
belonging to the private sphere, and thus that women had to leave suburbia for the city in order to experience modernity. This assumption stems
from a romanticisation of the city, especially Paris, in critical writings on
modernity. It also draws on rather rigid notions of 'separate spheres'; the
idea that women were confined to the private sphere of the home while
men predominantly acted in the public sphere of work. Women crossed
the boundaries of public and private spheres more easily and readily
than has been claimed by some.[18] Furthermore, spaces did not have
fixed geographical boundaries. Indeed, certain spaces such as department stores, shopping centres and exhibition halls (especially the Ideal

Home Exhibition at Olympia) had complex and conflicting identities as both public and private.[19] Moreover, such spaces were sites of consumption. The goods that they offered – the products of modernisation, although not necessarily Modernist – were taken back to the suburbs and consumed in the home.[20] As Meaghan Morris points out, 'the cultural production of "actual women" has historically fallen short of a modernity understood as, or in terms derived from, the critical construction of modernism'. We need to study, as she puts it, 'the everyday, the so-called banal, the supposedly un- or non-experimental, asking not, "why does it fall short of modernism?" but "how do classical theories of modernism fall short of women's modernity?"'[21] Similarly, in this book I identify a specifically suburban Modernism, and I trace its specific and exemplary manifestations by taking the interwar suburban house on its own terms, asking what it was that builders, retailers and homeowners defined as modern.

Modernity, however, was not welcomed by all. While some thought progress was inevitable, others thought its gains came at a terrible price and grieved for what Harris has called 'the memory of a lost domain'.[22] As Harris points out, some sought to reconcile modernity with the 'lost domain' and consequently 'remorselessly modern purposes were clothed by the fig-leaf of invented tradition'.[23] Such a reconciliation, I argue, was played out in suburbia. Furthermore, it is no coincidence, in the cultural theorist Bill Schwarz's words, that 'the emergence of a popular modernism also coincides with the deepening idea of English traditionalism'. As he suggests, 'the dynamic and recurring inventiveness of tradition may precisely have required a popular and carnivalesque projection of modernity and of the future in order to sustain the idea of the past'.[24] The specifically suburban blend of tradition and modernity was noted by a few contemporary commentators.

The architectural critic J.M. Richards' *The Castles on the Ground* (1946) is worth noting for his contemporary emphasis on the personal meanings that users invest in architecture. He said:

It takes all sorts to make the suburban world, and its essential quality lies in a mixture of familiarity and novelty, glamour and homeliness. The suburb is neither the refuge of dowdiness, tolerated for the sake of old associations, nor the playground of slick modernity, but is something of both and everything in between. The past jostles the present and pigeonhole conventions are no more often true than untrue. Familiarity breeds no contempt, liberty does not lead to license and the new wine improves in the old bottles into which it is consistently being decanted.[25]

A specifically suburban Modernism emerged in the interwar years, embodied most fully in the suburban semi-detached house. The suburban house displayed a series of polarities, yet negotiated a space between them. These oppositions include modernity and nostalgia; urban and rural; past and future; masculine and feminine; culture and nature; public and private. Suburban Modernism was the middle ground where such polarities could come together; contradictions are intrinsic to it.

The Modern Movement and housing in Britain

The influence of the Bauhaus, founded in Germany in 1919, was slow to reach domestic design in Britain. Le Corbusier's 1923 book *Vers une architecture* was not published in an English translation until 1927 when it appeared as *Towards a New Architecture*. Some English architects and critics saw Le Corbusier and Pierre Jeannaret's 'Le Pavillon de l'Esprit Nouveau' at the 1925 Paris Exposition des Arts Decoratifs et Industriels Modernes. The pavilion was an uncompromising Modernist display of a prototype dwelling that had been subjected to the forces of prefabrication and mass-production.[26] Together with the Bauhaus and the work of the American architect Louis Sullivan, it represented the beginnings of the 'International Style' (the name of an exhibition at the Museum of Modern Art in New York in 1932), with a machine aesthetic that influenced architects, designers and critics. However, many British critics and architects, such as F.R. Yerbury (the secretary of the Architectural Association who wrote several books and articles with Howard Robinson, principal of the AA), John Gloag and H.R. Birnstingl, viewed Modernism critically.

The social anthropologist Daniel Miller identifies several key terms that were used in the language of Modernism: Objectivity, Rationality, Formalism, Honesty, Functionalism, Science and Machine Aesthetic. These terms are enacted in the formal characteristics of architecture such as straight lines, flat roofs, absence of decoration, use of new materials and the exposure of structural elements.[27] The typical materials of Modernist architecture were reinforced concrete, glass and steel. Buildings tended to be asymmetrical, composed of cubic shapes, white flat roofs and white rendered walls, with horizontal windows making use of large planes of glass. All these elements were in sharp contrast with the characteristics of British suburbia.

The influence of Modernist architecture first appeared in British housing through individual private commissions. Peter Behrens' 'New Ways' for Bassett-Loake in Northampton in 1926 is usually thought of as the first Modern Movement house in England. However, it is arguable that this design was Moderne or Modernistic (which as I show later is a more critical term) rather than Modernist proper.[28] The same could also be said for Thomas Tait and John Burnet's garden colony factory town at Silver End in Essex for the philanthropist Francis Henry Crittall (of Crittall Windows Ltd fame), which was begun in 1926 (Figure 3.3). The influence of the Modern Movement proper did not really start in Britain until 1929 when Amyas Connell started work on 'High and Over', a private house that, again, was arguably more Modernistic than Modernist.[29]

Speculative builders began to experiment with the International Style, which had previously been associated with avant-garde patrons, by about 1933 when the market for speculative housing had reached saturation point in Britain. The style's simplified form and construction appealed to them as a way to reduce costs, as well as appealing to marginal market groups.[30] These developments were, on the whole, not very successful, and white-walled, flat-roofed houses of the Modern

3.3 House at Silver End, from *Modern Home*, 17, February 1930

Movement were not popular with the English housebuying public.[31] Flat roofs for sunbathing did not work in the English climate. White-painted outside walls became streaked from rain (as Lancaster pointed out in his depiction of a rain-sodden terrace) and render broke down, allowing damp to penetrate. Inadequate insulation in concrete houses was also a problem in the English climate. However, sunlight was thought to have desirable health-giving properties (the absorption of ultraviolet rays was positively encouraged) and suntans were fashionable. So Modernist and Modernistic houses were thought suitable for seaside architecture: the sunlight-bearing quality of white walls and curtain windows, together with flat roofs that could also double as sun decks, made them attractive. The estates of such houses that were developed by the sea, including at Churton in Devon built between 1933 and 1935 and designed by William Lescaze, and Frinton Park in 1934 designed by Oliver Hill, were curtailed because of poor sales. As Ian Bentley has argued, 'This is not surprising, for by now the Modern Movement was associated, in the minds of many people, with big businesses and big government.'[32]

For some critics there was also a sense that Modernism was not suited to the English character. Evelyn Waugh's novel *Decline and Fall* (1928) satirised the Modernist architect in the story of Professor Silenus, a young architect who designs a Modernist house for his client Margot Beste-Chetwynde:

> "The problem of architecture as I see it," he told a journalist who had come to report on the progress of his surprising creation of ferro-concrete and aluminium, "is the problem of all art – the elimination of the human element from the consideration of form. The only perfect building must be the factory, because that is built to house machines, not men…"[33]

While the British state used Modernism for public buildings, individuals largely rejected it for private housing. Indeed, Miller sees the conservatism, individuality and tradition of the suburban semi as in direct opposition to the communal and egalitarian values of Modernism. However, as he notes, individuals can experience a conflict of ideology within themselves, as evidenced by those in positions of power in the state who chose Modernist housing for the masses yet often chose semi-detached suburban houses for themselves.[34]

This is exemplified by Robertson and Yerbury who in their review of the 1927 Stuttgart exhibition, which was intended to be an object lesson in working- and middle-class housing, said that the radical departures of white walls, verandas and flat roofs were inappropriate for England, except perhaps for 'some sun-favoured nook on the southern coast'.[35] More importantly, they thought that Modernism was unsuited to the English character because behind it lay 'an idea which presupposes not only a change in architectural standards, but a change in the human personality of the sort of tenant for whom these houses are destined'.[36] For Yerbury and Robertson, then, architecture represented deeply held human values. Until the late 1920s they distrusted theory and lacked an understanding of the radical principles of Modernism, but they were sympathetic to Scandinavian architecture that was based on a modern reinterpretation of the classical tradition.[37] In the 1920s the English architectural press was very insular, and although Robertson and Yerbury saw what they did as reportage, they were perceived as radicals by some of their contemporaries just for covering new European architecture.

By 1929, however, when Yerbury and Robertson were at their most productive, there was a shift in the architectural scene and Modernist work began to appear in the British architectural and design press and at the Architectural Association. By the late 1920s Yerbury had begun to display a more sympathetic attitude to Modernism, publishing 'Modernism for Moderate Means: Some Small Town Houses in Paris' in 1929.[38] In 1932, three years later, Yerbury and Robertson made a more dramatic conversion to Modernism.[39] In an article entitled 'Quest of the Ideal', they compared Le Corbusier's villa at Garches with some nearby houses in an English Arts and Crafts style:

> One suddenly realises that 'English' houses are wrong, and that Le Corbusier's house is right. A motor-car stands before its door. One sees that the motor-car and the house are in tune, that the design of the house and car are in the natural harmony which has always obtained between manmade objects of any period which is truly an epoch. The coach has gone, the garb of its occupants, the house which filled them. Today, another vehicle, another dress, another architecture.[40]

As Alan Powers comments, 'it is at least an entertaining speculation that British intellectuals accepted Modernism not because they liked it but because it was sufficiently uncomfortable and self-righteous for them to feel at home with it'.[41] This also invokes Lancaster's image of the 'new Puritan' in his functionalist room (Figure 3.1).

Not all British critics were eventually converted to the Modern Movement. In 1944 John Gloag made a scathing attack on the Modern Movement as inappropriate for the English climate, character and love of ornament. He did not approve of those young architects who had been attracted by the 'glib, foreign phrase' of Le Corbusier's that a house was a 'machine for living in'.[42] He said that the 'modern movement does not yet speak English. It has so far been regarded, though not acknowledged, as a fashion.' Architects, he alleged, have tended to tell people how to live, rather than provide a background for living.[43]

Apart from a few Modernist experiments with private housing such as Erno Goldfinger's Willow Road, the Modern Movement had the greatest impact on public housing as blocks of flats in urban settings. Elizabeth Darling has recently described the attempts at Modernist reform, which did not necessarily result in actual buildings by named architects, as 'narratives of modernity', using such means as exhibitions, radio broadcasts, lectures and journalism to create a sympathetic audience for the eventual hegemony of the Modern Movement in architecture and design in Britain.[44] Exhibitions – from the reforming zeal of the British Industrial Art in Relation to the Home at Dorland Hall in 1933 to the populist Ideal Home exhibitions – became key vehicles for disseminating visions of the Modern Movement to popular audiences.

The house of the future

For all who stand in its garden and look at its somewhat metallic sheen, its definitely factory-made lines, and its air of challenge to eyes attuned to bricks and mortar, gables and gullies, there will be a shock similar to that which would have come to a cave man peering forward at the 'Laburnum Villa' of 1928.[45]

The modernity of the first 'house of the future' to appear at the Ideal Home Exhibition in 1928 was clear from its description in the show's catalogue quoted above (Figure 3.4). Designed by S. Rowland Pierce and R.A. Duncan, ARIBA, this was not a straightforward presentation of the Modern Movement. The house combined the emerging International Style for the exterior with ideas about the impact of colour on the emotions in the interior and 'Efficiency' style in the kitchen, imagining life

3.4 S. Rowland Pierce and R.A. Duncan's 'The House of the Future', at the Daily Mail Ideal Home Exhibition, 1928

in the year 2000 with electric servants, aero-cars and even a wireless international communication device. A feature in the *Illustrated London News*, which included detailed cross-section drawings of the house and its equipment, said 'This house is the first serious attempt to show in concrete form the prospective results of modern scientific inventions and discoveries.'[46]

It was envisaged that such a house would be built on a frame of hidden stainless steel supports. The frame would be covered by a material that had not yet been invented which resembled thin sheets of a horn-like substance that could be tough, yet capable of being cut and welded at high temperature. The material would come in any colour or pattern desired and would form both the inner and outer walls, as well as the floors.[47]

The interior of the house could be accessed by an outside staircase to the flat roof; inside, a lift was available. The space of the house was as adaptable as the furniture; four cabin-like bunk bedrooms could be converted into two double bedrooms by use of roller shutters. The beds were heated by electric-powered mattresses and heating throughout the house came from electric panels on the floor. Glass-covered pergolas on the roof provided 'sun-baths' with ultraviolet rays. The catalogue concluded 'It is a house not built to last a lifetime. It is such a house as goes out of date as your motor-car gets out of date, renewed in the same way.'[48] The house was decorated throughout in 'a colour to suit the temperament';[49] even the lighting was in various changeable hues. In Britain it was not unusual for a more restrained Modernist exterior to have a more exuberant 'modern' interior. Pierce and Duncan's house of the future was perhaps more similar to Raymond McGrath's 'Finella' (a remodelling of the interior of a Victorian building in Cambridge in 1928–29) and some of the more Modernistic work of British architect Oliver Hill.[50]

The kitchen was designed in long and compact lines like a dining-car and was furnished with a kitchen cabinet rather than fitted cupboards. It contained many novelties. For example, no washing-up need ever be done as disposable dishes, plates and cups would be used. Cooking and freezing would be done by electricity. Pneumatic chairs could be deflated and rolled up when they were not needed. A table in the dining room could be folded and wheeled into the kitchen. The study was fitted with a television, wireless receiver and transmitter, electric typewriter, 'tele-newsprinter' and electric piano.[51]

The house of the future presented a fantasy of domestic life where every-day household tasks would be automated, and presented Modernism as the rational labour-saving solution for life in the future. In 1928 a special edition of the *Daily Mail* was published, dated 1 January 2000, to celebrate the 'house of the future'. The paper declared that the servant problem was at last conquered by the 'domestic labour eliminator'. It also forecast atomic energy, colour television and the Channel Tunnel, but stated that interplanetary space travel had not yet been realised.

Arnold Bennett, the popular novelist, wrote an essay on the house of the future for the *Daily Mail Ideal Home Exhibition Catalogue*. He had experience of women's magazines, joining the staff of *Woman* in 1892, writing 'Gwendolen's Column' about dresses, household management and new developments such as central heating, and serving as editor from 1896 to 1900.[52] His interest in domestic convenience and labour-saving home design, which he wrote about in his novels, was mocked by intellectuals.[53] I would suggest that Bennett's emphasis on the revolution in home economy constructed a popular modernity that touched the lives of his readers more than the Modernist revolutions in art and literature.

Drawing, no doubt, on his experience at *Woman*, Bennett wrote about the four elements of comfort that needed to be borne in mind when planning the houses of the future: noise, foul air, darkness and cold. His recommendations paid little attention to architectural style. Instead, he concentrated on the levels of comfort that he believed could, and should, be achieved in the present day. Bennett was also concerned with the excessive permanence of homes and the value of colour to well-being. He proclaimed that furniture should, as much as possible, be built in. This would mean that people would be able to move and set up home far more easily and speedily. He welcomed change and declared that in the future 'pictures, furniture and other agreeable fal-lals' would be hireable in order to diversify and vitalise the 'interest of existence'. Similarly, the decoration of the walls should be changed to suit the owner's temperament and bring cheer. He recommended that brighter colours should be used; drabness was a medieval attribute.[54] Bennett's concerns were pragmatic and achievable within the realms of existing technology. His ideas were thus totally compatible with the concerns of the Ideal Home Exhibition, in that modernity could be embraced through technological change and improvements, particularly in the

3.5 Wells Coates and David Pleydell Bouverie's 'Sunspan' house, from the 'Village of Tomorrow' at the Daily Mail Ideal Home Exhibition, 1934

interior, rather than by wholesale adoption of Modernist architecture and aesthetics.

One of the most direct attempts at Modernist housing for suburbia in the Ideal Home Exhibition was exhibited in 1934's 'Village of Tomorrow'. Wells Coates and David Pleydell Bouverie's 'Sunspan' house (Figure 3.5) was the only house in the exhibition to have been fully equipped and furnished to architects' specifications and was influenced by Le Corbusier's concept of minimum dwellings and the 'house-machine'. It was related to Wells Coates's minimum flat, which had been shown at the British Industrial Art Exhibition at Dorland Hall in 1933. The architectural critic Morton Shand commented on the Sunspan house as 'Perhaps the first serious English contribution to domestic planning forms since that famous discovery of the "free, open planning" of the English country house took the Continent by storm at the beginning of the century.'[55] The builders E. & L. Berg built fifteen, some without Coates's knowledge.[56] Berg were certainly not committed to Modernism; in 1938 they exhibited a Tudorbethan-style house at the Ideal Home Exhibition. The exhibition tended to relegate Modernism to a fantasy vision of the future and kept it a distance, while audiences were likely to recognise the Modernistic as modern.

'Art Deco' and 'Modernistic'

The obvious answer to the question I posed at the beginning of this chapter about what it was that builders, retailers and homeowners defined as 'modern' is Art Deco. It is helpful here to have an account of the origins of the term 'Art Deco', first used as the subtitle to the catalogue of *Les Années 25*, an exhibition of interwar design at the Musée des Arts Décoratifs in Paris in 1966. According to the curator and design historian Bevis Hillier it was first used in English in November 1966 as a heading to an article in *The Times* and first appeared in book form in Osbert Lancaster's *With an Eye to the Future* (1967). Hillier popularised the term in his *Art Deco of the Twenties and Thirties* (1968) and subsequent 1971 Philadelphia exhibition and lavish catalogue.[57] As Hillier says, 'the term "Art Deco", like all stylistic labels, is a generalization which helps us to understand our visual history'.[58] It has become synonymous with the architecture and design of the 1920s and 1930s, incorporating decoration and the stylisation of images. The popularisation of the term was also aided by a revival of the style from the late 1960s and into the 1970s, when it became fashionable to collect original objects from the interwar period, many of which were mass-produced and cheaply and readily available.[59] New Art Deco influenced designs were produced, particularly in graphics, and influenced fashion.

The term Art Deco was abbreviated from the title of the 1925 Paris Exposition des Arts Decoratifs et Industriels Modernes. The sleek, softened and often voluptuous Modernism that appeared there had been a tendency in French design since before the First World War. Many of the products on display were luxurious, drawing on foreign influences and historical styles and made of exotic materials. Manifestations of this 'Moderne' Art Deco style spread internationally from high-end bespoke luxury to mass-market Woolworths. The term Art Deco now has widespread currency and is often used to describe anything that is modern but not Modern*ist*. In 2003 Hillier and Escritt defined Art Deco as 'a stylisation of modernity, a decorative response to modernity'. For them it is a 'total style', appearing on a range of designed media from 'packaging and posters to vehicle design and building', across national and class boundaries.[60] The same year there was a revival of interest in the style with an exhibition at the Victoria and Albert Museum and an exhaustive catalogue that explored Art Deco as a global phenomenon.[61]

One of the best-known exponents of Art Deco is the designer of ceramics Clarice Cliff, whose work epitomises the use of the term over the last forty years or so. As Hillier notes, 'the modernity of Art Deco was often seen in terms of frivolous commercial novelty, in stark opposition to Modernism's pious reforming zeal'.[62] Sometimes, however, there are slippages between the terms Modernism and Art Deco, and a designer such as the ceramicist Keith Murray gets assigned to both movements. Furthermore, the term Art Deco is often applied extremely loosely, just as the more recent terms 'retro' or the increasingly popular 'Mid-Century Modern' are applied to post-Second World War design.

And yet the term Art Deco excludes a whole range of domestic design that combines modern technologies, materials and forms with traditional – often invented – ones. I consciously avoid the term Art Deco throughout this book because it was not used in the interwar years and it is too broad for my discussion here. 'Jazz Modern', 'Zig-zag', 'Moderne' and 'Modernistic' were the contemporary terms for what now falls under the umbrella term of Art Deco.[63] Such designs in architecture, furniture and furnishings often borrowed from the formal language of one of the

post-First World War European Modernisms such as Cubism, Futurism
or De Stijl, especially two-dimensional painted sources. As the design
historian Paul Greenhalgh says, 'For many, the design process seemed
to entail no more than the application of two-dimensional images to the
surfaces of three-dimensional objects.'[64] In addition, the terms 'American
Streamline' and 'Streamlined Moderne' were used in interwar Britain to
describe American products that followed the streamlining originating
from the automotive industry.[65]

For self-professed Modernist critics, designers and architects, these
terms and the styles they described, especially Modernistic, were loaded
with negative connotations of decorative modernity rather than pure
functionalism and were also tainted by commercialism. The Modernistic
style was deemed as false as mock Tudor architecture and spurious
'reproduction' furniture. Modernistic is my preferred term in this book,
commonplace in interwar magazines and books with both positive and
negative connotations, according to the intentions and prejudices of
writers and audiences. Unnecessary streamlining was condemned when
used for products such as vacuum cleaners that had no need to be aero-
dynamic, and also brought with it Americanisation, which for some critics had negative and vulgar connotations.[66]

One of the most common motifs of the Modernistic style was a stylised sunrise or sunburst in a combination of red, yellow or orange, symbolising modern ideals of sunshine and health. The sunrise was found
in domestic architecture as a design for stained glass windows in bays
and on front doors. Front doors and garden gates in wood or metal
also depicted sunbursts (Figure 3.6). Tudorbethan-style houses sometimes had non-structural decorative beams on their façades formed into
a sunburst pattern. Sunrises could also be found on radiogram speakers,
as well as lighting, the backs of wooden chairs, doormats, rugs, textiles, ceramics, gas and electric fires, kitchen cabinets and packaging for
food and cleaning products. Even ice-cream wafers came in a sunrise
design.[67] In Lancaster's 'Modernistic' cartoon (Figure 3.2), the mirror

3.6 1930s 'Suntrap' house, New Malden, Surrey, 1948

over the mantelpiece took the form of a stylised sunrise and the shape also appeared on the radiogram.

One example of the Modernistic style in domestic architecture was the 'Suntrap' house, many of which included decorative sunrise features. Such houses were built with hipped roofs, often in green tiles, and with two-storey bay windows. A brochure for an Edgeware estate comprising such houses, dating from about 1935, urged its readers to 'Be Modern at

St Margaret's' (Plate 8). These houses combined uncluttered Modernistic elevations, complete with curved Crittall windows, under a familiar pitched roof executed in shiny green roof tiles instead of the usual red.[68] Metal Crittall windows glazed in rectangles came to signify modernity and were often installed in neo-Georgian cottages with traditional bays.

The Ideal Home Exhibition's 1934 'Village of Tomorrow' featured not only Coates and Pleydell Bouverie's Modernist Sunspan house but also a range of other houses designed in a Modernistic style. One example consisted of a mixture of cube and curved forms with flat roofs of varying levels, accessorised by shutters. The curved entrances and the chevron patterns that decorated them were more reminiscent of the Hoover factory than the restrained Modernism of the Sunspan house (Figure 3.5). 'P.B.', writing in the *Journal of the Royal Society of Arts* about the 1934 Ideal Home Exhibition, declared that 'whilst the ideal village contains some genuine modern architecture [...] ingenuity is proving that there is no difficulty in giving modern architecture a horrible, Ye Olde George V, trimming, between which and Ye Olde Tudor nastiness there is not a penny to choose'.[69]

In 1942 the critic Anthony Bertram decried such Modernistic architecture produced by builders as 'another kind of fancy-dress':

> The modernistic is bogus modern, as the Tudoristic is bogus Tudor ... what the modernistic builder does is to build an old-fashioned villa with the old-fashioned plan in the old-fashioned way, and then he 'streamlines' it, tacking on his modern features just as the Tudoristic builder tacks on his bogus beams.[70]

Both Anthony Bertram and John Gloag were concerned that the public too readily mistook the Modernistic for the Modernist.[71] It is likely that the general public did indeed see the Modernistic and the Modernist as being the same, and, moreover, that the two were collapsed together into one vaguely modern style. As Julian Holder points out, for much of the general public, Modernism meant simply the Art Deco style associated with the 1925 Paris Exhibition, and sunburst motifs formed part of the vocabulary of the speculative builder of the period. To many a Modernist this treatment, restricted to surface decoration, was as 'bogus' as the mock-Tudor and accordingly described as Modernistic, a derogatory term.[72]

The boundaries between Modernistic and Modernist were not so distinct as contemporary designers, architects and critics would have liked to have thought. For example, an architect such as Oliver Hill seemed to work quite comfortably in both idioms as well as in more straightforward historical revival styles. News of Modernistic designs reached a wider public via enthusiastic reports in women's and homemaking magazines. For example, in 1929 the 'Home Gossip' column of *Modern Home* reported on the home of the famous traveller Rosita Forbes, whose husband Raymond McGrath had designed their home: 'In the entrance hall [...] the walls are lined with squares and diagonals of black and white glass divided with leaded strips.'[73] McGrath, like Oliver Hill, was one of several British designers associated with variations of the Modernistic style.

Betty Joel, a self-taught British designer working in the Modernistic style, also received much attention in magazines. She was very successful, opening her own showrooms in Knightsbridge in the late 1920s, which sold her own designs and those of others, many of them French, in specially designed room-sets. She used curved edges in her furniture, to echo the 'feminine form', she said. She abolished all unnecessary mouldings and projections and introduced an innovative recessed drawer handle that she claimed reduced the number of surfaces that needed dusting. Women's magazines of the period praised her work as a female designer designing for women. Her work also reached popular audiences through the Ideal Home Exhibition, to which she contributed an 'Ideal Boudoir' in 1925.[74] In contrast, her work was not well received by the design press. For example, in 1935 she exhibited a curved bed mounted on a circular revolving platform at the British Art in Industry exhibition at Dorland

Hall. The bed offended the sensibilities of Modernist critics and was criticised as a 'dislocated hip bath'. Joel's work was thought for a long time to be 'rather low-brow, even kitsch'.[75] Her designs appear to have been denigrated as a particularly feminine form of the Modernistic, all the more so due to her sex.

The Modernistic style, as Lancaster's cartoon so vividly depicted, was found in the home across a range of furniture, furnishings, decoration and ornaments. Dining suites, sideboards, compact three-piece suites, coffee tables, display cabinets, cocktail cabinets and gramophones could all be purchased in a range of Modernistic styles that utilised curved and geometric forms and decorations. Many made use of exotic veneers, moulded Bakelite, chrome trims and painted decorations. The wireless radio, which appeared in Lancaster's cartoons for both 'Modernistic' and 'Functional', was widespread by the mid-1930s. It was one of the first electrical appliances that many people owned, and as well as being a source of entertainment in the home as the family gathered around it (Figure 1.6), it was a potent symbol of modernity. At first styled to look like traditional, wooden, cabinet furniture, later, smaller models were more streamlined and decorative and could be placed on a shelf to ornamental effect.[76]

The Modernistic style was thought particularly appropriate for the bedroom, especially the dressing table, which formed the centrepiece of the 'lady's boudoir'. The design of the dressing table was also influenced by the glamour of Hollywood films. Many, such as *Dinner at Eight* (1933) starring Jean Harlow, had scenes set at elaborate dressing tables made of exotic woods, chrome and mirror glass with elaborate drapes or fringing forming a skirt. This image of modern femininity was a recurring setting for publicity photos of actresses reproduced in advertisements and magazines. A sense of glamour and luxury was also provided by new artificial silks, rayons and satins used for curtains topped with painted pelmets, bedspreads and down quilts in Modernistic patterns created by stitching their padded filling, and cushions. Gloss-finished wallpapers

3.7 Mr and Mrs Beaver's bedroom, May 1937

were also used to add to the sense of luxury and Hollywood style in the English bedroom. This influence can be seen in the 1937 bedroom of Mr and Mrs Beaver, who I introduced in Chapter 1, which had a shiny, Hollywood-style counterpane (Figure 3.7) and a chrome Modernistic pendant light alongside their more traditional oak bedroom furniture and simple cotton drapes and restrained striped wallpaper.

It is worth sounding a note of caution here. Few consumers in interwar England invested in complete suites of new modern furniture, even with the increased availability and affordability of hire purchase. Many had to make do and mend, as indicated by the thriving trade in second-hand furniture. Furthermore, consumers tended to invest in more 'traditional' styles for large and expensive items, which were seen as an investment and expected to last for many years. However, this does not mean that

such traditional styles were installed in combination with equally traditional soft furnishings and ornaments; the Modernistic coexisted side by
side with the traditional in the interwar suburban home.

One example of a popular Modernistic object that provoked outrage
among designers and critics was the square clock, an example of which
appears on the mantelpiece of Lancaster's 'Modernistic' room (Figure
3.2). This can be seen to exemplify the tensions between Modernist
design reform and popular taste for the Modernistic. For example, in
November 1928 the newly launched *Modern Home* magazine, aimed at
the house-proud and modernising professional housewife and her husband, informed its readers: 'The square clock has certainly come into
its own. On the smartest mantelpieces and dressing-tables you see it,
as big as a photograph frame, or nearly as small as a wrist watch.'[77] The
square clock became readily available, sold by retailers such as Catesbys
(Plate 7).

Frank Pick, president of the Design and Industries Association, turned
his attention to the design of clocks in a talk broadcast on BBC radio in
1933 on 'The Meaning and Purpose of Design'. This was one of a series of
instructional talks on 'Design in Modern Life', which were revised and
published as a book in 1934. The talks were intended to educate listeners
in 'good design'. They took the form of a discussion between an expert
and a questioner who acted as 'the listener's friend'.[78] In the talks, design
reformers such as John Gloag and Frank Pick despaired at the application of so-called 'modern' shapes for decorative rather than functional
purposes. In his talk Pick said,

> Many of the common things which we use have had their design settled long
> ago. The face of a clock, for instance. The hands go round, and so the figures
> should be arranged in a ring. Yet in these days you get clocks which are tri-
> angles, squares and oblongs. The hands at one moment are trying to reach
> the figures on the margin, the next moment they entirely overlap them.
> There is only one right answer to the design of the face of a clock. Pity the
> wretched designer forced to improve on the best for the sake of novelty![79]

Rather than blame the designer for being, as he put it, 'so perverse', Pick railed against the consumer: 'If the "purchasing public", prompted by devils of fashion, would not buy them, then they would not be made.'[80] Design reformers sought to improve the public's taste and to create a demand for 'good design' to which manufacturers would have to respond.[81]

There was a fear among designers, architects and critics that the Modern Movement would be seen as just another choice of style, or else debased, rather than being regarded as the ultimate, rational aesthetic. Designers and reformers despaired of middle-class taste in general and lower-middle-class in particular. For example, Birnstingl saw them as being duped by the manufacturers of mass-produced goods who

> exploit a very easily aroused desire for change, for the novel, the crude, and the startling; [they] fill the world with ill-made and worthless objects; whose life is limited since they are both useless and badly made; objects that will remain unendeared to their owners, because their appeal is superficial. And so the home becomes a vulgar setting to vulgar people surrounded by vulgar objects exchanging vulgar thoughts and rejoicing in vulgar exhibitions.[82]

For many designers, architects and critics the way to improve manufactured products was to educate consumers to develop 'good taste' for 'good design'.

There was also a focus on women in debates about Modernistic 'bad design'. Some critics and designers saw women as reckless, infantilised consumers, easily swayed by novelty. It is no accident that a woman occupied Lancaster's Modernistic room. The Modernistic signified the luxury, escapism and consumer desires of the Odeon cinema and 1930s Hollywood, hinted at by Lancaster in the floor-length curtains with their stepped pelmet, reminiscent of the drapes of the silver screen. This appropriation of masculine rationalism as 'sham' Modernistic was denigrated as feminine and trivial. What is apparent from contemporary critics is a gendering of popular modernity. For example, in *English*

Panorama (1936) Thomas Sharp discussed women's supposedly inborn tastes, declaring that 'She has a sense of property and a desire to display it … that is far more highly developed than his, she is at once more conservative and more open to the appeal of small novelty: aesthetically she has few or none of the makings of a citizen.'[83] Women were thought by many to be outside what the artist Wyndham Lewis called the 'rough and masculine work' of Modernism,[84] yet were condemned for their modernity. Thus Lancaster's cartoons neatly conveyed the gendering of Functional and Modernistic as masculine and feminine respectively.

Metamorphic Modernism

The very small size of suburban semis that were below the Tudor Walters standards, but still accommodated a family of four who expected certain consumer standards derived from shop and exhibition displays, magazines, advertisements and films, led to manufacturers and retailers responding with multi-functional forms of furniture.[85] Modern suburban furniture also reflected a desire to incorporate the latest technologies. As an advertisement for the 'Majiik' 'modern table' in 1929 put it:

> As out-of-date as the bustle or the chignon is the old loose-leaf dining table. Modernity demands the newest and the best of everything … Here is the extending Table which represents the very spirit of modernity. Majik in name, magic in operation and efficiency. A touch at the ends and the table extends without rubbing. No loose leaves. No key. Nothing to go wrong.[86]

The advertisement featured a photograph of a table with Queen Anne style legs accompanied by a girl in a fashionable drop-waisted dress. Its typography was Modernistic in style. Technology was in itself modern and did not necessarily need a Modernist style in order to complement the modern home, a point to which I will return in Chapter 5.

New designs for furniture for 'modern' purposes also proliferated. For example, the telephone demanded special furniture for its accommodation, and small multi-functional units intended for the hallway – holding phone directories, umbrellas and canes – were popular.[87] Built-in furniture and storage was often rejected as inflexible. Instead, storage was often ingeniously built into small pieces of furniture. Bookcases, for example, were combined with armchairs and occasional tables (Plate 7). Arding and Hobbs' 1937 *Beautiful Homes* catalogue depicted a '"Novelty" adjustable easy chair' that offered 'reclining back adjustment' and was 'fitted with bookcases on one side and flap forming cushion on the other'.[88] Frederick Lawrence's 'combined oak bookcase and coal cabinet', for example, was promoted as 'A real need in every home' (Figure 3.8). The advertisement continued: 'Substantially built, well finished rich Jacobean brown, 2 bookcases each end, centre compartment has galvanised removable lining for coal, and is hinged at bottom to pull out at convenient angle for easy access.'[89] This particular item was designed in a geometric style that nodded to Modernism, yet its finish was Jacobean. Such furniture with built-in storage suited the

3.8 Illustration of combined oak bookcase and coal cabinet, from *Frederick Lawrence Ltd., Inspirations for Modern Homes, c.* 1930s

compact space of the interwar suburban house, where every inch had to be used as effectively as possible. Indeed, furniture catalogues were careful to include the measurements of such items.

The interwar period witnessed a revival in the design of 'metamorphic' furniture that had originated in the Regency period.[90] For example, the *Daily Mail* commented that 'A striking feature of the new furnishings for the modern home is a grandfather clock with a fully equipped cocktail bar within' (Figure 3.9).[91] This was a way for suburbanites simultaneously to buy into the modern fashionable craze for cocktails and to have the status symbol of the grandfather clock, which nodded to tradition. This offended Bertram's notion of 'form follows function'; he included a drawing of an example of a combined grandfather clock and cocktail cabinet as an object lesson in 'bad design', captioning it 'This case was to hide works, not drinks.'[92] As Judy Attfield has noted, the cocktail cabinet was 'an article of display', noting that it was often empty and performed a symbolic rather than practical function.[93] As Attfield notes, the emergence of combination sideboard and cocktail cabinets shows how '[m]anufacturers hedged their bets by combining traditional with contemporary features and several pieces of furniture in one'.[94] Another example was an 'intriguing' Jacobethan-style 'oak settee that can be instantly converted into a table', described as 'ideal for the small home' and exhibited at the Ideal Home Exhibition in 1929.[95] The drop-side sofa proved a practical solution to the need for a spare bed in smaller homes, and 'bed-chairs' were also available.

Such devices were both 'olde-worlde' and modern. A similar blend, as Lancaster pointed out, could be found in houses designed in historic styles such as 'Stockbroker's Tudor'. For Lancaster this was a step too far:

> the greatest ingenuity was displayed in providing the various modern devices with which they were anachronistically equipped with suitable olde-worlde disguises. Thus electrically produced heat warmed the hands of those who clustered around the Yule-logs blazing so prettily in the vast hearth; the light which shone so cozily from the old horn lantern was

3.9 Grandfather clock cocktail cabinet at the Daily Mail Ideal Home
Exhibition, 1934

> obtained from the grid; and from the depths of some old iron-bound chest
> were audible the dulcet tones of Mr. Bing Crosby or the old-world strains
> of Mr. Duke Ellington.[96]

These new types of 'metamorphic', multi-functional furniture emerged as a direct response to the extremely small spaces of local authority and speculatively built houses occupied by the new respectable working classes and lower middle classes. Despite being reviled by Modernist critics, these examples of metamorphic furniture were understood as 'modern' by manufacturers, retailers and consumers, and fitted neatly into interwar spaces and popular narratives of suburban Modernism in interwar England.

The 'English compromise' and 'good design'

Residents of interwar suburbia were addressed by influential narratives of 'good' and 'bad design', produced by critics and organisations that attempted to promote a distinctly English version of Modernism in architecture and design. Continental Modernism was rejected by writers such as Gloag and Birnstingl who bypassed the excesses of the Victorian period to claim a long lineage of simplicity and good proportions from the Georgian period for 'good design'.[97] For Birnstingl, the Georgian style had 'a simplicity and grace that was at once elegant and inextravagant'.[98] It was this, together with the Arts and Crafts movement, which influenced the design of Welwyn Garden City and London County Council's post-First World War municipal housing, which met with Birnstingl's approval (Figure 2.5). He described them as 'little groups of houses, well-built, well-grouped, and well-equipped … with some consideration for the wonderful traditions of English architecture'.[99] He also claimed them as essentially Georgian:

> Here it is to be seen exhibiting the first and essential of urban virtues; good
> manners. It realizes that, as a member of a community, it is unbecoming

to attract attention to itself, to shout and make faces at its neighbours, as it were. And so these schemes have about them an air of dignity and reticence, they exhibit, in fact, urbanity, a quality as becoming to the small, four-roomed house as to the large mansion. In this respect they may be said to be Georgian, for urbanity was surely the keynote of all the immense building activity of that epoch.[100]

Thus for some architects and critics, the Georgian period became the model for modern English 'good design'.

Other designers and critics looked backed to the simplicity of the medieval period. The historian Michael T. Saler posits the idea of 'Medieval Modernism' in relation to the ideology of Frank Pick, chief designer of the London Underground, derived from the simplicity, honesty and lack of ornamentation of the Arts and Crafts movement.[101] A peculiarly English Modernism emerged. Some English designers, architects and critics both looked back to an idea of the rural vernacular cottage and also drew on elements of Georgian design for principles of proportion and symmetry, as well as the Arts and Crafts movement. The design historian Paul Greenhalgh describes this as an 'English compromise' in design, which 'put a stable, better past into the future tense'.[102] In practice this meant furniture derived from the Arts and Crafts movement with pegged joints made without the use of glue, simple and plain forms often drawing on vernacular styles invoking 'Old England', combined with simple geometric carved decoration.

Similar ideals of 'good design' were promoted by organisations such as the Design and Industries Association (DIA), which was formed in 1915 to improve the quality of design in British industry. The DIA campaigned under the Arts and Crafts 'fitness for purpose' maxim for better design. The Association's early aesthetic principles followed W.R. Lethaby's Arts and Crafts ideals, focusing on the traditional 'art industries' of ceramics, textiles and furniture; in other words, hand-made and short-run products with a traditional craft base and an established market.

In 1920 the DIA contributed a domestic 'Chamber of Horrors' to the 1920 Ideal Home Exhibition, warning visitors about what to avoid when decorating or furnishing a home. The messages of the DIA were promoted within the Ideal Home Exhibition not only as lessons in 'good design', but also as warnings on 'bad design'. The DIA aimed to demonstrate 'fitness for purpose' by showing the 'approved pattern' and the 'horrible example' in pairs 'to enforce the moral', in order to emphasise and illustrate its message. The DIA's sense of morality spilled over into the language that was used to describe the exhibit: 'There is a depraved china milk-jug, for instance, with a hollow handle which fills with milk. The handle can never be properly cleaned and acts as a poison-centre. A virtuous, sensible milk-jug will keep it company.'[103] Such a description constructed a moral geography of the kitchen. It seems no coincidence that the words the DIA used were also those employed to describe the desirable and undesirable conduct of women, at a time when reformers were concerned with the attainment of good mothering for the future of the English 'race'.[104]

The 'English compromise' was practised by designers such as Gordon Russell, who furnished Berg's show home of Coates and Pleydell Bouverie's Sunspan house in this style. Instead of the functionalist bent ply and cantilevered tubular steel and glass furniture that the house's Modernist interior might suggest, Russell's simple modern style, derived from the Arts and Crafts movement and in line with DIA ideals of fitness for purpose, was a forerunner of the wartime Utility furniture scheme.[105] Such furniture could also be found in the interiors of the Modernist houses at Silver End (Figure 3.10). Birnstingl's notion of 'good modern furniture' is enlightening here; he described it as 'good in its materials and in its workmanship, and aiming at an ideal which is neither absolute beauty not absolute usefulness, but which strives to combine with these a new quality, that of labour-saving'.[106] Thus the discourses about the 'English compromise' of Modernism in the context of the home were combined with a concern for labour-saving and efficiency that I will explore in the next chapter.

3.10 'Delightful cottage' interior, Silver End, from *Modern Home*, 17, February 1930

Some suburban dwellers and designers were attracted to a 'restrained Modernism', a term coined by Finn Jensen to describe a building style with a plain brick elevation rather than crisp, white rendering.[107] This was seen, for example, in the winning flat-roofed, brick-built design of the 1930 'House That Jill Built' competition at the Ideal Home Exhibition, designed by housewife Phyllis Lee and realised by architect Douglas Tanner, which will be discussed in more detail in Chapter 4. There are also echoes of Elisabeth Scott's Royal Shakespeare Theatre at Stratford-upon-Avon, the result of the first competition in the world for a public building won by a woman, and Dora Gordine's Dorich House. The brick-built, massive, largely unadorned forms of both these examples have usually been explained in terms of their similarities to both industrial structures and German Expressionism. Saler's notion of 'Medieval Modernism' might be a more apt categorisation.[108]

For many architects, designers and critics, Nikolaus Pevsner's

Modernist definition of 'good design' – functionalism – held sway.[109] This was a moral belief in the potential of simple and functional design to enhance people's lives. Pevsner set the debate about Modernism and provided both its chronology and lineage, from which British design was largely excluded other than the Arts and Crafts movement, which he saw as proto-Modernism. Critics such as Pevsner made little attempt to come to terms with the aesthetic of 'bad design', or to explore its cultural meanings and resonances. Much of the writing on design reform in the interwar period displays a tension between 'good design' and 'bad design'. 'Good design' was thought to be 'simple', 'straightforward', 'decided by utility' and 'fit for purpose'. Underlying much design reform was a notion that educating consumer taste would create a demand for modern design that manufacturers and house builders would be forced to fulfil.[110] Art and design historians and critics such as Anthony Bertram wrote relatively little on popular taste except to condemn it. Suburban Modernism was seen as the opposite of 'good design': as Modernism's other.

Modernisation

In media discourses on homemaking in the interwar years there was much emphasis on modernising the home. Consumers were influenced by the proliferation of homemaking and women's magazines, many of which were aimed at the respectable working and lower middle classes. *Modern Home* magazine was launched in October 1928; published monthly and aimed at the house-proud and modernising professional housewife and her husband, it continued until 1939 (Plate 3). The February 1929 issue contained not only an account of Rosita Forbes's house discussed above, but also an article by a Mrs Wilfred Ashley on 'What I think of modern furniture', in which she gave her opinion on 'the modern trend in furnishing and decorating'.[111] The 'modern home' of the magazine could blend old comforts with new technologies. For example, a feature on 'Other people's homes' noted how 'This little thatched cottage on a

Sussex common looks really old, but captain P.A. Barron lets us into the secret of its up-to-date equipment.'[112] Modern homes were often newly built and efficient to keep. Another feature described 'a modern home you can build for £930 and run without help'. The house combined a traditional pitched roof with a Modernistic geometric façade reminiscent of the houses at Crittall's Silver End.[113] The sense of modernisation was also enhanced by the magazine's use of a Modernistic typeface for some article titles.

Modern Home readers were often advised to modernise their homes by changing the fireplace and the mantelpiece. New 'Devon' tiled fireplaces, consisting of tiled surrounds in a stepped pattern (Figures 1.5 and 4.2; Plate 7) or tiled inserts with wooden surrounds, could be fitted to replace old wooden or cast-iron ones. These tiled fireplaces were supplied in pre-formed sections and were easy to fit in new houses or as part of a modernisation scheme in an old one. They remained popular well into the post-war period. The tiles were usually a mottled beige or cream colour, sometimes combined with a coloured border and smaller inset tiles in orange. Blues and greens were also available. These tiled fire surrounds usually contained an open coal fire. Lancaster's Modernistic sitting room with a tiled mantelpiece displaying a Modernistic mantel clock and stylised ceramic dog, with an unframed and angled mirror above it, was typical (Figure 3.2).

Aside from the kitchen, the most modern room of the interwar home was usually the bathroom. The indoor bathroom, with a plumbed-in, fixed bath, large rectangular handbasin on a pedestal or brackets and a toilet, which was sometimes located in a small adjacent separate room, was the height of luxury and modernity.[114] Bathrooms were sometimes located downstairs to save on plumbing costs. For first-time homeowners and the occupants of the new local authority estates, the indoor bathroom liberated them from the tedium of filling a portable bath by hand in the kitchen or the combined kitchen/living room. It also spared them a trip to the public baths, making bathing a private activity. In the case of new houses, buyers often had the opportunity to choose bathroom fixtures and fittings at the point of purchase. For those living in older houses, installing a modern indoor bathroom was a potent symbol of modernisation and modernity.

In most suburban bathrooms white sanitary ware and tiles were standard. Cleanliness and hygiene were of paramount importance. This was reflected in the use of glazed tiles, chromium fittings, panels enclosing the bath, linoleum on the floor and the predominance of white. The opportunity to introduce colour and decoration into the bathroom was afforded by the tiling of walls to whatever height finances permitted. White tiles were standard but were often combined with edging and decorative inserts in other colours. Tiling gave builders and home-owners an opportunity to let rip with a riot of colour and Modernistic design, typically geometric, stepped patterns creating a sense of luxury and glamour. Decorative effects could also be created through the use of special patterned wallpaper with water-related scenes such as the seaside, fish or seabirds, or decorative linoleum. Coloured suites were available and enthusiastically marketed by manufacturers. For example, Twyford offered its customers coloured bathroom suites in celadon green, lavender blue, old ivory and black with the insides finished in white (Plate 12). Taps had a more simplified, streamlined design than previously and a multitude of matching accessories were available, including mirrors with coloured frames, bathroom cabinets, shelves, toothbrush holders and soap and sponge trays. The extending, circular, chrome shaving mirror attached to the wall was a popular feature.

Textiles, linoleum, rugs and wallpaper were viewed as a cheap way of modernising the home with less risk than the purchase of an item of furniture that would be expected to last for many years. Modernistic patterns in bright colours that combined stylised florals with geometric 'cubist' forms were popular (Plate 14). Simple, more restrained abstract patterns and plainer, textured and woven fabrics in neutral colours were available for those with more Modernist tastes. Catesbys sold a range of colourful linoleum in striking Modernistic designs that were intended to be installed as unfitted 'Linola squares' like rugs, rather than fitted from edge to edge in rooms (Plate 7). Wallpaper manufacturers came up with elaborate schemes with border and feature papers that were designed to make a picture-frame effect on each wall (Plate 13). Wallpaper was available very cheaply and replaced frequently, a convenient way to cover up damp and add colour to the home. Although it may seem incongruous to present-day eyes, it was common to combine Modernistic wallpaper or borders with traditional furniture, as was seen, for example, in a photo of a show home in a Morrell prospectus for Countryside Estates in the 1930s (Figure 3.11).

For Birnstingl, this unfettered use of pattern and colour was the result of the 'Efficiency' aesthetic where labour-saving was paramount,

3.11 Sitting room, from Morrell prospectus for Countryside Estates, *c.* 1930s

leading to mouldings and other decorative details disappearing. He claimed that women were seduced by colour, particularly in textiles and cushions, because they had sacrificed form in the attainment of their labour-saving ideal.[115] This may be a caution against the Moderne or Modernistic stylised geometric and floral patterns in bright colours accented with black which in 1927 were beginning to appear in textiles and wallpapers – always seen as the bottom of the hierarchy of design and associated with women – having first been evident in clothing. Birnstingl also predicted that colours would acquire 'specific health values' and 'the decoration of the home will pass from those whose qualifications are connected with art to those trained in chromatic therapeutics' who would determine colour schemes, with 'art shade' replaced by 'health shade'.[116] This prediction was soon to come true; as I have discussed above, the 1928 House of the Future at the Ideal Home Exhibition used changing coloured lights against a white background to enhance the mood of its occupants.

Coloured paint also offered homeowners opportunities to express their modernity. In one extreme example, homeowner Sidney Campion was determined that his new house should be modern.[117] He achieved this by turning it into what he called a 'Temple of Colour'. He said, 'Now that I had a house of my own I could at last surround myself with gorgeous colours, and break away from the accepted traditions of brown and grey and graining.' His kitchen was painted with '[a]n apple-green dado and pale pink wallpaper covered with thousands of vari-coloured petals', which contrasted with black woodwork with 'a glossy finish like the sheen of a raven'. His lounge was painted in sunshine yellow, 'the dominant colour of a large bookcase covering one wall', with highlights of pale pink and pale blue, and these colours were repeated in satin wallpaper. A fawn carpet had a 'bold blue pattern'. Campion revelled in his friends' reactions to his bold colour scheme: '"Certainly very novel", observed friends, and I am sure that only good breeding precluded them from adding devastating comment.'[118] His wife restrained him from carrying out his love of colour on the exterior. He wistfully ended his account with his longing for the Modernistic: 'If ever I am rich and can build a house in the country, it will not only be a Temple of colour, but also a Temple of Curves.'[119] Campion's modernity was of his own making, and contrasted with Modernist notions of good taste and design that turned towards plain surfaces and restrained, neutral white, off-white and beige tones.

Home crafts offered women particular opportunities to modernise their homes.[120] The pages of women's and homemaking magazines were full of instructions on how to make such items as cushions and tray cloths decorated with applique and embroidery. From 1929 Modernistic motifs became increasingly common in such designs. For example, the April 1929 issue of *Modern Home* magazine included instructions for a 'raffia cushion with jazz border … for sun-parlour or garden use'.[121] Again, cushions appear in Lancaster's 'Modernistic' cartoon (Figure 3.2).

While some middle-class homeowners relished original antique furniture and features in their property, others were keen to banish any traces of Victorian furniture, taste and style. This became evident from the late 1920s in homemaking magazines. The desire to modernise furniture and decoration sometimes led to a do-it-yourself approach – albeit with somebody else's labour – as evidenced in the advice column of *Modern Home* magazine. In February 1929 the magazine printed the first enquiry from a reader asking how to modernise an item of furniture. Mrs Hile of St John's, Worcester, asked: 'Is there anything I can do to an old-fashioned black and white brass bedstead to make it suitable for a modern bedroom?' The writer of the advice column replied, 'I should advise you to have the ends covered with very thin sheets of plywood – any small carpenter can undertake the job for you. Then make loose covers for the ends in a flowered cretonne, furnishing taffeta or similar material, to match the decorations in your bedroom.'[122] This covering up of old-fashioned styles with sheets of ply was a frequently advised strategy for thrifty modernisation.

Another problem for owners of older property was what to do with original features that had fallen out of fashion. In June 1929 Mrs L.M. Illard of Plymouth asked for advice: 'We have taken a rather nice roomy flat of the old-fashioned type, so we are confronted with one horror! An old-fashioned coal range in the room I wish to make the dining-room. Can you suggest a camouflage?'[123] With the abandonment of the traditional arrangement of kitchen/living room, where heating and cooking was done on a traditional coal-fired range, for a separate kitchen with modern gas or electric cooker, this was a common problem. The magazine advised: 'If you do not wish to have the range removed, why not have the front filled in, flush with the surrounding wall, with Poilite [sic] or asbestos sheeting, to simulate a paneled or tiled effect and have a modern gas fire fitted in front of this?' When 'Mr G' of Belfast enquired in April 1929, 'Can I paint over the ugly multicoloured tiles in my hall floor?', he was advised to cover them with a 'hard-wearing paint'.[124] Such correspondence suggests that householders made personal investments in the modernisation of their homes and were actively involved in carrying them out themselves.

The better-off middle classes who lived in old houses but wanted to be modern could employ architects and professional decorators to help them modernise. Homemaking magazines were full of accounts of such projects. An article in *Good Housekeeping* in 1935 described 'A Victorian room transformed' by Mr Maurice Adams, and included before and after photographs. 'Modern' 'streamline' furniture was built into recesses and an electric radiator replaced the old fireplace. The picture rail was removed and the room was papered to the ceiling in pale grey and lemon yellow horizontal stripes. Parquet squares were laid over the floorboards and topped with a hearth rug. Curtains, 'block-printed artificial silk in design of nigger [sic] and sepia on a yellow ground' in a geometric 'cubist' pattern, were drawn across the whole room.[125] While such modernisation projects were beyond the means of many, features in magazines appealed to the aspirations of a wider social group of homeowners.

In their desire to be modern, consumers could also take inspiration from displays at events such as the Ideal Home Exhibition and at retail showrooms. For example, Catesbys had a huge furniture and furnishings retail showroom on London's Tottenham Court Road. One of their catalogues documented their exhibition of 'comparative furnished rooms' displaying a series of 'before' and 'after' rooms, comparing the 'dull' and 'out-of-date' with the modernised (Figure 3.12). As the catalogue noted, 'Although many people begin to feel their homes are very out of date, very few can afford to discard all their old furnishings and replace them with something entirely new.' Their exhibition offered 'countless suggestions for modernizing your existing furnishings at very little cost'. Thus a sitting room furnished in a traditional style with a three-piece suite covered with a traditional jacquard fabric was re-upholstered in modern diagonal stripes. As the catalogue proclaimed, 'The suite is NOT new – the old one has been remodelled!' Other furniture was new; the dark-stained, barley-twist leg occasional table was replaced by a lower, circular coffee table in a lighter finish that stood on a single, fluted column. Other changes included swapping a free-standing gramophone for a wireless set placed on a new built-in ledge installed across the width of the room. This was built under the new short curtains, again in diagonal stripes, which replaced floor-length jacquard curtains and nets. The aspidistra on a tall plant stand was replaced with a free-standing cigarette lighter. The tall sideboard with mirrored whatnot (a stand with small shelves for objects) was replaced by a simple, low, modern, square console table. The only antique in the room was a chair that suggested the timeless tradition of English good taste. Busily patterned wallpaper was replaced with a modern paper trimmed with a striped border paper at picture rail height, which was also used in the contemporary fashion to frame the new feature ledge shelf. A patterned Axminster carpet topped with a rug with a 'cubist pattern' – the only nod to modernity in the old room – was replaced with a plain carpet. Instead of an Art Nouveau overhead lampshade, the room was now lit with a simple table lamp. The new room combined a

3.12 Front cover of promotional brochure by Catesbys, 'How to modernise your home at little cost', c. 1930s

restrained 'English compromise' with the Modernistic.[126] Elsewhere in the Catesbys catalogue, furniture was featured in a plethora of styles from 'Unit furniture' designed for the 'modern small house' (which would have been recognised as 'good design' by the most hardline Modernist) to a 'Jacobean dining suite', which fused traditional form with Modernistic carved decorations.[127] The suburban Modernism of the interwar home included traditional and modern styles without contradiction.

Making modern choices: Marks and Tillie Freedman

The biggest opportunities for householders to be modern came with the purchase of a new house. Builders often allowed purchasers to choose their own fixtures and fittings (Figure 3.13). It was standard practice for

3.13 Homebuyers at Jack Cook's Estate Agents, Kidbrook Park, London, *c.* 1930s

house buyers to be given a budget for decoration (paint and wallpaper) and features such as fireplaces, usually to be spent at the builders' nominated supplier and then installed as part of the purchase price. The consumer possibilities offered by the purchase of a new home are vividly illustrated in the following story of the purchase in 1934 of a semi-detached house at 1 Burleigh Gardens, Southgate, in the borough of Enfield in north London, from the builder A.T. Rowley of Tottenham, by Marks and Tillie Freedman from Walworth in south-east London.[128]

At a price of £1,020, the house was by no means the cheapest option at the time. Its cost represented about four years' wages for Marks Freedman, who listed his occupation as 'engineer' in his mortgage application, on a wage of £5 a week.[129] The Freedmans paid an initial deposit of £5 to secure the house. The balance of the deposit – £97 – was to be paid on signing the contract.[130] A mortgage of £400 was obtained from East Barnet Valley Urban District Council under 1923 legislation that allowed local authorities to lend up to 90 per cent for the purchase of houses valued up to £1,500.[131] The sum was to be repaid in quarterly instalments over twenty years at an interest rate of 3.75 per cent.[132] The Freedmans also had to pay surveyors' fees of £2 2s.[133] The couple seemed to have the rest of the money needed for the purchase available in cash.

Quite why the Freedmans decided to move to Enfield is unclear, but it may have been due to Marks's work as an engineer. Certainly it represented a significant relocation for them both, away from their families. Marks was born in Whitechapel, east London in March 1901, the eldest son of Nathan Freedman (b. 1876), a ladies' mantle maker originally from Russia, and his wife Leah (1877–1945), originally from Poland. The family subsequently lived in the same area and in the 1911 census family fortunes had increased enough for them to have a general domestic servant resident. In December 1933 Marks married Tillie Goralick, and the couple moved into a house in Walworth with her brother.[134] The Freedmans' purchase of a new house in Enfield represented middle-class aspirations (Plate 9).

The Freedmans' new semi-detached house comprised two reception rooms, kitchen, scullery, hall and landing, three bedrooms, a WC and a bathroom. As the first house on its side of the road, it benefited from a large corner plot with gardens extending to the side as well as the front and about 100 feet (30 m) to the back. Its interior dimensions were relatively generous. The house had a red, tiled roof and bay windows in both front reception room and master bedroom, with hanging red tiles between them. The façade was built of red brick and rendered on the first floor. Although not half-timbered, it gestured to a Queen Anne historic style. Seen in the broader context of the full range of designs on offer, this was quite a restrained and modern style.[135]

There was extensive correspondence between Marks Freedman and the builder, A.T. Rowley. The Freedmans had considerable freedom in choosing fixtures and decoration for the house. In many instances they exceeded the allowances in the purchase price and paid extra for additional features. For example, they paid £3 3s for the fitting of coloured leaded lights to the fanlights on the front elevation.[136] The Freedmans' correspondence with the builder reveals their intense desire to make modern choices, such as an electric point in the bathroom to illuminate a shaving mirror. However, the letter with the quote of 25 shillings for the cost of the work was annotated in Marks's handwriting, 'phoned them, not required'.[137] Time and time again throughout their correspondence, the Freedmans reined in their consumer desires. They even tried to cut costs by omitting a wardrobe cupboard in a bedroom and picture rails.[138] What is unclear is whether this intense scrutiny of details was a joint enterprise by the Freedmans: all the letters were signed by Marks; Tillie was only mentioned once in the correspondence.

The Freedmans' relationship with the builder became particularly strained over their choice of fireplaces. The purchase price of the house included the choice and fitting of fires and fireplaces to the value of £20, which could be chosen from Messrs Cakebread Robey.[139] The company's showroom in Enfield was housed in a distinctive modern building, in geometric form, reminiscent both of the factories on the Great Western Road described in J.B. Priestley's *English Journey* and buildings from exhibitions such as the 1924 British Empire Exhibition.[140] Modern suburban consumers like the Freedmans were exposed to modern design in their workplaces and their leisure activities, including shopping and the cinema, as well as learning about it in women's magazines and the new housekeeping magazines, popular newspapers and domestic advice manuals.

For the two reception rooms and two of the bedrooms the Freedmans spent a total of £31 8s 6d on fireplaces, over 50 per cent more than the builder's allowance.[141] By the mid-1930s gas and electric fireplaces had become popular with householders, who preferred them to coal fires, which were perceived by some as great harbourers of dust and disease. Built-in gas and electric fires also offered new forms of living that meant that households were not confined to one room in the evening and at weekends.[142] The Freedmans' choice of fireplaces for downstairs were particularly modern for the time; a similar fireplace appeared in Lancaster's 'Functional' room (Figure 3.1). This choice was perhaps influenced by Marks Freedman's training as an engineer, which led him to appreciate new technologies. He wrote to the builder that in the front reception room he wanted 'Portello 3-unit gas fire with wall panel. Since this has no hearth and is well above the floor, the floorboards should be continued up to the wall and the skirting also continuous, in a similar manner to the illustration in your possession of a Portcullis gas fire' (Figure 3.14).[143] Portcullis gas fires were first shown by Bratt, Colbran & Co. in the autumn of 1932. The architectural historian and critic Nikolaus Pevsner commented approvingly that the 'radiants form a grid or gridiron of portcullis shape, an artistic improvement of great consequence'.[144] Pevsner felt that this was preferable to a gas fire that imitated a coal fire flame effect. The portcullis shape increased energy output, as well as being aesthetically pleasing. As Pevsner noted, they were at first 'too new and unusual to be commercially successful',[145] and it took at least a year

PORTCULLIS GAS FIRES

No. 793. Wall Panel in San Stefani Marble, overall size 25½″ × 35½″ high, slabbed into one piece 2 15 0

		£ s. d.
In Napoleon Marble	£2 7 6	
In Light or Dark Swedish Green Marbles ...	3 6 0	
In Sycamore Onyx Marble	2 17 6	
In Portuguese Beige Marble	2 10 0	
In Golden Fleury Marble	2 12 6	

"Portello" 2 unit "Portcullis" Gas Fire in Lustral Colour with Gold or Silver relief, overall size 15½″ × 24½″. Automatic Ignition 4 2 6

6 17 6

No. 793. Wall Panel can be supplied 3″ wider, i.e., 28½″ × 35½″ high for 3-unit "Portello" Gas Fire.

In San Stefani Marble	2 18 6
In Napoleon Marble	£2 10 0
In Light or Dark Swedish Green Marbles ...	3 11 0
In Sycamore Onyx Marble	3 1 0
In Portuguese Beige Marble	2 12 6
In Golden Fleury Marble	2 15 0

"Portello" 3 unit "Portcullis" Gas Fire in finish as above, overall size 18½″ × 24½″ high. Automatic Ignition 4 15 0

7 13 6

No. 793. Wall Panel can also be supplied 31½″ wide × 35½″ high for 4-unit "Portello" Gas Fire. Prices upon application.

PRICES OF GAS FIRES ARE SUBJECT TO CURRENT ADVANCES

BRATT COLBRAN LIMITED, 10 Mortimer Street, London, W.1
TELEPHONES   MUSEUM 9411 & 9311   10 LINES

54

3.14 Portcullis gas fire, from Bratt Colbran catalogue, *c.* 1935

for retailers to stock them, let alone for the public to purchase them, which suggests that the Freedmans made a progressive and cutting-edge choice.

For the back reception room, the Freedmans originally specified a combined gas and coke fire with a brown porcelain finish, but after seeing a sample of it at the showroom they changed to chromium plate. Marks wrote to the builder: 'To take this fire I have selected a tiled fireplace with electric clock inset.'[146] To his consternation, when the builder installed the fireplaces it was not done to Marks's satisfaction and he wrote to complain:

> With regard to the fireplace and gas fire in the back reception room, I am surprised to see that the gas pipe has been carried along the hearth, instead of downwards through the hearth which is of course the correct way as shown in the enclosed leaflet from the makers [sic] catalogue. Seeing that I have spent £13 on this fireplace, it seems a pity that its appearance has been spoilt by the fitting, and I consider that it should be put right.[147]

There followed a protracted correspondence over who should bear the cost of correcting the placement of the pipe.

How typical the Freedmans were of interwar homeowners is hard to ascertain. While I have discussed here their more modern choices, they also exercised more traditional tastes in other areas of the house, which I discuss in Chapter 5. What does seem clear is that it was possible to select both modern and traditional designs without any apparent contradiction.

Conclusion

The critics and practitioners of Modernism in architecture and design in interwar Britain were uncomfortable with the popular taste of the suburbs. As I have argued here, a further problem with accounts of this period by design historians is the idea that there was a universal notion of Modernism and 'good design'.[148] For some critics, both historical and recent, the absolutism of a Modernist aesthetic framed their judgements; they neither engaged with popular taste on its own terms, nor looked outside Modernist doctrines for a notion of what the 'modern' might be. The suburban Modernism examined in this chapter shows how it might be more helpful to think of *Modernisms*; a multiplicity of responses to modernity including and exceeding the strictures of the Modern Movement in architecture and design, responses that negotiate with tradition as well as newness. This, however, taps into the fears of Modernists that Modernism would be seen as just another choice rather than a rational, totalising aesthetic beyond style and fashion. Such concerns have also influenced design-historical accounts that see the history of twentieth-century domestic architecture as a linear narrative, going through phases of proto-Modernism and Medieval Modernism before arriving at Modernism proper around 1930. As this chapter has shown, a whole variety of Modernist styles coexisted, and the boundaries between them were blurred and much less well-defined than some design historians have claimed. Furthermore, while such categories may have exercised designers, architects and critics, they had little impact on the general public.

While the Modernistic had only limited popularity among the public as a style of architecture, it was highly successful in the domestic interior. Indeed, it was common for the interiors of interwar suburban houses not to stick consistently to one style. A Tudorbethan semi might be decorated and furnished in Modernistic abundance. Many suburbanites looked backwards to a romanticised hybrid Old English, Jacobethan or Tudorbethan tradition in the dining room and sitting room and also forwards to Hollywood glamour, most often in the bedroom. It was desirable for the kitchen and bathroom to contain the most 'modern' fittings and appliances available. Like speculative builders, most manufacturers and retailers were not fully paid-up Modernists, and produced a range of diverse styles to cater to popular taste, which will be discussed in more detail in Chapter 5.

In this chapter I have attempted to reveal some of the influences on the modern choices that interwar consumers made in the design and decoration of their homes. The case study of the Freedmans reveals interwar owner-occupiers as discriminating consumers actively engaged in the formation of suburban Modernism. While suburbanites may have eschewed the rational and improving Modernist ideas of architects and design reformers, they did not reject modernity. Rather they can be seen as negotiating and discriminating between the plethora of choices available, mediated by magazines, suppliers, retailers and builders. For many, modern and traditional decoration and furniture could exist happily side-by-side.

4

Efficiency: labour-saving and the professional housewife

A new identity of professional housewife emerged in suburban estates in interwar Britain. This is illustrated vividly by the front cover of the *Daily Express* publication *The Housewife's Book* (*c.* 1935), which uses a collage of photographs of the professional housewife at work (Figure 4.1) and a further 324 drawings and photographs inside conveying her duties in minute detail.[1] New methods of housework using labour-saving appliances emerged alongside new spatial configurations for the kitchen and the scullery. As Meaghan Morris puts it, 'modernity crept in through the back door, via the kitchen'.[2] The home, I argue in this chapter, was not a separate sphere outside of modernity; rather, it was a dynamic site of rapid change in which women experienced major shifts in spatial organisation, domestic practices and technologies and their own roles and identities. Drawing on international ideas of efficiency adopted from industry, especially time and motion studies, the idea of the modern labour-saving home gained momentum in the interwar housebuilding boom through the discourses of household advice manuals, magazines, advertisements and exhibitions as the habitat of the professional housewife.[3]

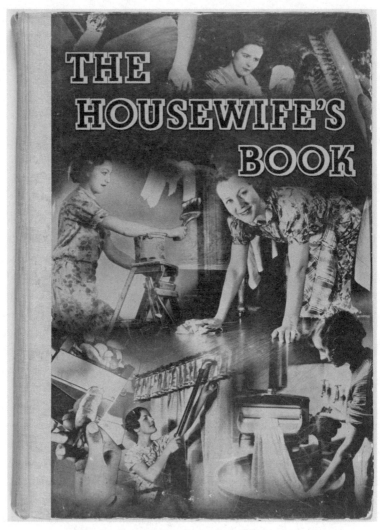

4.1 Front cover of *The Housewife's Book, Daily Express*, c. 1930s

Everyday housework:
Mass Observation's Respondent 082

The everyday experiences of interwar housewives were often far removed from the idealised discourses of efficiency and labour-saving. Fascinating first-hand accounts of the minutiae of daily life, including housework and cooking, can be found in the Mass Observation archive. Women participated as diarists and compilers of day reports, as interviewees and respondents to questionnaires. Their accounts and answers reveal differences and anxieties about everyday practices such as the nomenclature of the kitchen and the location of meals.

One of the most fascinating eyewitness accounts in the Mass Observation Archive can be found in the day surveys of 38-year-old Respondent 082 from Marlow, Buckinghamshire, written in 1937–38. She lived on a hill leading out of Marlow in a small, new, semi-detached house with five rooms and a bathroom, and a 'good garden' where some of the family's food was grown: 'the surroundings are lovely'. There were clear social divisions within the town: 'Many of the wealthier people have houses in Marlow, who with the church, dominate the peasant mentality, causing a medieval atmosphere.'[4] Some of the men worked in the neighbouring towns and most of the others worked on the land.

Respondent 082's day surveys reveal that her respectable suburban semi in Marlow was a step up in the world from the circumstances in which she had grown up and in which her siblings still lived. All this was manifested through her descriptions of domestic practices. Respondent 082 was from an 'extremely poor', large family: 'the mental attitude was that we were not margarine eaters. We hadn't sunk as low as *that*. Although I am puzzled to know how we could have sunk much further, being as we were only one step removed from destitution.'[5] For her, margarine was an indicator of social status: 'I connect the constant use of margarine with a social grade lower than the one I move in.'[6] She described her mother as having 'dominating traits. Bound by tradition

& dogma.' She was more negative still about her father: 'I cannot write anything coherent about him. Due perhaps to his being associated with strong unpleasant emotions during my childhood.' She had three sisters, one of whom had died while another still lived with her parents, as she was deaf and dumb and could not read or write, though despite this she worked in a West End dressmakers. Her third sister had 'no interest outside her four walls' and was married to a man who was 'consciencous [*sic*]' but 'ignorant himself and does like educating people'. Her brother was 'plebian, down-at-heel and usually unshaved. Almost always on the dole', a 'born gambler' and teetotaller with three children. His wife not only had a 'Vacuous smile. Face like a full moon. Fat and illiterate' but was judged wanting in some, but not all, of her domestic accomplishments: 'Seldom cooks anything. Children look neglected. But home (2 rooms) spotless.'[7] A former neighbour was said to have a 'Dirty home' as well as 'Never having any money except to back horses with.'[8] Respondent 082 judged the respectability of family, friends, acquaintances and neighbours by their standards of housework.

In contrast to her family, Respondent 082's husband was 'Well bred. Educated at a boarding school. His grandfather used a coat of arms […] Offered a commission during the war and refused it. Mentioned in dispatches.' He had originally trained before the war as an engineer, but could not secure a job in his profession except for labourer's wages because he was over forty.[9] He was reduced to working as a bus driver, often on late shifts, which meant that their meals and her housework were organised around his hours so as not to disturb him while he slept late in the morning. Her husband struggled to cope with his reduced social circumstances; he 'Cannot adapt himself to the indignities of working class life. Somewhat neurotic.'[10] She suggested that he had lowered his standards: he 'doesn't wash or do his hair before breakfast (except when he is staying in his mother's house)'.[11] She described his mother as 'The world's prize snob' who had never been to visit them.[12] Throughout her day reports, Respondent 082 describes a struggle to keep up appearances

4.2 Mantelpiece photographed by Respondent 082, Mass Observation Day Survey, 14 September 1937

and standards of living, especially when confronted by her husband's more middle-class family. This is evident in her description of the snapshot she sent Mass Observation as part of the 1937 mantelpiece survey (Figure 4.2) where the vase is off-centre. She said, 'Although a family secret I think that I should mention that the flowers are always arranged so as to hide a crack in the mirror.'[13] Respondent 082 was acutely aware that appearances were not always what they at first seemed.

Women in new suburban houses evolved their own ways of performing their duties as housewives. *The Housewife's Book* included plans of work for 'a mistress and one helper' and 'a small servantless house'. These give an idea of the kinds of ideal housework routines that were expected. For the servantless housewife, the plan advocated rising at 7.00, stripping the bed, airing the rooms, unlocking the house, stoking the boiler and lighting the living-room fire (if needed) and preparing breakfast. From 8.00–9.00, breakfast should be taken and cleared away, washing-up done and children taken to school. From 9.00 to 10.00 the porch and steps should be swept, the sitting-room fire laid, the dining-room and sitting-room carpets vacuumed and the surrounds mopped and the rooms dusted. From 10.00 to 11.00 beds should be made, upstairs rooms mopped and dusted, the bathroom cleaned and the stairs swept. From 11.00 to 12.00 preparations should begin for the main midday or evening meal and shopping be done. Lunch or dinner should be served at 1.00. After washing-up, tidying the kitchen and scullery from 2.00 to 3.00, the housewife should change out of her working clothes. From 3.00 to 4.30 she might have some free time: 'Recreation, resting, visiting or special duties such as ironing, gardening, needlework according to season. Minding young children if necessary.' Tea should be prepared and served and washing-up done between 4.30 and 6.00. Then from 6.00 to 7.00, food was prepared and cooked for supper or dinner. Children should be put to bed at 7.00 and dinner served at 7.40. The meal should be cleared away at 8.00–8.40: 'Wash up if liked, but this can be deferred until the morning.' From 8.40 there was time for 'Reading, recreation, letter writing, accounts.' In addition, it was recommended that laundry be done on Monday, the dining room be turned out on Tuesday and the silver cleaned, two bedrooms turned out on Wednesday, the sitting room turned out on Thursday, thorough cleaning of the bathroom and WC on Friday together with baking, and on Saturday special cleaning of hall, kitchen and scullery.[14]

Respondent 082 ran her house without servants or casual help but shaped her housework routines around her own needs and interests. She organised her housework around her 11-year-old daughter's school day to ensure she could spend time with her, but she also gave herself breaks in the day when she could read books, which was clearly a source of pleasure, satisfaction and self-improvement: 'I usually arrange my work so that I can do my reading while I am alone in the house.'[15] Books she mentioned included the recently published and popular novel *The Citadel* by A.J. Cronin, which influenced the founding of the NHS and the Labour party landslide of 1945,[16] and Mass Observation co-founder Tom Harrisson's non-fiction anthropological study *Savage Civilization* (1937), which she had access to via her brother-in-law who was employed by a firm that did work for the publisher Victor Gollancz.[17] Other books she borrowed from the library, often ordering them in especially. During meals: 'We all read at table Eileen included. I know she shouldn't, but I can't stop her if I do it myself. I have explained that it is considered bad manners, and that she mustn't do it anywhere else.'[18] Reading was clearly very important to Respondent 082's sense of identity and she frequently judged others on their reading matter. Other women attempted to differentiate their own identities within the category of 'housewife' by emphasising their creative homemaking skills over the 'rough' work of household maintenance through 'home craft' activities such as needlework, felting, knitting and interior decoration (Plate 16).[19]

Respondent 082 cooked a roast dinner on Saturday rather than Sunday so that she could take Sundays off from her household duties. She ensured that the roast was large enough to eat cold on Monday when she did her laundry so that she did not have to cook then. Her day reports detail exhaustively her cleaning routine, which involved dusting, sweeping the hearth, polishing floors, shaking out rugs, sewing, and even distempering walls. One of her most arduous tasks was to lay and light the fire. She longed for new appliances that could save her labour. On seeing an advert for Gamages in a newspaper she said, 'I want a small electric fire for the sitting room. Coal fires make such dirty work.'[20]

The timing of the main meal of the day varied, as *The Housewife's Book* explained:

> As meal-times [*sic*] vary considerably in different families and in different parts of the country, according to the nature of the husband's work the principal meal is sometimes taken in the middle and sometimes at the end

of the day. As a general rule, when the husband's work is near at hand and he can take meals at home, the principal meal is taken at midday, and the housewife's morning will necessarily be busier, but she should have more leisure between tea and supper.[21]

As Respondent 082's husband worked locally as a bus driver he usually took his dinner at home at midday, although his shifts sometimes meant that his meal was taken in mid to late afternoon. In her day reports she detailed preparations for dinner and the evening supper, in which she seemed to take little pleasure. She made frequent use of convenience and pre-prepared foods such as corned beef, tinned beans, crisps (served as a side vegetable) and custard powder, supplemented with home-grown vegetables such as cabbage from her garden. Visits from family members for meals were often a source of stress for Respondent 082. Her late sister's husband was an 'Egoist [...] Remotely related to Mrs Siddons [...] Regards women as an inferior species.' She complained about one of their visits: 'They all sit around waiting for me to dish up the dinner. I feel an insane desire or is it a sane one to put on my coat and walk out of the house, but I go on dishing up the dinner.'[22] Fantasies about escaping her domestic duties recur throughout her day reports.

Mass Observation also undertook extensive interviews with women for *An Inquiry into People's Homes*, a report for the Advertising Service Guild prepared in 1943. It surveyed 1,100 people, 90 per cent of whom were housewives, in twelve locations including garden cities and municipal housing about their existing homes and what they wanted for the future.[23] Satisfaction with homes was highest on the housing estates (80 per cent) and lowest in old houses (62 per cent).[24] These Mass Observation reports and surveys serve as correctives to idealised discourses of efficiency, labour-saving and the kitchen found in magazines, exhibition catalogues, domestic advice manuals and advertisements.

The 'servant problem'

The contemporary discourse of advice manuals, magazines and advertisements of the interwar years identified a 'servant problem'. This in turn justified a need for 'efficiency' and 'progress' in homemaking. The 'servant problem', which was discussed in the media before 1914, was primarily a concern with the quantity and quality of available servants.[25] The middle and upper classes had long complained about servants but they now feared the emergence of a more assertive working class who behaved more like organised industrial workers than compliant servants.[26] The young women who once went into service preferred the freedom, better pay and conditions of the occupations they entered during the First World War, such as making munitions, mill and shop work, to 'skivvying'.[27] Within months of the outbreak of war, servants disappeared from middle- and upper-class households.[28]

After the war, some female former servants worked in assembly industries making labour-saving goods that middle-class women bought. These occupations paid better wages than domestic service and enabled working-class women to purchase goods and products to ease their own domestic labour.[29] However, many of the women employed in wartime industries were demobilised and forced back into domestic service after the war. By 1921, government grants given to the Central Committee on Women's Training and Unemployment (set up during the war) were tied exclusively to domestic service training.[30] In 1922 the new Insurance Act stipulated that applicants were to accept any job which they were capable of doing, and that they no longer had any right to a job with comparable pay and conditions to their previous employment.[31]

Consequently, women were forced back into domestic service through legislation and economic expediency. Although domestic service declined in the interwar years, it still represented the largest occupation for women. In 1911 there were 2,127,000 women in domestic service in Britain; ten years later the number had fallen to 1,845,000, but this figure still represented 32.5 per cent of the female workforce.[32] Moreover, in 1923 domestic servants were still the largest single group of employees in Britain.[33] However, by the 1920s over 70 per cent of households that employed servants had just one: a maid-of-all-work, who often had to look after children as well as do housework.[34] Increasingly, only the upper middle classes could afford to employ live-in servants, and there was a shift away from residential servants to 'dailies' (typically an older local women) and the casual employment of 'chars' and other household help, especially among the less well-off middle classes. Furthermore, with post-First World War inflation in the 1920s, many 'New Poor' middle-class families struggled to maintain their pre-war standards of living.

By 1931, there was a momentary increase of 15 per cent in the number of female indoor servants, caused by high unemployment and the economic recession as well as the housebuilding boom. However, due to the increased number of houses there was actually a shortage of domestic staff.[35] Moreover, '[t]he conspicuous numbers of factory and shop workers able to enjoy their independence meant that domestic service was increasingly seen as menial work, only undertaken by children from the poorest families and the most rural backwaters'.[36] The 'New Rich' respectable working-class and aspiring lower-middle-class residents of the new suburban estates also bemoaned the lack of servants. In fact, some of them may have once been servants themselves. The 'servant problem' touched all levels of society as a reality, a lived experience and an aspiration. Women from both the 'New Poor' and the 'New Rich' used the discourse of the 'servant problem' to mask the fact that their income could not stretch to domestic service, or, if it did, not beyond casual help. There were new one-to-one relations between mistresses and servants in smaller houses. As Selina Todd has argued, young, bob-haired, female servants 'became symbols of a new assertive modernity, fashioned by mass-produced clothes and cosmetics which suggested a girl could escape her place, if only fleetingly'.[37] As Nicola Beauman says, the 'servant problem' featured frequently in women's novels:

> In the early part of the period it was to most middle-class women merely
> an unavoidable annoyance ... but one they were unsuited to deal with ...
> As time went on, the shortage of domestic help became an accepted fact
> of life, although most middle-class women never really understood why
> young girls preferred to work in a factory.[38]

This was reflected in middlebrow women's novels such as Lettice
Cooper's *The New House* (1936). For some middle-class women such
as Virginia Woolf, a life with fewer servants was imagined as a libera-
tion. On her return to Bloomsbury in 1924, she fantasised about her new
house 'entirely controlled by one woman, a vacuum cleaner, & electric
stoves'.[39] The reality was somewhat different; Woolf's former maid-of-all
work Nellie became a 'cook general' and the two developed a tempestu-
ous relationship, with Nellie frequently giving notice as a means of get-
ting her own way.

As households struggled to recruit and hold on to good servants, pay
and conditions improved and there were more liberal conditions for
some, such as more informal uniforms. The housing boom of the mid-
1930s meant that the 'servant problem' remained. In 1937 the Ministry of
Education concluded that the shortage of servants was due to an increase
in demand rather than a decrease in supply.[40] Increasing numbers of
foreigners who came to Britain as refugees initially found work as servants, some through domestic servant permits.[41] Domestic service was
still the largest source of employment for women in 1945. By 1951, the
numbers had fallen by more than 750,000 to 343,000.[42] However, these
figures may mask the employment of women on a more casual and ad
hoc basis.[43]

The idea of the servantless home ruled over by the professional housewife meant different things to different women and several models coexisted, from households with reduced staff, to those with casual staff, to
those with none at all. Indeed, in some advertisements it was difficult
to tell whether it was a servant or a professional housewife depicted
(Plate 10). The 'servant problem' prompted calls for more efficient,

labour-saving homes that could be run with a reduced staff and led to the professionalisation of the middle-class housewife.

Scientific management and the labour-saving home

Take your minds for a moment from the home to a modern, well-managed factory, where every movement of the worker is considered with a view to saving unnecessary labour. In a factory you cannot afford to waste human energy. That is the system we want applied in our homes. Do not misunderstand. We do not want to turn our homes into factories. Our homes must be homes – places of peace, contentment and happiness; but because they are homes we do not want to waste our energies and work in them.[44]

These words were spoken by the domestic advice writer Constance Peel in a lecture on the labour-saving kitchen in 1920. She showed a series of lantern slides to demonstrate 'how time is wasted and labour increased in preparing meals'. One of her diagrams showed how 'in the average middle-class home […] a girl has to walk 350 ft. over the process of laying tea. By a proper arrangement of cupboards and dressers, this could be reduced to 30ft.'[45] A similar diagram was used by Mrs Guy, a member of the Ministry of Reconstruction's Women's Advisory Sub-Committee on Housing, to accompany an article in the *Daily Mail* in 1919 (Figure 4.3).[46] The new discourse of scientific home management thus equated the home with the factory, referring to the housewife (or her servant) as a worker, the kitchen as her workshop and labour-saving appliances as her tools.[47]

Constance Peel was influenced by American domestic advice writers who adapted ideas from scientific management techniques for use in the home and promoted the use of labour-saving appliances. Like the factory owner, the householder was advised to make an expensive investment in specialised machinery that would reduce costs in the long term. Christine Frederick published *The New Housekeeping: Efficiency Studies in Home Management* in 1914, which she followed a year later with

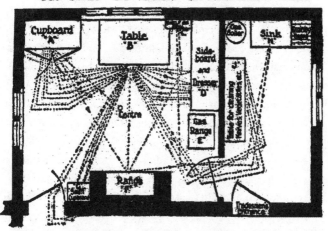

The kitchen in which the worker walked 350 feet to make afternoon tea.

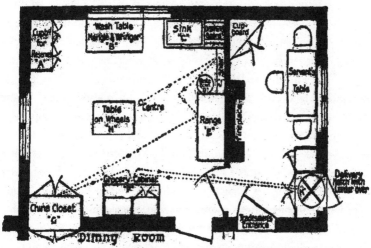

The same re-arranged in which the worker walked only 50 feet.

4.3 Diagram by Mrs Guy of 'Steps to make afternoon tea', from *Daily Mail*, 16 August 1919

Scientific Management in the Home: Household Engineering. Frederick adapted what might be called the 'ideology of efficiency' developed by F.W. Taylor in his *The Principles of Scientific Management* and Lillian Moller Gilbreth and Frank Bunker Gilbreth's *Applied Motion Study* (1917), which had been used in factories (notably by Henry Ford), to rationalise the home. Frederick suggested that when housekeeping was reformed according to the principles of efficiency, it would turn house-wives into professional managers of household affairs. Lillian Moller Gilbreth's *The Homemaker and Her Job* (1927) took Frederick's ideas further to professionalise housework and make the homemaker an exec-utive engineer, drawing on her expertise in motion studies and stress-ing the 'psychological and physical pleasures that efficient work might bring'.[48]

The idea of a 'labour-saving home' was addressed in Britain from the turn of the twentieth century by writers of domestic advice manuals such as Peel. She addressed women's need to run their homes efficiently with fewer servants during the First World War in her book *The Labour Saving House* (1917). In a similar vein, social reformer Clementina Black, of the Women's Industrial Council in Britain, published *A New Way of Housekeeping* in 1918. Rational housekeeping ideas also rapidly became assimilated into women's and homemaking magazines and newspapers.

Women's organisations called for 'homes fit for heroines', particu-larly for war widows and women who had undertaken munitions and other war work, often at a terrible cost to their health.[49] The Minister of Reconstruction, Dr Christopher Addison, set up the eleven-strong Women's Housing Sub-Committee in 1917, largely at the urging of the highly politicised women's organisations that had fought for suffrage. This was the first time that women were systematically asked about their housing needs. The Women's Committee represented the needs of a diverse group of women. It included Labour, Liberal and Co-operative women, as well as local suffrage societies, professional groups such as the Association of Women Property Managers, mother and baby welfare groups, and 'ordinary', unmarried women represented by members of the typing pool of the Savoy Hotel in London.[50] The Women's Committee, chaired by Gertrude Emmott, Liberal president of the parliamentary and legislation committee of the National Council of Women, included Constance Peel. Only one woman, Sybella Branford, had any architectural training.[51]

The Women's Housing Sub-Committee reported on the needs of working-class housewives. Much of their focus was on the kitchen and housework. As part of their extensive research, the committee visited specimen houses built by the Ministry of Munitions during the war. They used questionnaires, leaflets, lectures and exhibitions to canvass and represent working-class women throughout Britain. In their reports of 1918 and 1919 they advised on post-war housing for the working classes, with special reference to the convenience of the housewife. Their recommendations were very thorough: they advocated a separate scullery for food preparation and cooking, which they thought should be taken out of the traditional kitchen/living room arrangement. They believed that features that aided labour-saving such as deep sinks and easily cleaned corners should be an integral part of the design of the house. Most importantly, they stressed that a hot-water supply was essential and that a cheap electricity supply was highly desirable.

In the Women's Housing Sub-Committee there was conflict over the possibilities that cooperative and communal laundry and kitchen facilities offered. Many of the women on the committee thought that these would ease the lot of working-class housewives, but the latter were fed up with the involuntary sharing they had endured during the war and hated anything that smacked of communal arrangements. Despite their detail and representativeness, the recommendations of the Women's Housing Sub-Committee met with a hostile reception from local authorities who deemed them too expensive, and they were only published in a limited form. Moreover, the design of the houses that were actually built did not include many of the Sub-Committee's suggestions and some of the women who occupied them were subsequently disappointed. It was not only women from the Labour Party who participated in the debates about housing. There was a long tradition of philanthropy among women activists in the Liberal Party. The Conservative women of the Primrose League also campaigned on the importance of the domestic sphere and women's conditions.[52] Women's organisations such as the National Federations of Women's Institutes and Townswomen's Guilds also campaigned on housing issues.[53]

Peel's lecture was given as part of a conference on labour-saving in the home attended by delegates representing women's organisations from all over Britain held at the Ideal Home Exhibition in 1920. Speakers included several members of the Women's Housing Sub-Committee. The conference encompassed a diverse range of interests, from those who feared that labour-saving state housing would be too expensive for the poorest to afford, to those concerned with the needs of the middle-class servantless housewife. Many of the delegates expressed their frustration that women's views on housing were not listened to.[54] The delegates were united in a belief that women's duties in the home were work and that all women deserved a labour-saving home.

Other sources of advice on the labour-saving home were reforming organisations such as the Committee of Scientific Management in the Home, the Electrical Association for Women, and Women's Gas Council.[55] Much of the advice given by women experts on housing took the form of model rooms and houses, and demonstrations at exhibitions. Following the founding of the Electrical Association for Women in 1924, there was an 'All-Electric' house at the 1925 Ideal Home Exhibition.[56] Influences also came from Europe; the Congres Internationaux d'Architecture Moderne discussed the issue of the efficient planning of the kitchen at a meeting in Frankfurt in 1926. The venue for the meeting provided a valuable object lesson with the kitchens of its recently completed mass housing scheme, which had been subjected to time and motion and ergonomic studies, resulting in Grete Lihotzky's Frankfurt

Kitchen. The Women's Gas Council, established in 1930, took on some of the ideas from the Frankfurt Kitchen.[57] It also influenced Elizabeth Denby, one of the designers of the Gas, Light and Coke Company's model dwelling Kensal House, built in West London in 1936 as an object lesson in labour-saving, economical design.[58] In 1937 the Council of Scientific Management in the Home (set up by the National Council of Women in Great Britain) created a model kitchen that toured the country. Housework was also professionalised through the domestic science movement; training colleges were set up to teach girls the principles of time-management, economy and nutrition.

Ideals of labour-saving and efficiency in domestic life were also a strong feature of the Ideal Home Exhibition, which provided a key focus for housing issues. It was an important source of information for women's organisations, such as the Women's Institutes, who visited it annually in the interwar years. Furthermore, the exhibition had an enormous influence on the thousands of new houses that were built in the interwar years by both local authorities and speculative builders. The exhibition brought women's ideas about housing from all kinds of perspectives – from those who campaigned against the insanitary conditions of the poor to those who advocated a labour-saving house as a solution to the 'servant problem' – into the mainstream.

In the late 1920s talks about efficiency and labour-saving and the home were broadcast on BBC radio. One of the pre-eminent broadcasters was Nancie Clifton Reynolds, a Girton College educated economist who became an expert on housework. She wrote regularly for *The Listener*, *Country Life* and women's magazines, and published *Easier Housework by Better Equipment* in 1929. With her husband Clifton Reynolds, she was the proprietor of a shop called 'Easier Housework' in Streatham, south London. Nancie was an accomplished public speaker and demonstrated labour-saving appliances at the Ideal Home Exhibition, regional exhibitions and department stores around the country, supervising 'a gang of pretty tough women "demonstrators"'.[59]

In 1929 Nancie Clifton Reynolds gave a series of lectures at the *Daily Mail*'s Better Housing and Housekeeping Exhibition in Hull City Hall. A reporter commented: 'She is a most interesting woman, and not only has she been educated in economics, and their various uses in life to-day, but she is backed by very practical experience, being a wife, and mother herself.'[60] She made eight BBC radio broadcasts on domestic science, known as 'Household Talks', between 1927 and 1930. The *Radio Times* noted that Reynolds' own home was 'equipped with every modern convenience and labour-saving device'.[61] Her talks included 'Planning an Ideal Kitchen'[62] and 'Alternative Ways of Cooking'.[63] Writing in the catalogue for the *Daily Mail*'s 1922 Ideal Home Exhibition, Reynolds noted:

> Since the first Ideal Home Exhibition opened its doors in 1908 the progress of home-making has greatly accelerated. Woman's striving for more freedom, for self-expression, has probably been the greatest factor in this speeding up of the march towards the Ideal Home, and nothing has done more to bring the perfect home nearer than woman's determination to be freed from the thraldom of domestic duties carried out in archaic and inefficient ways.[64]

For Reynolds, labour-saving appliances were a necessity. Her husband's 1947 *Autobiography* gives an account of how she struggled to combine her working life advising women on labour-saving in the home with her own domestic duties at home as a wife and mother of two young children, unaided by servants. This eventually led to her separation from her husband. Had it not been for her untimely death, aged only 28, in 1931, she might have been even more influential.

Women were also educated in efficiency in housework by an expanding mass media. Approximately sixty different women's magazines were launched in Britain between 1920 and 1945, catering for a wide range of women.[65] These magazines drew on the talents of professional 'experts' and writers of household management manuals, such as Constance Peel and Nancie Clifton Reynolds. Homemaking was simultaneously constructed as a duty – an expression of love and respect – and a demonstration of professional skill, as well as a source of pleasure and fun. These magazines presented a new role for women as professional housewives, justified by ideas of 'progress' and evolution.

Under the influence of domestic reformers such as Peel and Reynolds, ideas about efficiency and labour-saving became popular. Forty-nine per cent of people surveyed by Mass Observation on their 'Ideal Home' wanted to live in a house with a garden. This was envisaged as a 'small modern house with plenty of labour-saving devices, self-contained and as private as possible'.[66] For many women, however, the reality was far from the labour-saving ideal.

Saving labour?

For domestic advice writers, magazines and advertisers, labour-saving devices were seen to be essential. However, they were not necessarily powered by electricity. An account of one such device appears in Denis Mackail's 1925 novel *Greenery Street*, which follows the trials and tribulations of Felicity, a newly-wed, middle-class housewife setting up home in a rented house in Chelsea. She attends a labour-saving week at a department store and makes a new purchase that she tries to explain to her husband:

> "I bought a thing that the man showed me that – well, I can't quite explain it to you until you see it, but you hang it up in the kitchen and it's got lots of little spaces, and it shows you just what you ought to order. The man said it would pay for itself in no time."
>
> "I don't understand," said Ian. "Do you mean it's a kind of machine?"
>
> "Oh no. Just a sort of thing – with a lot of little flaps. The cook's supposed to twaddle them all round whenever she runs out of anything."
>
> "What happens then?" Asked Ian.
>
> "Oh, don't you see. Then she looks at it and it shows her."
>
> "Shows her what?"
>
> "You are stupid, Ian. You'll see the idea at once as soon as it arrives."[67]

4.4 Unattributed photograph for Barnaby's Studios of a 'household wants' indicator, *c.* 1930s

Felicity's purchase was a shopping or household wants indicator, a list of household goods such as food and cleaning products painted on a tin or wooden plaque (Figure 4.4). Beside each item was a small, coloured tab that was flipped as the household ran short of a commodity to enable a shopping list to be easily compiled either by the housewife or perhaps her cook. Made by companies such as Chas. Letts & Co. (better known for their diaries), writers of domestic advice manuals in the 1920s suggested that they should be placed on the scullery or kitchen door.[68] Sometimes they were found already fixed to the inside of the doors of kitchen cabinets made by companies such as Easiwork, whose very name conjured up ideas of efficient housework.

One of the most popular non-electrical labour-saving devices was the mechanical Ewbank carpet sweeper. Housewife Mrs Beaver (who I introduced in Chapter 1) is depicted using one in a photograph (Figure 4.5). *The Housewife's Book* recommended carpet sweepers: 'these handy little labour-savers should be used for a few minutes after every meal or wherever crumbs or litter make an appearance'.[69]

The notion of labour-saving devices also extended to include furniture, fixtures and fittings. In 1920 a group of housewives and designers who made up the Household Appliances Committee of the Design and Industries Association (DIA) judged a competition organised by the *Daily Mail* for 'the best individual labour-saving suggestions that could be compressed on a postcard'.[70] One of their commended designs was for an 'artisan scullery' that consisted of the adaptation of 'the usual type of scullery sink' with a shelf to hold a washing bowl, and a draining board. Above the sink there was a draining rack for plates, and situated beside it a shelf to hold plates, and beside it a pot stand, thus ensuring that everything was in easy reach.[71] Such a simple design would have appealed to the DIA not only for its rudimentary labour-saving arrangement, but also for its plainness and undisguised functionalism.

Trays, sometimes with tiers, service or dinner wagons or trolleys and serving hatches, all of which conveyed food to the table, were said to be labour-saving and even to be able to take the place of servants.[72] Folding two-tiered trays were useful in houses where rooms were simply too small to allow a trolley safe passage or where there were steps between kitchen and dining room. Service hatches could be built into the wall between kitchen and dining room or even installed at a later date (Plate 11). However, they were only effective if they saved steps in the loading of food on either side.[73] They were a way of negotiating the threshold between kitchen and dining room both physically and symbolically, allowing food to appear as final dishes at the end of the production line, not just saving but hiding the labour of preparation behind the kitchen door or the serving hatch.

Arguably, for many it was the utilities of gas and electricity that most contributed to a labour-saving home by allowing small cookers that were

4.5 Mrs Beaver cleaning the carpet in her dining room with a Ewbank carpet sweeper, 1937

much less laborious to run than a traditional range. Cooking had traditionally been done on coal-fired ranges, which had the added advantage
of heating the kitchen and providing hot water.[74] Free-standing gas or
electric cookers became popular because they were easier to use and keep
clean. Cookers were installed in most new houses, sometimes in addition
to ranges, and eventually superseded them altogether as ranges fell out of
fashion. And, of course, many simply did not have the space for a range
in a compact kitchenette. Whereas the range was built to last by iron
founders, the new gas and electric cookers, predominantly secured by
hire purchase, placed more emphasis on price and appearance than on
durability. They were made out of pressed steel panels covered in mottled grey or black enamel that was easy to clean. The introduction of the
'Regulo' thermostat in 1923, together with its cheaper price, enhanced the
popularity of gas over electricity.

Consequently, for some women cooking became a high-status leisure activity enabling self-display and self-improvement that was too
interesting to be left to servants. Nicola Humble argues that a new sort
of fashionable cookery book appeared in the interwar years: 'Written
by society hostesses and famous restaurateurs, expensively produced
with elegant typefaces and specially commissioned artwork, these books
offered a new vision of domesticity as elegant and creative rather than
tedious drudgery.'[75] They presented cooking as a choice rather than a
necessity. Such books often suggested that the housewife should pass
recipes on to the cook but, in reality, they were providing her with the
information she needed to do it herself. The notion of the hapless new
housewife struggling to follow instructions was satirised in a 1932 *Punch*
cartoon depicting a husband peeking into the kitchen to see smoke pouring out of the gas cooker. His wife, clutching a cookbook, says 'Only
another five minutes, darling, and the book says the meat will be done'
(Figure 4.6). However, for Respondent 082, cooking was clearly no joke.
During a dinner that she had found particularly arduous to prepare, her
brother-in-law suggested: 'Perhaps in years to come people won't eat

"ONLY ANOTHER FIVE MINUTES, DARLING, AND THE BOOK SAYS THE MEAT WILL BE DONE."

4.6 Cartoon of a young, middle-class housewife coping without servants, from *Punch*, 1932

meals as we do now, but will take tablets of concentrated food. I almost said "hurrah" when he continued "By that time I hope I shall be dead.""[76]

The provision of running water, especially if there was a means of heating it, also had a profound labour-saving effect, especially for laundry. One of the housewife's 'most detested but most implacable of tasks' was laundry, usually done weekly in the kitchen, scullery or kitchenette, or sometimes the bathroom.[77] As Christine Zmroczek says:

> each batch of washing meant soaking, scrubbing, usually boiling, several rinses, several wringings, mangling, and hanging up to dry, followed later by ironing, airing, folding and putting away. Each wash involved a great deal of physical exertion, much bending and lifting, and carrying of water and heavy wet washing.[78]

For Miriam Kingham, the 'Ideal Type Boiler', gas copper and 'deep butler's sink', supplied by builders Smith Bros as part of the specifications for her Edmonton house, would have helped hugely with her domestic work.[79] The copper, usually situated in the kitchen, was either a large, built-in tub with space underneath to light a fire, or free-standing and powered by gas or electricity to heat the water. Gas and electric coppers were more efficient and cleaner than coal but expensive. Coppers took up a lot of room in small kitchens and caused problems with condensation.[80] Whites were scrubbed and then boiled in the copper, stirred and agitated by hand with a stick called a dolly. The steaming clothes were then hauled out of the copper with a long pole or tongs, which could be a dangerous process. Some whites were then blued or starched. Next came rinsing and wringing by hand or with a mangle or a smaller portable Acme wringer, which was very hard work.

Washing machines were one of the aspirational labour-saving devices on display at the Ideal Home Exhibition (Figure 4.7). Operated by electricity or by hand, many combined the functions of washing and wringing. *The Housewife's Book* made washing machines appear commonplace, advising that it 'is almost a necessity, and as one can be bought to-day for

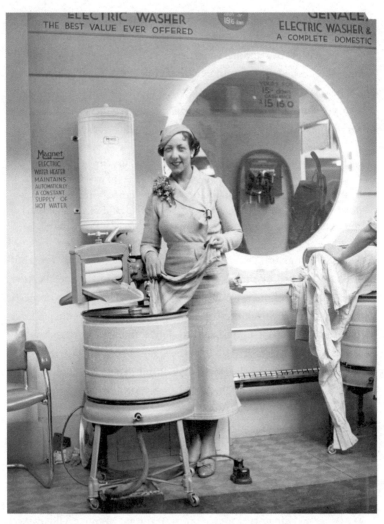

4.7 Actress Ellen Pollock trying out an electric washing machine at the Daily Mail Ideal Home Exhibition, 1935

a very modest sum, its purchase is a wise investment'.[81] They were actually prohibitively expensive to buy and run, involved a lot of labour still and were not very efficient.[82] In fact, just 4 per cent of UK households had a washing machine of any kind in 1938.[83] Moreover, those who could afford a washing machine could also afford to pay for help. Of more impact were soap powder brands such as Rinso and Oxydol, which for some women replaced bars of Sunlight soap. However, some thought that this was not as effective.

Drying ideally took place outdoors but this was often a haphazard business because of bad weather, which meant washing had to be dried indoors. Airing cupboards were much desired by Mass Observation respondents.[84] After the laundry was done there was a lot of clearing up because everything became wet, steamy and soapy, especially the floor. Some laundry was done outside the home in a public wash-house, by commercial laundries and local washerwomen, especially sheets, shirts and collars.[85]

For Respondent 082, laundry, done every Monday as was customary for many women, was an arduous task often thwarted by bad weather. She gave an account of one laundry day. She got up at 5.20 to make her husband breakfast before he went to work on an early shift: 'I am not going back to bed as we usually do when we get up quite early, as it is washing day, and looks like being a wet one. Dismal prospect.' By 6.45: 'While clothes are boiling I sweep & dust kitchen.' At 7.30 she woke her daughter. At 9.40: 'Washing nearly done, but it still rains steadily. Have a cup of coffee and glance at the paper.' At 11.10: 'Stopped raining. I take the clothes into the garden, hang up a few articles and it starts raining again.' At 11.00 the baker calls and at 12.10 she has a cup of coffee and bread and cheese as her husband's shift means that dinner will be served at 4.00. At 1.00 she washes and changes and writes to the library to order a book. At 3.25 she cooks potatoes to go with cold meat for dinner. At 3.35 the milkman calls and at 4.25 she goes into the garden to cut a lettuce and discovers that it is raining again: 'So I bring in the clothes just a degree dryer than when they were put out this morning.'[86] The clothes that she hung on the line were also subject to the scrutiny of her neighbours, of one of whom she said: 'Very seldom see her except on washing days, when she is very interested in the articles hanging on my clothes line.' Respondent 082 also scrutinised others' laundry for signs of respectability or otherwise: 'Absence or presence on clothes lines can be very revealing. In the lowest strata of society for instance the men never wear pyjamas. They go to bed in their day shirts.'[87]

The use of electrical labour-saving devices was limited in the interwar years primarily because of their high cost and the inconsistencies of an electricity supply that was not standardised. There were still numerous different AC and DC systems in use in the late 1930s, even within the same towns.[88] This meant that appliances might become obsolete even if the household moved only a few streets away. Furthermore, as manufacturers had to make different models of appliances for different voltages, prices were very high. The appliances that were most used tended to be the smaller ones such as irons, which were little changed in design other than being wired for electricity, which made them easier to operate. Nevertheless, in 1935 only 33 per cent of households had an electric iron.[89] Despite being a suburban homeowner, Respondent 082 did not have an electric iron; she heated her iron 'on the gas' (her gas cooker).[90] By 1939, however, 60 per cent of homes had electricity, which created a market for labour-saving appliances.[91] Thus nearly three-quarters of those with electricity had electric irons, which had become more affordable in the intervening years.[92]

Furthermore, as Sue Bowden and Avner Offer have noted, since the 1920s, 'households on both sides of the Atlantic have consistently given priority to leisure appliances [such as radios and televisions] over housework durables' (Figure 1.6).[93] They partly ascribe this to the low value placed on women's time and hence on time-saving. They attribute the demand for appliances among middle-class women to 'the perceived ability of the appliances not only to alleviate the domestic servant problem but also to permit middle-class women to become "better" housewives, to permit them to do work their grandmothers and mothers would have delegated to servants'.[94] Most working-class women used appliances only in their capacity as part-time and casual servants in middle-class homes, rather than in their own.[95]

Recent historians have argued that labour-saving appliances were not as widespread as has been previously thought, although the evidence that survives in the form of magazines, advertisements and domestic design advice literature might encourage historians to think otherwise.[96] Furthermore, it is probably testimony to the expense and value placed on such objects that some have survived and have been donated to museum collections.[97] Moreover some households which could have afforded labour-saving appliances preferred to employ a 'skivvy' for a pittance, who, in the words of Winifred Foley, who herself entered domestic service at the age of 14, was 'a creature that would run on very little fuel and would not question her lot'.[98] This, then, poses some particular problems for the design historian in terms of evidence.

For housewives, labour-saving appliances were suggested to be – or so advertisers told them – a solution to the 'servant problem', as if they were electric servants that actually replaced human labour. Furthermore, many advertisements showed a mistress with her maid, implying that it would be the latter who would actually use the appliance. Paradoxically, early domestic appliances were usually so expensive that only the more affluent households that could afford to keep servants could purchase them.

It was also debatable whether many so-called labour-saving appliances actually did save any labour. According to Bowden and Offer, advertisers used three main strategies to market electrical appliances. First, servants who used electrical appliances would be more productive and ease the transition from the live-in to the daily. Secondly, servants would rather work in a household with the most up-to-date appliances and so they were used as an incentive to make servants' jobs seem more attractive in the face of the 'servant problem'. Thirdly, electrical appliances were less trouble than servants.[99] As Bowden and Offer argue, although electric appliances had the potential to alleviate the 'unskilled, hard physical labour involved in many household tasks', the opportunity to install and use them was not taken up in interwar England.[100]

Even though their use was not widespread, electrical appliances and other gadgets were one of the most popular features of the Ideal Home Exhibition. In 1934 the Sunbeam Mixmaster was demonstrated at the Ideal Home Exhibition by a woman in a white laboratory coat (Figure 4.8). The audience were shown how it did everything from mashing potatoes, cleaning cutlery, and mixing cakes to making ice-cream. Some contemporary Modernists were scornful of such labour-saving appliances, especially those that they regarded as 'gadgets'.[101] Modernists also

4.8 A woman demonstrating an 'electrical cooking apparatus' at the Daily Mail Ideal Home Exhibition, 1934

objected to the application of what they thought of as superfluous surface decoration to appliances, where form certainly did not follow function, although this undoubtedly made them attractive to consumers. Later in the 1930s they also objected to the use of streamlining, inappropriate to the function of appliances.[102]

In *Lares et Penates or the Home of the Future*, H.J. Birnstingl recognised the necessity for labour-saving in the home but cautioned against the indiscriminate use of the term by manufacturers:

> The phrase at once became a hall-mark, but it was a hall-mark without an assay-office and anyone could apply it ... to the well-made and to the shoddy ... For the credulity of woman knew no bounds, moreover she was utterly devoid of any standard of workmanship, or of any power for appraising the practicality of mechanical devices. Her love of spending money, too, was a factor on the side of exploiters.[103]

Birnstingl saw women as undiscriminating consumers who were easily duped by poor-quality labour-saving devices. His view suggests that while the primary function of appliances was to save labour, this was not necessarily the outcome.

Feminist critics such as Ruth Schwarz Cowan have argued that labour-saving appliances did not save labour but instead enabled work to be done to higher standards of cleanliness, thus increasing work for women and allowing them less time for leisure, despite the discourse of efficiency.[104] They have noted, first, that appliances were largely aimed at middle-class women who did not previously work in the home. Therefore, they increased labour for (some) women. For example, laundry might previously have been done outside the home by commercial laundries; the advent of washing machines meant that this task could now be done inside the home. Furthermore, professional laundries depended upon the labour of working-class women, which meant that appliances often merely substituted one woman's labour for another's. Labour-saving appliances can, then, be said to create more work. This is particularly true of tasks concerned with hygiene, which appliances enable to be performed to ever-higher standards. For example, vacuum cleaners replaced sweeping and beating and meant that higher standards of cleanliness could, and therefore should, be attained. However, such critiques have been informed by the same concerns with functionalism and efficiency as those of Modernist design historians who, when considering aesthetics, concentrate on the question of whether or not an object adheres to the Modernist maxim of 'form should follow function'.

For many interwar women, the application of scientific management techniques and the use of labour-saving devices in the home was an implicit recognition that the home was, too, a site of production. Thus, labour-saving furniture and appliances operated in the realms of the symbolic and social rather than the rational, economic and productive.[105] A further interrogation of the advice literature that eschews an emphasis on the rational and scientific goes some way towards suggesting an alternative reading of the modern housewife. For example, Nancie Clifton Reynolds wrote in 'Making Housework a Pleasant Game':

> The modern housewife has discovered that, if she uses the correct household appliance for her work, if the right tool is used for every task, she can have a perfect home, and at the same time, plenty of leisure … Housekeeping can become a game. It can be played to time, with pauses for rest and periods of effort.[106]

She suggested that scientific principles of household management could be fun, but only if the housewife had purchased the appropriate appliances: 'It can provide endless interest and be the subject of daily experiment but, without the saving help of the correct household appliances it loses its glamour and becomes dull and wearisome.'[107] The appliance was not, then, valued just for its labour-saving potential. It was also valued for the image that it projected; it could invest a boring and tiresome task with glamour. Thus, the modern identity of housewife depended upon the possession of the most up-to-date appliances and products. This can be seen in advertisements, such as those for Electrolux, which used Modernistic graphic images and lettering to depict a desirable and dynamic image of a glamorous, modern, professional housewife (Plate 10).

This is not, however, to suggest that all women actually felt glamorous and fulfilled when they did housework. For many women, housework was a source of real frustration. For example, Respondent 082 said: 'Dislike the dirty part of housework and find myself doing unnecessary jobs, just to put it off.'[108] After dinner with family visitors she says, 'I start washing up. I loathe the sight of dirty pots and dishes.'[109] On another occasion while having family visitors she says, 'Having to be maid-of-all-work and hostess combined and looking after two boisterous children can be very exhausting.'[110] She felt especially pressured to keep up the standards to which her husband's family, who were better off and of higher social standing than her own, were accustomed when they visited.

The professional housewife was just one identity for women in the interwar years when the idea of 'woman' was a shifting signifier.[111] Added into this were transformations and shifts in class identities, which were literally displayed in women's homes, in their activities as housewives and homemakers. Thus, supposedly labour-saving furniture and appliances were used to mark out and perform these new identities, to create an impression. For example, vacuum cleaners, previously largely the preserve of houses with servants, became more popular in the 1930s as their price fell due to changes in construction and lighter materials.[112] As Paul Oliver has pointed out, many women were careful not to let the possession of a vacuum cleaner convey the fact that they no longer hired domestic help:

> But though the sound of the vacuum cleaner could be heard in the street, emphasising that the house was clean and kept in good order, the housewife preferred not to be seen actually engaged in the process; while she was unseen there was still the possibility that someone else was employed to do the housework in her well-run home.[113]

The housewife, therefore, kept the vacuum cleaner stowed away in the cupboard under the stairs. It was 'a complex symbol of the transitional position of the middle class'.[114] For some women, questions of function were not paramount; gadgets operated as souvenirs of stages in their life histories, such as memories of setting up home as young brides, and acted as what the anthropologist Janet Hoskins has called 'biographical objects'.[115] Their possession could also be part of a collective sense of identity. There is a subtle difference between keeping up with the Joneses and wanting to be like them. As Amanda Vickery argues, envy is not the sole motivating force in women's consumer practices.[116] Whatever the reason for labour-saving devices, Mass Observation reported in *An Inquiry into People's Homes* that 'Labour-saving devices are much appreciated, and are constantly asked for if absent.'[117]

The 'Efficiency' style

The concern with labour-saving extended to the design of the home and, as Birnstingl said, 'became a touchstone by which the desirability of houses was appraised'.[118] An 'Efficiency' style in architecture and design emerged in Britain, the constituents of which were standardised building techniques, harnessing some elements of Modernism such as rounded corners and an absence of mouldings and decoration. Influences included both the Deutsche Werkbund and the 'fitness for purpose' maxim of the British Arts and Crafts movement. Seen by some recent architectural historians as a form of 'modernity without modernism' or a 'proto-Modernist' stage, in the discourses of magazines and household advice manuals the 'Efficiency' style was modern and ran parallel to other Modernisms, being of particular interest to the professional housewife.[119]

A key element of post-war reconstruction and the provision of 'homes fit for heroes' by the state was the adoption of standardised building techniques, which allowed the use of less skilled labour and lowered costs. In his chapter on 'Bricks versus Offal' in *Lares et Penates*, Birnstingl railed against the use of imported, non-vernacular/local materials: 'timber from Canada, tiles from Marseilles, cement from Belgium, bricks from Peterborough, all these materials are available at any place and at any moment'.[120] He imagined a future of standardised houses, 'which can be ordered like a new rowing machine, a rose tree, or an enamelled bath'.[121] Steel came in for Birnstingl's particular criticism, and he predicted a dystopian future in 1987 when there would be a serious outbreak of rust in the town of 'Steelville'.[122] Architects such as S.D. Adshead pioneered the development of construction systems using brick and concrete over a light steel frame, which was produced as the 'Dorlonco' system after the First World War by the Dorman Long steelworks. It was used for about 10,000 houses built by local authorities all over Britain.[123] London County Council's Downham Estate, built in 1925, included steel-framed Atholl houses (Figure 4.9). In the case of speculative housing,

4.9 Atholl steel house, Downham Estate, London, 1925

standardised techniques contributed, along with other factors discussed in Chapter 2, to the reduction in prices after 1932. Such houses have been criticised for being modern on the inside but traditional on the outside, in apparent contradiction.[124]

The attitudes that Birnstingl displayed towards the contemporary home were typical of a certain kind of English writer on the 'English compromise' of 'good design' in architecture and design, schooled in the Arts and Crafts tradition. Birnstingl was especially keen to retain a notion of beauty in the home and a sense of decoration, which he feared that an excessive preoccupation with labour-saving and efficiency would banish. He cautioned against a future of rusting, standardised, steel houses that could be bought from catalogues and women who rejected beauty in favour of a labour-saving 'Efficiency' style that gave them more time for leisure pursuits. Tellingly, he imagined a future when women would go on strike against beauty and the threat of the introduction of dust-trapping mouldings by boycotting the cinema. However, despite his scepticism he did accept that a labour-saving home would bring real benefits. He also hoped that with the increased use of electricity rather than coal the amount of dirt would be lessened and the dread of dust accumulation would pass, and beautiful forms could be evolved that would 'not be constantly harassed by the dust bogey'.[125] Underlying his idea of beauty in the home seems to be a very traditional idea of the woman as the 'angel in the house' rather than the modern professional housewife with time for leisure and her own interests.

Notions of efficiency derived from industry also appealed to Modernist organisations such as the Design and Industries Association. The organisation advised manufacturers to pay careful attention to the time and motion studies of F.W. Taylor and the Gilbreths. In the 1920s the DIA organised a consumer education programme through a series of exhibitions and publications. One such exhibition in 1920 consisted of a series of eight domestic rooms filled with what it called the 'Efficiency' style, based on the simple forms of Scandinavian applied arts.[126]

The DIA contributed an essay on 'The Equipment of the Ideal Home' to the book of the 1920 Ideal Labour-Saving Home competition. Here, the DIA explained the Arts and Crafts 'fitness for purpose' maxim that it had adopted in its campaign for 'good design' thus: 'a thing must first "do the job" for which it is made, and that decoration which conflicts with this end is simply bad design'.[127] The essay was an exhaustive study of the minimum standard for each item that was needed to ensure efficiency in the home. In DIA discourse, its 'Efficiency' style was presented as the logical labour-saving solution: 'All ordinary commonsense people want every article of use in the house to be so pleasant to look upon in shape and colour that no further decoration is needed.' The cleanliness and the brightness of the simple, everyday crockery on the dresser were all that was needed to decorate a small room, said the DIA. Thus, in such surroundings housework would be lessened and cheered and become 'more of a pleasure than a drudgery'.[128]

The DIA strongly recommended simple, cheap, painted furniture, devoid of so-called superfluous decoration: 'What is to be specially noted is the absence of all "attached" and "pretentious" decoration, all applied mouldings and other irrelevant complications.'[129] In case the furniture it advocated should seem too 'severe', the DIA advised: 'like all simple, rightly designed things – that is, designed for their purpose – they grow on one, and make one impatient of fussy, irrelevant, dust-collecting excrescences or degradations, such as machine-carving and other shams'.[130] The furniture seemed modern and, indeed, shocking to the public of the Ideal Home Exhibition. Ironically, such designs were influenced by the Arts and Crafts movement, which drew on historical vernacular traditions. Consequently, what was thought of as 'modern' looked both backwards and forwards. Wealth and social status were more clearly signified by decoration for the aspirational middle-class audience. Furthermore, such furniture may also have had undesirable connotations of working-class culture and 'making do'.

Most domestic advice writers thought that the labour-saving home could only be achieved through the adoption of the most efficient techniques and technologies of house planning, architecture and housework. Modernist critics were as quick to disparage what they called 'sham' Modernistic domestic architecture and interiors as they were to condemn the old-fashioned and nostalgic. Scientific management techniques resulted in developments such as improvements in internal planning, heights of work surfaces, fitted cupboards and the use of electricity and gas instead of dirty soft coal. The resulting 'Efficiency' style concerned Birnstingl because he saw every ledge and moulding as 'a potential thing of beauty', but women, he said, just saw them as potential dust retainers.[131] All this, according to Birnstingl, resulted in an 'unconscious striving after the public lavatory ideal' in which 'woman seized with delight upon the white tile'.[132] This started in the bathroom where it could be 'tolerated' and spread to the scullery, kitchen, halls, nurseries and even to sitting rooms as tiled skirtings; 'The final triumph will be when it lines the walls of the master's study.'[133] For Birnstingl, 'Efficiency' was a gendered style, most suitable for the bathroom and the kitchen. To some extent, this was also how it was viewed by the wider public.

The kitchen

To the housewife, the kitchen is her workshop. In particular, it is the place where she cooks, and prepares meals. Other things are also done in kitchens, such as eating, washing and listening to the wireless, but the distinguishing mark of the kitchen is that it is cooked in.[134]

Thus, Mass Observation's *An Inquiry into People's Homes* identified the kitchen as the housewife's primary place of work. It concluded, 'Kitchens are a very important factor in housing satisfaction; people possessing a convenient kitchen like their home very much more than people with kitchens they dislike',[135] reflecting the fact that 90 per cent of people interviewed for Mass Observation's enquiry were housewives.[136]

One of the biggest difficulties the Mass Observation investigators faced

1 Sitting room of 17 Rosamund Road, Wolvercote, Oxfordshire, 1995

2 Kitchen of 17 Rosamund Road, Wolvercote, Oxfordshire, 1995

3 Front cover of *Modern Home*, November 1931

4 Poster for the National Building Society, *c.* 1935

5 Poster for Woolwich Equitable Building Society, *c.* 1935

6 Illustration of 'Axminster' linoleum in 'Catesbys one-piece linola squares', from *Catesbys Colourful Cork Lino*, 1938

Within the illustration:

Catesbys
ONE PIECE
LINOLA
SQUARES

SIZE.	£	s.	d.
7ft. 6in. × 9ft. 0in. ...	1	8	6
9ft. 0in. × 9ft. 0in. ...	1	13	6
9ft. 0in. × 10ft. 6in. ...	1	19	6
9ft. 0in. × 12ft. 0in. ...	2	5	0
10ft. 6in. × 12ft. 0in. ...	2	15	0

DESIGN ILLUSTRATED is No. KL.680.
Other "LINOLA" designs post free;
write stating colour and size required.

7 Illustration of 'Modernistic' linoleum in 'Catesbys one-piece linola squares',
from *Catesbys Colourful Cork Lino*, 1938

BE MODERN

at St Margaret's

8 Front cover of brochure for St Margarets Estate, Edgware, *Be Modern at St Margaret's*, c. 1935

9 Front cover of brochure for Goodchild's Enfield Town Estate, *c.* 1935

10 Advertisement for Electrolux appliances, from *Homes and Gardens*, December 1929

—THE MODERN SERVICE HATCH

Manufacturers : OSTENS (Byfleet) Ltd.
Atlantic House, 45 Holborn Viaduct, E.C.
Works : Byfleet, Surrey

11 Advertisement for dining hatch, *Ostens Servway: the modern service hatch, c.* 1930s

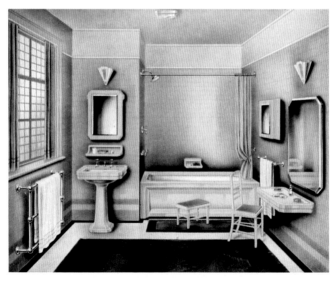

12 Illustration of bathroom, from Twyfords, *Booklet No. 489: Coloured "adamant" sanitaryware catalogue of bathroom fittings,* 1935

"Cactus"

Sheer delight in wallpaper decoration—where originality of motif comes without a hint of freakishness. The decorative beauty of the Cactus Design is an inspiration —and an innovation as well ! No small part of its distinction lies in the use of the companion papers and the border to build up alternative schemes.

Lower Filling. 2600	... ...	6/- per piece
Upper Filling. 2601	... ...	4/6 per piece
2¼ inch Border. B.2601	... ...	3½d. per yard
Pair of Subjects, respectively 17 ins. wide by 36 ins. high, and 36 ins. wide by 20½ ins. high. Ready cut out. (Only supplied in pairs.) B.2602	... ...	16/6 per pair
Green Mottled Ceiling Paper, 2603	... ...	3/6 per piece

13 Illustration of decorative scheme, from catalogue by T. Whatley & Son, *Studies in Harmony: a Prelude to a Brilliant Season*, 1937

14 Modernistic wallpaper sample (detail), *c.* 1930s

15 Dutch tile wallpaper sample (detail), *c.* 1920s

16 Front cover of *Feltcraft by Penelope* depicting a galleon, *c.* 1940

17 Illustration of the 'Henry VIII' dining-lounge, from *Bolsom's Furniture Catalogue*, *c.* 1935

18 Sample of 'Bedroom paper, H 1095, 1/3 per piece' (detail), from *Ideal Papers for Ideal Homes, Crown Wallpapers*, Ideal Home Exhibition, 1927

19 Detail from front cover of *The Book of the Home* depicting ebony elephant, *c*. 1920s

20 Illustration of mantelpiece featuring teak elephants, from *Claygate Fireplaces*, 1937

in talking to respondents about the kitchen was difference in nomencla-ture. Like so much of the language related to the home, verbal differences were indicative of social class and associated customs and practices. In their previous homes, many 'New Rich' suburban homeowners would have cooked, eaten and lived in one room with a range as both the source of heat, oven and hob for cooking, and hot water supplier. This kitchen/living room symbolised home and as well as a table and chairs it often con-tained an armchair or two. However, typically for the respectable working classes and lower middle classes, rooms for cooking and eating were sepa-rated. Herein, as Mass Observation noted, there was considerable 'verbal confusion': 'Some people call the room where they cook the kitchen and the room where they eat the living room. Others call the room where they cook, the scullery, and the room where they eat, the kitchen. Yet others cook in a kitchenette or a back kitchen, and eat in a living room or a kitchen.'[137] To clarify, Mass Observation defined the kitchen as 'the place where cooking was done, irrespective of whether the housewife called the room a kitchen, a back kitchen, a kitchenette or scullery'.[138]

From the mid-nineteenth century, in medium-sized houses of seven or more rooms there was a separate scullery (sometimes known as a back kitchen) for dirty work such as washing-up and cleaning food, a kitchen for cooking, and a dining room for eating.[139] Bigger houses had a morning or drawing room for sitting in after meals were eaten. In the new suburbia, householders often found themselves with a combined modern kitchen-scullery for cooking and washing-up. This was com-monly known as a 'kitchenette' and suited the compact space of new suburban houses built to minimum Tudor Walters' standards in either a small, lean-to, square extension or a narrow galley. For example, the Kinghams' galley kitchen measured 11 ft 2 in. by 5 ft 7 in. (3.4×1.7 m).[140] Its small size was justified by builders as 'labour-saving', but in reality it was to save space.[141] Meals were usually taken in a separate room, typi-cally a rear reception room, which tended to be known as the living room by households with working-class backgrounds and as the dining room by the middle classes. This was sometimes also accessed from the kitchen via a serving hatch. Day-to-day living tended to be done in the living room, with the front reception room kept for best and known as a parlour, sitting room or lounge. Despite being used less frequently, the parlour was often bigger than the living room. For example, the Kinghams' front reception room was the largest room in the house, measuring 15 ft 9 in. by 12 ft 2 in. (4.8 × 3.7 m). The rear reception room was 11 ft 11 in. by 8 ft 11 in. (3.6 × 2.7 m), considerably smaller than the front room.[142] It is likely that this room combined the functions of dining with day-to-day living.

There were tensions between housing reformers about whether there should be a combined kitchen/living room or a separate scullery. For example, at the 1920 conference of women's organisations at the Ideal Home Exhibition, Eleanor Barton proposed that 'The living-room should be the living-room, and not the workshop of the home. The work of the house should be done in the scullery, and the wife and mother should be able to sit down with her family away from her utensils. This means that in the scullery there must be a cooking stove.'[143] However, confining cooking to the scullery meant that it could not be combined with other duties such as looking after children.

The new kitchen-scullery was a novelty for better-off middle-class women too, who had been accustomed to having live-in servants before the war and rarely worked in the kitchen themselves. Many of those who lived in older houses where kitchens were traditionally in basements moved them up to the ground floor. In *Good Housekeeping* in 1925, Mrs C.D. Rackham advised on 'Banishing the basement bogey'. On remodelling her tall, narrow, terrace house built in the 1820s, the first thing she did was to 'abolish the basement kitchen':

> On the ground floor was a long room running right through the house divided into two by folding doors. The back half of this was converted into the kitchen leaving the front for the dining room; the folding doors were removed and replaced with a service cupboard. This was made by adapting an ordinary dresser sideboard which we possessed already.[144]

This ingenious transformation created cupboards and a drawer that were accessible from both the kitchen-scullery and the dining room, as well as a service hatch to save labour. Although Mrs Rackham still had a servant, it was clear that she aimed to create a labour-saving house with a vastly reduced staff.

Some householders still had the traditional living room arrangement. Mass Observation's Respondent 082 described her kitchen in 1937: 'It is really a living room with washable gas-stove & tiled sink. It has large windows which look out onto the garden. Furniture consists of sideboard, 4 dining chairs and table and 2 fireside chairs. Curtain green & gold. Quite a nice "kitchen".'[145] The house had a separate sitting room.

Housewives were advised to have kitchen walls painted in a light colour. Yellow was popular to give the illusion of sunlight. Tiles were recommended around the cooker and the sink, and preferably to waist height all around the kitchen. Smith Bros, builders of the Kinghams' Edmonton house discussed in Chapter 2, boasted in their promotional brochure of a 'tiled kitchenette'.[146] Sometimes the illusion of tiles was given by two colours of paint separated by a black-painted border, or wallpaper could be hung that imitated tiles (Plate 15). Traditional stone flags and red tiles were thought to be unhygienic and cold. Linoleum floors were recommended for hygiene and warmth and they had the advantage over tiled floors of protecting against breakages. Nancie Clifton Reynolds advised a small check pattern in black and white to hide dirt and step-marks, or an imitation red-tiled linoleum in older kitchens to preserve the character. Rising damp was often a problem and cork underlay was advised. Some householders improvised from the cork packaging that lined greengrocers' boxes of fruit. Sheet rubber was another alternative.[147]

It was typical to have a larder or pantry for food storage. Smith Bros noted the provision of a larder in their promotional brochure.[148] Although ideally the larder was installed in the space where food was prepared, in reality it was often in the sitting room or even in the hall.

Food was kept cool in the larder, preferably on a marble slab or a piece of slate. It was essential for the larder to be well ventilated, with a gauze-covered window to admit air and keep out flies. Larders built into small homes were often inadequate, and in many semis such as 17 Rosamund Road they were located on south-facing, sunny walls, making them very warm.[149] It was recommended that a refrigerator should be located inside the larder but they were prohibitively expensive for most. An ice box or chest was a good compromise. Some were made of wood and insulated with compressed cork slabs. A food safe, which worked by evaporating water, could also be used, especially to store meat.[150]

Domestic writers advised on how to enhance efficiency through kitchen design. Nancie Clifton Reynolds described the ideal layout 'if steps and fatigue are to be saved' thus:

> First in the row should come the larder, ice box or food store; secondly, the table or surface where the food is prepared; thirdly, the cooking stove; and lastly, the service place. Then the preparation of a meal should not entail endless cross walking to and fro, but should merely mean an ordered progression on the part of the housewife from one stage to another.[151]

Domestic experts recommended the installation of a built-in or free-standing dresser to store china and cutlery. A free-standing table (a porcelain or enamelled top was more desirable than scrubbed deal) was often placed centrally to be used for food preparation and other tasks. This arrangement gradually fell out of favour and the central table was replaced by one or two small, side surfaces, influenced, said Reynolds, by 'the American atmosphere of many household magazines'.[152] Many kitchens were simply too small for a central table. Pans could be hung above the cooker or placed on a free-standing pot stand. A deep porcelain Belfast sink should preferably be placed under the kitchen window with a wooden or porcelain draining board to the left or even on both sides (with the right used for stacking dirty dishes). It was preferable that there should be a drying rack for plates above the draining board on the left. As discussed in Chapter 1, for women like Cecilia Collett at 17 Rosamund Road the lived reality was often very different to the ideal, despite the discourses of labour-saving and efficiency in advice manuals and magazines.

From kitchen cabinet to fitted kitchen

Ideals of efficiency led to new designs for furniture such as the kitchen cabinet or 'commodious cupboard'.[153] More commonly known in Britain as kitchen cabinets, they were produced in compact form for smaller suburban houses in a range of prices by companies such as Easiwork Hygena, Ladymaid, Quicksey, Simplette and Savework (by Manuel Lloyd and Co. Ltd) (Figure 4.10). Steel cabinets from the American company Royal Ossco were also imported.[154] By the mid-1920s most furniture

4.10 A woman demonstrating an Easiwork cabinet, *c.* 1925

retailers sold at least one style of kitchen cabinet, which were available in a wide range of sizes, prices and specifications. Some kitchen cabinets were made of oak, others painted deal or even aluminium or steel. They took the form of a single, free-standing cupboard with multiple doors and drawers. They were organised into compartments to allow for the storage of food and equipment associated with food preparation and sometimes cleaning equipment. They usually incorporated a flour sifter, flour bin, metal-lined bread drawer, rolling pin, 'shopping or household wants reminder', bin for sugar and storage jars. There was a sliding or fold-down worktop for food preparation and also a meat safe; larger ones even included built-in ironing boards. For example, the Easiwork 'Empire' had a shelf for proving bread and a notice that suggested menus and information on weights and measures and the care of the cabinet itself. Some retailers even supplied kitchen cabinets fully stocked with food. Many builders, such as H. Smith Bros, who constructed the Kinghams' Edmonton house, installed kitchen cabinets (in this case by Hygena) in the kitchenette as part of the purchase price.[155]

The British kitchen cabinet had its origins in the American Hoosier cabinet, first manufactured in Indiana from the late 1890s until the 1930s, with production peaking in the 1920s when more than one in ten American households owned a Hoosier-brand cabinet.[156] Easiwork appears to have been the first company to sell kitchen cabinets in Britain. The company was based in London, with a factory in Shepherd's Bush and a showroom in Tottenham Court Road. It was founded by G.E.W. Crowe, a Canadian who originally imported refrigerators and space-saving kitchen cabinets from Canada. Easiwork created the market for kitchen cabinets through their advertising, their endorsement by the Good Housekeeping Institute and participation in exhibitions such as Dorland Hall and the Ideal Home Exhibition. They also introduced porcelain-topped kitchen tables, the first stainless steel sink, first chromium-plated steel furniture and first automatic-lighted, enamelled gas cooker.[157]

The design and utility of the kitchen cabinet was a subject of much concern to Nancie Clifton Reynolds.[158] She devoted several pages of her 1929 *Easier Housework* to a detailed discussion of the pros and cons of all the features of the kitchen cabinet. She discussed matters such as the sliding action and linings of drawers, paint and enamelled finishes, the quality and materials of fittings, door latches and hinges.[159] She claimed that: 'The cabinet is really the best solution of the problem of combining efficiency with space saving.'[160] However, she warned that it

> may make a perfect kitchen possible for its owner. It should also be remembered that it opens up vistas of untidiness ... Unless the user is tidy in the first place and anxious to possess a tidy kitchen, the result will be disastrous. Whoever uses a cabinet must put everything back in the right place after use, must keep the contents of the drawers and shelves clean.[161]

Reynolds spoke from personal experience, as she had an Easiwork cabinet in her London home, photographed at the beginning of her book complete with cluttered surfaces (Figure 4.11). The kitchen cabinet is thus best understood through a dynamic network of actors in the interwar suburban house, including the cabinet itself, the compact space of the kitchen and the housewife. It may speak the discourse of labour-saving and easier housework, but only if certain sets of actions are performed. Nevertheless, it could also signify the professionalisation of the housewife and her modernity, and the partial recognition of her labour.

It was a short step for Easiwork to move from the production of kitchen cabinets with additional side unit extensions to modular kitchen units, which they produced from the early 1930s. These were a part of a range of modular furniture that they commissioned from designers and architects in Britain such as Wells Coates and Erno Goldfinger.[162] These modular kitchens were reminiscent of the Frankfurt Kitchen and developments in Sweden and the United States in the interwar years. However, the era of the commodious cupboard lasted well into the postwar period in Britain. Kitchen cabinets were produced under the Utility

4.11 Nancie Clifton Reynolds' kitchen in London, from *Easier Housework by Better Equipment*, 1929

furniture scheme in wood and, later, surplus aluminium with an enamelled finish. They continued to be produced until well into the 1950s in Britain.[163] Fitted kitchens took much longer to catch on and were not commonly found in smaller homes until the early 1960s.

'The house that Jill built'

Manufacturers used Mass Observation surveys and other market research to ask women about their ideal kitchen and bathroom. In 1929 the *Daily Mail* took this one step further by calling on 'ordinary' housewives to become architects and to participate directly in the design of 'The House That Jill Built' through a competition 'to discover the requirements of the intelligent woman in connection with modern homes' (Figure 4.12).[164] Women readers were asked to submit the specifications and rough plans of 'the house they would build for themselves if they had a free hand to do so'. With a significant budget of £1,500, this was very much an ideal home. The competition attracted thousands of entries from 'women of all classes in all parts of the country'.[165] It was won by Phyllis Lee, a Croydon housewife with no training in architecture, who received a prize of £250. She said that she had her own family in mind when she planned the house and 'put in everything I would like to have myself in my own home'.[166]

Although the house was described as 'a woman's challenge to the architects and builders who are providing the homes of to-day', it was a male architect, Douglas Tanner, who designed the house from the winning plans.[167] Nevertheless, Lee helped in the specifications of the equipment for the 'house of her dreams', which was built by the Universal Housing Co. at the 1930 Ideal Home Exhibition. While it is difficult to tell how closely Tanner's designs followed Lee's original scheme, it is possible and instructive to compare the ways in which each of them described the house, particularly in terms of ideas of efficiency, health and labour-saving.

4.12 Feature on 'The House That Jill Built', designed by Phyllis Lee, at the Daily Mail Ideal Home Exhibition, from *Modern Home*, June 1930

Lee gave her thoughts on her ideal home, 'which puts into solid form the domestic dreams of thousands of women', in an interview with *Modern Home* magazine. She made it clear that the house was aimed at women who had to run a home and bring up small children without the help of a maid. Consequently, Lee complained about the poor design of the interiors of speculatively built houses: 'I think it was because I rebelled so much against the inconvenience, the pokiness and the lack of space in the average small house in the endless rows of suburban houses that I planned my dream house.'[168] *Modern Home* gave little attention to the exterior of the house, other than remarking that after the 'simple exterior of deep red brickwork with its steel casement windows has been admired', one enters the house.[169]

Lee's ideas went down well with Tanner because he could easily accommodate them within a Modernist architecture. It was Tanner, rather than Lee, who wrote the essay on the house in the Ideal Home Exhibition catalogue. In it he commended her design, saying that it demonstrated that 'the argument that women are conservative in their ideas about their home which they have to manage is entirely fallacious'.[170] In a clear echo of Le Corbusier, he told the *Daily Mail*: 'I call it a living machine … everything is designed for the purpose which it has to serve, with a primary view to efficiency and labour-saving in maintenance.'[171] He commended the house for its plainness and simplicity and approvingly noted that it demonstrated that 'women are no longer satisfied with the pretty, but inconvenient, house so dear to the heart of the speculative builder, but are beginning to appreciate the beauty and dignity of design which is devoid of superfluous ornamentation'.[172] Unlike Lee, Tanner's criticisms of speculative builders were focused on the exterior design, rather than the interior planning. The exterior, he said, had 'plain, well-proportioned and vigorous lines'. He was eager to reassure visitors that the absence of the usual pitched roof did not detract from the pleasing appearance of the house. Visitors had, anyhow, been introduced to a harsher, white, Modernist style two years previously in the 'House of the Future' (Figure

3.4), which formed part of 'Sunbeam Town'. The simplicity of Jill's house was softened by its being brick-built, rather than concrete; any tendency towards monotony was removed by the use of multi-coloured bricks for the facing in varied arrangements and the use of steel casements in wood frames. The house, Tanner said, was homely precisely because there were no 'fussy mouldings or striving after effect'. Furthermore, it adhered to the Modernist principle of 'fitness for purpose' in its planning: 'Every room is used for the purpose for which it is planned and there are no "best rooms" used for special occasions.'[173] Moreover, the position of the house in the Village of Ideal Homes stressed its modernity; it was sited between a 'Jacobethan' manor house and a grand neo-Georgian house.

Lee focused on the interior of the house; she suggested integral design features to ease the burden of the housewife. While Tanner approved of what he perceived as Modernism in the design of the house, Lee was interested in the design of the house inasmuch as it aided labour-saving. So, for example, Tanner might have approved of the open-plan design of the house for aesthetic reasons, but Lee arrived at her arrangement of a large living room with windows at each end, and a kitchen with a meals alcove (rather than the usual arrangement of a dining room with two small living rooms), because it meant that only one fire was needed. This solution meant that the separate parlour (which most women usually defended) was effectively eradicated. The meals alcove had a long, low, fitted seat under the window and another against the wall, necessitating few chairs. The table was long and narrow to take up as little space as possible. There was a lot of built-in storage space; for example, there were lockers under the window seats. There were also plenty of wardrobes, cupboards and kitchen fittings. This did not mean, however, that Lee advocated that the house should be devoid of personal possessions; indeed, the lockers were expressly to accommodate 'those innumerable small things that help to make life pleasant'. Furthermore, she said, 'built-in furniture means less work every day in the week and consequently more leisure time for the homemaker'.[174]

Labour-saving was Lee's top priority and she sought to make housework as easy and pleasant as possible. Thus, she used materials that could be easily cleaned. Washable paint on walls reduced the frequency with which complete redecorating needed to be carried out. Unpainted doors with no mouldings needed only 'daily dusting and a slight polish ... from time to time'.[175] The handles and latches were untarnishable and only needed dusting, which was an advance on polishing. The kitchen and bathroom were tiled in cream and black to a height of four feet, which aided hygiene. Lee took much care to ensure that the design of the house would not tire women, and she arranged the kitchen as 'a really efficient workshop and the position of each fitting has been most carefully worked out. The gas cooker, porcelain topped table, sink and cooking cabinet are placed so that there is practically no need to walk more than a yard or so between them.'[176] The ideas of advocates of scientific management techniques in the home, such as Guy who had suggested a similar arrangement ten years earlier (Figure 4.3), clearly influenced the arrangement. Lee also took advantage of the latest technology and included a large cabinet and refrigerator for storing food, instead of the usual larder, as well as an electric washing machine. The equipment of the kitchen was expected to give pleasure to women; a photograph of the kitchen was captioned, 'How women would enjoy working in this kitchen!'[177] Tanner commended the house for embodying practical labour-saving, remarking that 'Mrs Lee has made a sincere and original endeavour to evolve a home where the work of the household could be a pleasant undertaking and far removed from the monotonous drudgery which the average small house places upon the woman who is responsible for its maintenance.'[178] Tanner's ideas about women's work were more conservative than Lee's; nowhere did he acknowledge that a labour-saving house would give women more time for leisure, something Lee stressed. However, both agreed that housework was a more pleasant undertaking in a well-designed, labour-saving home. Furthermore, Lee's design drew on her own personal experience as a housewife and mother.

'The House That Jill Built' engaged with the language of Modernism, not as an ultimate rational aesthetic, but as an aid to labour-saving and health. The interior was designed in the 'Efficiency' style, with rounded corners, and simple, fitted furniture was promoted because it was less likely to collect dust and could therefore save the labour of the housewife and aid hygiene. The house also reflected the middle-class shift towards a home that could be run by the housewife without domestic help. Nevertheless, the chairman of the Royal Society of Arts was not impressed, commenting: 'Good so far as it goes – even necessary – but was there anything in the home that removed the woman's daily and hourly task of cooking and cleaning up afterwards? If that home really represented what woman today wants, it can only be because she has not really thought of the possible.'[179] Many Modernists and social reformers thought 'the possible' to be collective facilities such as restaurants and laundries, that took some of the laboursome tasks outside the home.[180] Such facilities had come into being during the First World War, but were roundly rejected afterwards.

'The House That Jill Built' articulated the idea that there was a specific woman's point of view on housing as well as the idea that this point of view was especially concerned with efficiency, health and labour-saving. This was not lost on speculative builders. For example, a 1936 advertisement for the newly built Goddington Court Estate, headlined 'Planned from the woman's point of view', claimed: 'Every woman knows *exactly* what constitutes her idea of the perfect home, so the interior of each house … has been planned to earn the unstinted admiration of the ladies. But we also have much to show mere man who will appreciate the fine materials and workmanship which are so plainly visible.'[181] This was a view from the interior. Like many advertisements of the period, it suggested that the woman's point of view was confined to the interior of the home and the man's to the exterior. Furthermore, 'house' conjures up a picture of the exterior of a dwelling, whereas 'home' conjures up its interior. While this division would appear to reinforce the idea of separate spheres of public and private for men and women respectively,[182] it does not suggest that women were trapped within the interior; rather, it offers women active opportunities to influence and make their own spaces according to needs arising from their own experiences.

The house that Heath Robinson built

In 1934 the new commercial culture of efficiency and labour-saving in suburban England that the Ideal Home Exhibition had helped to create was sufficiently established for the show to poke fun at it. The show's centrepiece was a Tudorbethan house named 'The Gadgets' designed by the cartoonist Heath Robinson (Figure 4.13). The house was nearly twenty feet (6 m) tall and stood on a site measuring fifty by thirty feet (15 × 9 m). It was peopled by Mr and Mrs Glowmutton and more than twenty moving figures, together with cats, hens, birds and a cow. The house had an open front, like a doll's house, allowing visitors to see four main rooms, as well as an entrance hall, bathroom, study and attics. All the rooms were fitted with a variety of moving, labour-saving gadgets, as were the gardens.

In the entrance hall, a rotary foot wiper avoided the inconvenience of tripping over the doormat. Next to the entrance hall was the kitchen where the kitchen maid could be seen simultaneously peeling potatoes and operating the W.H.R. patent custard-making machine with her foot. Next door in the living room, Mr and Mrs Glowmutton descended to breakfast, alerted by the parlour maid operating the rotary breakfast gong. Their weight combined simultaneously to turn on the radiogramophone, give the cat its milk and serve eggs for breakfast. In the bedroom above, the beds were so arranged that the happy couple could each warm their feet on a hot water bottle heated by a strategically placed candle. Without leaving her bed, the lady of the house could extinguish the candle by turning a handle, while her husband, making use of a similar handle, could provide himself with a nightcap of whisky and soda. Mr Glowmutton washed himself in an attic bathroom, which, due to what Heath Robinson called 'a temporary derangement of the hot-water

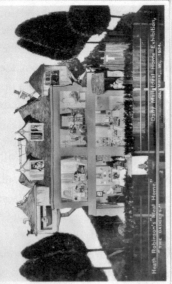

4.13 Postcards of 'The Gadgets' by Heath Robinson at the Daily Mail Ideal Home Exhibition, 1934

system', splashed his visitors in the garden.[183] The nursery was decorated with a frieze of Heath Robinson figures in silhouette. A number of devices enabled a single nurse to look after four babies. While she employed a baby-bathing machine, one of the other children was rocked to sleep by the pendulum of the nursery clock. Another child was fed from a suspended bottle, while a fourth child was amused by a mechanical toy.

Outside in the garden, Mrs Downbristle, the washerwoman, was seen winding out the washing on a moving washing line to give it an airing, assisted by Mrs Fitzwilliam, the mangle lady. Elsewhere in the garden, Sandy Willie, the gardener, was seen directing the nozzle of the weed-killing machine on to the thistles, while Jake, the garden boy, pulled the lever that worked the bellows that pumped the poison that made the thistle whistle. Mr Welwyn Sprozzle, the sunbather in a hammock on the wash-house roof, adjusted his sunshade by means of a string, while Harold, the under-gardener, drove the combined lawn-sweeper, mower and roller. Another gardener dealt with pests by spraying them with Heath Robinson's pedal-driven grub-killer. A remarkable amount of labour was needed to operate these supposedly labour-saving appliances.

This was Heath Robinson's first foray into the labour-saving home. Two years later in 1936 his seminal book *How to Live in a Flat* appeared. The joke of the work depended upon the existence of the culture of efficiency and homemaking that he lampooned. Heath Robinson relished the opportunity to see visitors' reactions to 'The Gadgets' at the Ideal Home Exhibition. However, he recalled that his ideas did not appear entirely far-fetched to some visitors, and not everyone got the joke: one 'earnest visitor' condemned it as 'impracticable'.[184] Most visitors to the Ideal Home Exhibition who gathered around Heath Robinson's Ideal Home participated in a collective, knowing and joyful experience of consumer culture and modernity similar to that found in the cinema. Ideas of efficiency and labour-saving in the home were not only ubiquitous, but also a mixed blessing, fraught with anxieties about the proper place of technology and the changing roles of men, women and servants in the home.

Conclusion

By the mid-1930s a commercial culture of homemaking was firmly established in Britain. The labour-saving home was thought to be achieved only through the adoption of the most efficient techniques and technologies of house planning, architecture and housework. However, as the testimony of Mass Observation's Respondent 082 demonstrated, homemaking and housework still brought with it considerable drudgery along with anxieties about gender and class roles. The 'real' kitchens of most women in new suburban homes consisted of a small room containing a Belfast sink, a draining board, a central deal or enamel table and a freestanding or built-in dresser like the one I encountered at 17 Rosamund Road and as depicted by London County Council in a 'sub-standard' kitchen in 1962 (Figure 1.4).

In post-First World War England, the term 'efficiency' had a broader appeal, promising not only to liberate housewives from the drudgery of housework, but also to get the economy back on its feet. The term 'labour-saving' came to signify a suburban modernity in the interwar years that was far removed from the dictums of the Modern Movement in architecture and design. Moreover, the motive for the acquisition of labour-saving goods could be to participate in a shared sociability.

Labour-saving furniture and appliances were potent symbols of modernity in the home, valued as much for their symbolic status, which evoked the accompanying consumer discourse of the modern housewife, as for their actual functionalism and efficiency. Specifically suburban and feminine forms of Modernism emerged that did not radically alter the exterior of the home but instead entered through the back door, via the kitchen. In the interwar period the kitchen was a major site of experimentation and modernisation, ruled over by the idealised figure of the professional housewife.

Nostalgia: the Tudorbethan semi and the detritus of Empire

Why are you, or perhaps your neighbours, living in an imitation Tudor house with stained wooden slats shoved on the front door to make it look like what is called a half-timbered house? Those slats have nothing to do with the construction of the house. They are just applied as ornaments. The house does not look like a real half-timbered house and it never can. It has been built in quite a different way from a real Tudor house. Why do we live in this sort of half-baked pageant, always hiding our ideas in clothes of another age?[1]

John Gloag, the novelist, historian and writer on design, made these comments in 1934.[2] While he was by no means a committed Modernist, Gloag despised the imitation Tudor, or 'Tudorbethan', for its inauthenticity, seeing it as inappropriate for modern life. Ten years later, Gloag complained that the 'twentieth-century Englishman's castle had become a museum of flimsy parodies of things used generations earlier'.[3]

Like Gloag, the Modernist critic Anthony Bertram thought it was wrong for modern people to surround themselves with styles from the past that were not even authentic. Bertram included an illustration by G.A. Wise to explain the Modernist maxim of 'fitness for purpose' in his book *The House: A Summary of the Art and Science of Domestic Architecture* (1935) (Figure 5.1). The diagram suggested that the baronial castle style was originally intended for a crusading knight and that it was

5.1 Diagram of 'Fitness for Purpose' by G.A. Wise, from Anthony Bertram, *The House: A Summary of the Art and Science of Domestic Architecture*, 1935

incorrect to adapt it as 'bijou baronial' for the bowler-hatted man who worked in the city. Similarly, the Tudor cottage was intended for the serf who lived in an age when water had to be fetched in buckets, and it was therefore incongruous that the Tudorbethan semi be built for the modern man with a car at his disposal. Inspired by Le Corbusier, Bertram proposed instead the 'house-machine' that would gain its beauty from its functionalism, rather than applied art.[4]

In this chapter I explore the reasons why nostalgia for an imagined Old English past, so bemoaned by Modernist critics, took hold in the architecture, design and decoration of the suburban interwar home. 'Nostalgia' is a deeply resonant word for my purposes. Its Greek origins are a compound of *nóstos* (to return home) and *álgos* (pain, ache). It has been described as 'a social and cultural phenomenon which, in the memorial culture of contemporary western societies, can denote melancholic pleasure. In common parlance, nostalgia refers to notions of lost innocence, beauty and apparently simpler times.'[5] Svetlana Boym distinguishes between 'restorative' and 'reflexive' forms of nostalgia: she argues that while the former is reactionary and desires to restore an imaginary past, the latter can be playful and ironic, and acknowledges that all representations of the past are constructions of a sort.[6] I would argue that reflexive nostalgia is particularly useful as it gives agency to both the producers and consumers of nostalgia.

I will investigate the reasons why suburbanites such as Ronald and Miriam Kingham chose to live in a 'half-baked pageant'. For first-time homeowners like the Kinghams, there was safety, as well as comfort and modernity, in the architecture and design of the past. I discuss the appeal of 'Old England' and nostalgia for simpler imperial, rural times. I focus in particular on the architecture of the Tudorbethan semi and the taste for antique and reproduction furniture, furnishings and decoration in its interior. This includes a discussion of how the detritus of Empire was washed up in the interwar home, in the form of objects such as the ebony elephant.

Old England: Tudorism and Tudoresque

Like many Modernists, Bertram was frustrated that the English looked backwards to the past in the architecture and decoration of their homes, rather than forwards to the future. In 1938 he put forward negative reasons for this:

> Probably the popular love for the Tudor, whether genuine or bogus, is based on fear and a wish to escape. When I was broadcasting I had many letters that said quite frankly, 'The suggestion of those quiet old days gives us the restful atmosphere we seek in our homes.' This is a self-deception, because, of course, the old days were far from quiet, but it is not surprising. These are insecure and frightening times and I believe the economic depression and the fear of war are the chief promoters of the Tudoresque.[7]

Bertram's thesis has much going for it. In the interwar years, the Tudor and Elizabethan periods were consistently represented as the crucial moments in the formation of British national identity. The British, or perhaps more accurately the English, have had a long-standing love affair with the Tudor period. From the eighteenth century, this was manifested across a range of visual and material culture – including architecture, furniture, ceramics, textiles, stained glass, advertisements, paintings, murals, theatre, tableaux vivant, pageants and exhibitions – that continued into the 1920s and beyond. It was found not just in Britain but also in the furthest-flung corners of the British Empire. Many of these examples of Tudorism were Tudoresque invented traditions that made little attempt at historical accuracy. Furthermore, the Tudor was so popular and became so appropriated across a range of cultural forms that it became a kind of vernacular, especially in architecture.

There was no single concept of Tudorism for interwar homeowners; multiple versions existed. Spectators, viewers, listeners and users had agency and were not duped by the hegemony and invented traditions of Tudorism. As Tatiana String and Marcus Bull argue, 'we should never underestimate the sophistication of those … who appropriate the

Tudor. The idea of Tudorism, or Tudorisms, emerges [...] as a series of interplays between persistent cliché and fine discrimination, and between enduring tropes and constantly shifting cultural adaptations.'[8] For design historians, this points to the endless recycling, reinterpretation and hybridisation – including the reinvention of reinventions – of Tudoresque styles of the past.

The popularity of a vision of rural England in politics and ideas stems in particular from the 1880s and needs to be understood within the context of a general crisis in urban, industrial society. This produced a cultural response in the form of a ruralist vision of a specifically English culture in art and letters, music and architecture from the 1890s and 1900s that was widespread by 1914.[9] As the historian Patrick Wright says, 'the idea of the golden age or the rural idyll seems always to have spoken to the constrained condition of everyday life'.[10]

It has further been suggested that the mid-Victorian turn towards the Tudor and Elizabethan periods was motivated by a desire for a more sophisticated, nationalist, aggressively expansionist and more Protestant 'Merrie England'. This vision of the national past was seen as more appropriate to the Victorian age of empire than that of the medieval village, which was based on the Church and Latinate culture and which was seen as too international and radical.[11] The historian Alun Howkins suggests that such a construction was not concerned with the actual Tudor dynasty (1485–1603), but was based on 'the later years of the reign of Elizabeth, lasting until the 1680s but with gaps, especially the 1650s'.[12] The attraction towards 'Merrie England' of 'Good Queen Bess' may also have been motivated by a desire to see echoes of her age in Queen Victoria's reign and parallels between the two women. As Howkins notes, late nineteenth-century historians such as J.A. Froude played an important part in elevating the notion of an Elizabethan 'Golden Age' peopled by manly English explorers and degenerate French and Spanish, which was imperial, rural and anti-industrial.[13] The establishment of an alternative imperial tradition for the British Empire – the Tudor and Elizabethan

– bypassed any uncomfortable comparisons that might be made with the Roman Empire. The historian Peter Mandler emphasises the 'importance of new technologies in animating and disseminating Tudor history to mass audiences – steel engravings, lithography, stereotyping, and above all the steam press', which meant that between the 1820s and 1840s, 'broader swathes of the population were being incorporated into the imagined communities of the nation'.[14] This led to Tudorism reaching lower-middle and autodidact artisanal classes.

Another important component of this vision of 'Merrie England' was a constructed English literary tradition. In particular, before and during the First World War there was a revival of interest in Shakespeare's work and the Shakespearean past. Stratford-upon-Avon became a popular tourist destination.[15] Shakespeare was thought to speak patriotically for the 'English race' and was invoked during the First World War because of the claimed call for 'national unity' in his work.[16] Indeed, Shakespeare was adopted in a variety of popular media, including guidebooks, history books, photographic volumes and exhibitions.[17]

A newly invented tradition of spectacular local historical pageants emerged in 1905 with Louis Napoleon Parker's Sherborne Historical Pageant and was developed by Frank Lascelles and others, becoming very popular. Inspired by medieval and Elizabethan masques, they told the history of places in outside settings and featured prominently Tudor and Elizabethan scenes, acted by large amateur casts that could consist of thousands.[18] They often took huge liberties with historical facts, with many of them including a 'Good Queen Bess slept here' scene. Historical pageants retained their mass appeal into the interwar period and Gloag's comment about 'living in a half-baked pageant' was clearly made with the pageant movement in mind.

Hollywood turned to Elizabethan and Tudor subjects in the interwar years, notably in *Drake the Pirate* (also titled *Elizabeth of England*, 1935), based on a 1913 pageant-play by Parker, and *The Private Lives of Elizabeth and Essex* (1939), starring Bette Davis and Errol Flynn.[19] Tudor was also a desirable style for film stars to associate themselves with in their private lives. In 1936 the Ideal Home Exhibition contained a replica of Mr and Mrs Clive Brook's Tudor lounge in a display of 'Homes of the Film Stars'. Clive Brook was a distinguished British leading man of stage and screen who usually played perfect gentlemen. By 1936 he had appeared as Sherlock Holmes in several films.[20] It was fitting, therefore, that somebody with such a persona should choose a traditional English Tudor lounge rather than Hollywood 'Moderne', which was well known to audiences through films and magazines. The Tudor interior was thought to be classy and aspirational. The 1936 Odeon cinema in Faversham, Kent, was even built in full-blown Tudorbethan style rather than the usual Moderne.

The Tudor period held a particular appeal for popular forms of entertainment and leisure. For example, half-timbered constructions were erected on a number of piers. As the historian Paul Readman has pointed out, 'the past could even play a part in holidaymaking in brash, self-consciously "Modern" resorts'.[21] The suburban golfer could socialize in Tudorbethan clubhouses, and it was also a common style for the new 'roadhouse' pubs.[22] Even shopping could be conducted in Tudor surroundings: Liberty & Co.'s department store was rebuilt in the 1920s with a half-timbered rear exterior and a galleried interior with wood taken supposedly from old naval warships. Tudorbethan was also a prevalent style for suburban parades of shops.[23] The appeal of 'Merrie England', seen as part of a rural idyll, was also linked to the popularity of the countryside as a site of leisure, with activities such as rambling, which reached its peak in the interwar years.[24]

The work of illustrators and architects was particularly important to the formation of the new vision of 'Merrie England'. The architect John Nash, for example, published books that, in Raphael Samuel's words, 'elevated the stately home to a pinnacle of romantic esteem while at the same time making the Elizabethan the morning star of the indigenous'.[25] By the mid-1870s Gothic was contaminated by its association with industrialisation, and architects turned to 'Queen Anne'.[26] The Tudor revival and half-timbered, tile-hung, 'Old English' imitations of manor houses emerged in the late nineteenth century.[27] Reginald C. Fry was the supervising architect for the layout of the Park Langley Estate in Beckenham and built many houses in such styles, including one that won a competition and was exhibited at the Ideal Home Exhibition in 1912. The architect George Devey tried to make new buildings appear as if they had been built and adapted over centuries and inherited rather than commissioned.[28] The 'cottage home' – a small country house – as a form of architecture emerged along with notions of domestic comfort that implied a rough equality between classes. This notion of the 'Olden Time' contrasted with the medieval Arts and Crafts utopianism of those motivated by socialist politics.

This architecture was the forerunner of what by the mid-1900s was known as 'English taste', which was synonymous with the southern English vernacular and its lowest common denominator, the 'Tudor' style.[29] The Tudor vernacular was popular because of its association with a rural, manorial and Protestant 'Merrie England'. It represented a specifically English architectural tradition as against the 'foreign' classicism of Greek and Roman architecture. The Tudoresque was exported and manifest overseas as an expression of Britishness, even becoming exotic.[30] The taste for the rural embraced the vernacular architecture of southern England as part of an ideal landscape. The years immediately following the First World War witnessed a middle-class fashion for restoring dilapidated country cottages and farmhouses, which could be purchased relatively cheaply in the 1920s, with some of their rural locations submerged into new suburbs and access to work made possible by new rail links and motor cars (Figure 2.10). Some better-off homeowners built new houses in a cottage style, influenced by the Arts and Crafts ideals of the Garden City movement. This was part of a popular interest in preserving the rural past in the 1920s.[31] For example, following a revival of interest in John Constable's paintings, Willy Lott's house in

Flatford, East Bergholt, Suffolk, which features in *The Hay Wain*, was preserved in 1926.[32] The embrace of the Tudoresque by architects was often reflexively nostalgic rather than historically accurate.

The Empire at home

As I have noted, in the interwar years it was comforting to hark back to an imagined 'Merrie England' in which the country led literature and the arts, commanded the oceans, explored the globe and had a natural governing class. While the Victorians were keen to see a parallel in the aggressive expansionist activities of the Elizabethan age to their own, the vision of 'Merrie England' had different connotations in the first half of the twentieth century in the face of social unrest, economic instability and anxieties about imperial decline. The mock Tudor or Tudorbethan was thought of as inherently imperial, symbolising England's glorious Tudor and Elizabethan pasts as a world power. Bungalows, both abroad and at home, were often built in Tudorbethan style. Bungalow was a Bangladeshi word and was particularly associated with Anglo-Indians.[33]

Images of the sea and of Britannia ruling the waves were part of national self-consciousness and were expressed in all kinds of cultural forms. The ship was a symbol of the navy, which represented Britain's greatness and was the link with the far-flung Empire. In the interwar years one of the most popular motifs was the Tudor galleon. This image could often be found adorning the stained glass panel on the front door of the Tudorbethan semi. Many of them were personally chosen by house purchasers, as it was common for builders to let them choose the stained glass themselves and for it to be installed at the point of construction. Galleons were also found on wall plaques, ashtrays and other decorative objects and were a common motif for home crafts (Plate 16).[34] The ship also brought back the spoils of Empire – which filled the ideal home in the form of Persian rugs, elephant-foot umbrella stands and the like – through trade and returning passengers.[35]

In the late nineteenth and early twentieth centuries both imperial and trade expansion stretched the geographical boundaries of Britain. As the historian Jose Harris has pointed out, Britain was

> a society without determinate boundaries, where internal social arrange-
> ments were highly localised and fragmented; which embraced four differ-
> ent national cultures and not just one; which was affected by transnational
> forces common to all European societies; and which traded with and gov-
> erned much of the world.[36]

Thus it is important, in Harris's words, to 'give some sense of a "soci-ety" that stretched from the village street to the African veldt, from the parish to the globe'.[37] Moreover, the idea of 'home' in an imperial context embraced the microscopic, in the form of the individual dwelling, and the macroscopic, as the mother country, looking outwards to the wider shores of the Empire.

By 1900 Britain possessed the largest Empire the world had ever seen.[38] As schoolchildren were constantly reminded, over a quarter of the globe, some 12 million square miles, was coloured pink, and Britain ruled a quarter of the world's population. Yet by the interwar years there were obvious signs and worries about a decline in Britain's imperial spirit and economic and military strength. Paradoxically, as the design historian Paul Greenhalgh has suggested, it was when Empire was in decline that imperial display, notably at exhibitions, became more overt, as can be seen for example in the 1924 British Empire Exhibition and the 1938 Glasgow Exhibition.[39]

In the interwar years many British people were very 'at home' with the Empire. It provided outlets for employment, enterprise and adventure, and the possibility of gaining status and prestige. While some had direct expe-rience of the Empire through employment or travel, others were linked through family and friends and the consumption of imported goods. The *Official Guide* to the 1924 British Empire Exhibition at Wembley referred to the event, with a domestic flourish, as a 'Family Party of the British

Empire'.[40] This kind of familial and domestic description can often be found in the catalogues of British international exhibitions that historians have often thought of as primarily concerned with trade propaganda.

Furthermore, it is worth noting that as well as showing the world the immense power, wealth and resources of Britain and her Empire, the British Empire Exhibition had a secondary purpose: to show the new life that the dominions and colonies offered to settlers. The glimpses of life overseas offered by these exhibitions encouraged so-called surplus women to emigrate to the colonies to become pioneer homemakers.[41] The female surplus consisted of single women whose personal need for a home and family, it was thought, could be fulfilled by carefully controlled emigration that would also serve the cause of colonial expansion. One of the major appeals to women of this new life in the Empire was the availability of cheap domestic labour at a time when it was increasingly difficult to find competent, reliable and affordable servants at home. Throughout the interwar period many British people emigrated, with numbers reaching a peak of 256,000 in 1923.[42] People worked in the colonial civil service, the colonial branch of their firm, tea or rubber planting or teaching and mission work. Others spent spells in the Empire as part of army or navy service. Those who settled in Britain's colonies sought to familiarise and domesticate the landscape. Women had particular responsibilities to make 'home' in the Empire.[43] Many, then, had a familiar and domesticated relationship to the Empire, seeing it not as an exotic 'other' but as an extension of 'home'.

Many interwar larders contained imperial products. For three-quarters of a century it was scarcely possible to buy anything without being reminded by its packaging of the idea of Empire.[44] Britain's relationship with the Empire allowed food and raw materials to be imported cheaply and the Imperial Preference system allowed Britain to give tariff protection to its own industry in 'home' and Empire markets.[45] In the early twentieth century the British Empire was a site for both the production and consumption of goods.[46] Propaganda from the government-funded Empire Marketing Board between 1926 and 1933 encouraged British consumers to buy Empire produce.[47] Buying goods from the Empire was part of a patriotic call to 'buy British' that had been prevalent since the 1890s. This was believed to be both a solution to economic competition and a way of justifying the continued support of the Empire. Furthermore, as Richard Price has suggested, imperial patriotic unity was the conservative version of socialist collectivism which was gaining popularity as an answer to economic inefficiency. Patriotism, and jingoism, he argues, called for a collectivism of spirit and sacrifice for the nation against the selfish individualism of the Little Englander who refused to be part of the unity of a national consensus. Patriotism for home and Empire especially helped calm the insecurities the lower middle classes felt about their social status and gave them respectability and a sense of belonging. It also encapsulated the 'clerkly' good values of selfless duty, sacrifice and obedience.[48]

Moreover, as Todd Kuchta has argued, there was an internalisation of Empire in suburbia itself. First of all suburbia was seen rather like a colony, with the metropolis as the centre of Empire. The pioneers of the new housing estates were seen as colonial settlers, establishing new social conventions and traditions, in much the way that colonial settlers were able to remake their identities.[49] This idea was not lost on the building firm New Ideal Homesteads, whose advertising campaign depicted new suburbanites as colonial pioneers (Figure 5.2). Imperial resonances were also to be found in the topography of suburbia through streets named after iconic figures from the height of the British Empire, such as Livingstone and Stanley. The British Empire's favourite poet, Rudyard Kipling, was asked to choose names for the streets that were developed around the Wembley exhibition site. Suburban dwellers could also drink in pubs with names such as 'The Lord Napier'. Empire was so familiar that it was part of home.

However, as suburbia grew and Empire declined, interwar suburbanites came to be seen as subjugated 'natives' rather than imperial

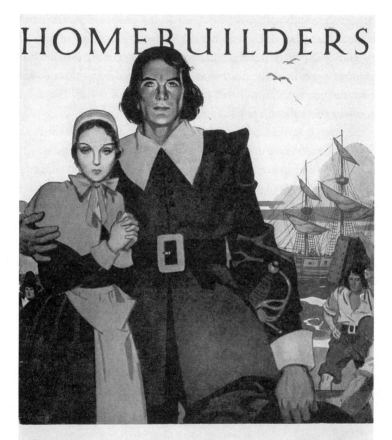

5.2 Front cover of New Ideal Homesteads brochure, *c.* 1930s

conquerers. Suburbanites were subject to the same kind of racialised language that characterised earlier depictions of the slums of 'Darkest England', with their residents likened to a degenerate, inferior race. Suburban men, in particular, began to be depicted as feeble and weak in novels such as George Orwell's *Coming up for Air* (1939). There were even fears that suburbia would form new slums.

The lives that British expatriates lived abroad in the Empire and colonies often had a kind of amplified and outdated Englishness, with conventions and customs from several decades earlier, often altogether made up. They mixed English ornaments with local crafts and souvenirs of pastimes such as big game hunting.[50] Many imperial and colonial settlers retired to England, especially to the Home Counties. They sought familiarity in their new surroundings; for example, the rolling hills of Surrey could remind them of the tea plantations of Kenya. Returned imperial Britons often named their houses after the places they had been. For example, John Gloag's 1923 *The House We Ought to Live In* showed a variety of lettering for houses, including 'Babadori': 'a name plate for a Country Cottage with decorations reminiscent of the West African village with which the name is associated'. To the left of the name, a coastline with palms was depicted, and to the right were grass huts.[51] Even that most archetypal and mocked of suburban house names – 'Dunroamin' – could, in this context, have imperial undertones.

The professional housewife's preoccupation with cleanliness also had specifically imperial undertones.[52] Imperial branding was found on a wide range of household goods and appliances associated with cleanliness that were produced in the interwar years. One such example is the Ewbank empire carpet sweeper (Figure 4.5). Made with an oak casing instead of the usual metal, which gave it an air of traditionalism and even resonances of Englishness and mock Tudor, large gold letters spelled out 'Ewbank Empire' across the front of the sweeper mechanism, together with a transfer-printed lion topped with a Union Jack. It is possible that this object might have been made to cash in on the popularity of the British Empire Exhibition in 1924. It is also a reminder of the women who made modern homes in the Empire as well as the idea of the 'imperial suburb' where the housewife cleaned her Persian carpets and dusted her ebony elephants in her Tudorbethan semi.

The Tudorbethan semi

Ronald and Miriam Kingham's house in Edmonton, north London, discussed in Chapter 2, is a typical example of what was commonly referred to as Tudorbethan, the most characteristic style of speculative builders. The façade of the Kinghams' house had non-structural half-timbering applied to the first floor, bay windows to the front reception room and front bedroom, a white, Atlas cement rendered finish and a red, tiled roof (Figure 2.1). The front door was situated on the right-hand side of the elevation, sheltered by an overhanging canopy porch.

'Tudorbethan' is an invented term that describes a hybrid architectural style loosely based on an amalgam of features from the Tudor and Elizabethan periods.[53] Many contemporary architects, designers, novelists and critics saw the Tudorbethan house, with its mixture of the traditional and the modern, as *ersatz* and backward-looking; the antithesis of Modernism. Such neo-Tudor houses were also described by a number of less flattering adjectives and epithets.[54] The poet and campaigner for the preservation of architectural heritage John Betjeman damningly tagged them as 'sham'.[55] Others described them as 'mock' Tudor or 'Jerrybethan'[56] or as a 'bogus style'.[57]

Critics despised the Tudorbethan for its inauthenticity and seemingly random bringing together of disparate architectural styles in an approximation of the past. Osbert Lancaster identified the two predominant speculative builders' styles as 'By-Pass Variegated' and 'Stockbroker's Tudor'.[58] Lancaster was very critical of 1930s spec-built suburbia:

One can amuse one's self by classifying the various contributions which past styles have made to this infernal amalgam; here are some quaint gables culled from Art Nouveau surrounding a façade that is plainly Modernistic in inspiration; there the twisted beams and leaded panes of Stockbrokers Tudor are happily contrasted with green tiles of obviously Pseudish origin; next door some terra-cotta plaques, Pont Street Dutch in character, enliven a white wood Wimbledon transitional porch, making it a splendid foil to a red-brick garage that is vaguely Romanesque in character.[59]

These Tudorbethan houses were decorated with pebbledash, leaded panes and mock Tudor timbering, with tiled roofs rather than the more expensive slate. Modern building techniques allowed builders to create a diversity of 'by-pass variegated' styles and adornments. As Ian Bentley points out, the Tudorbethan 'made reference to *many* historical architectures, achieving a rich variety of associations through a complex additive aesthetic, using elements such as bays, porches, gables and dormers to break up the overall building mass'.[60] The application of surface decoration, which bore no relation to the house's underlying structure, broke the Modernist maxims of 'form follows function', 'truth to materials' and 'fitness for purpose'. The details of Tudorbethan houses tended to be symbolic of the Tudor period, rather than imitative or descriptive. As well as combining the charm and character of the old with the convenience of the new, the Tudor cottage style was used by speculative builders to stress individuality, although many critics saw the overall effect as depressingly uniform.

Some builders of Tudorbethan houses claimed to use traditional building techniques. In 1922 John I. Williams & Sons advertised a Tudor cottage in the *Daily Mail Bungalow Book* which they claimed was 'a faithful reproduction on traditional lines', built according to traditional methods of construction with authentic materials. It could be built in any part of the world and could be modified to suit the wishes of the clients, 'providing they are not antagonistic to the period character'.[61] Williams described another of their Tudor cottages as having 'old characteristics happily welded to modern equipment for comfort and convenience'.[62] However, most builders made no pretence of being authentic. The Tudorbethan semi was no mere wattle and daub reconstruction of the past. Instead it was constructed from the most up-to-date materials. Speculative builders set out to demonstrate that they could improve on what the Tudors had done. In 1927 the Tibbenham Tudor Construction Company boasted of its modern methods of construction: 'the ideals of ancient craftsmanship have been combined with the utility of modern methods and materials' and 'Tibbenham Tudor houses combine oak half-timbering and concrete instead of brick and wattle. Thus, speedy construction is possible and even greater strength is assured.'[63] Builders were reflexively nostalgic, wanting to combine the comforting spirit of Old England with modern living.

It was commonplace for Tudorbethan-style houses to be described as 'modern' in advertisements by builders. For example, an advertisement for Modern Homes & Estates Ltd, accompanied by an illustration of a pair of semi-detached Tudorbethan houses, declared 'The best of them all is a "Modern Home"' (Figure 5.3). It continued:

> For solid construction, for outside appearance, and for the high quality and completeness of interior equipment, you will find it hard to beat these all-electric Modern Homes at Motspur Park. This estate is sure to appeal to all potential buyers of homes of this type. It adjoins the station and an up-to-date shopping parade, and electricity is cheap.[64]

The headline and the copy, with its emphasis on the 'all-electric' and 'up-to-date', might lead the reader of today to assume that it advertised houses built in a Modernist, or at least a Modernistic style. Although the Tudorbethan style might today seem incongruous and at odds with the copy, for the interwar house purchaser this mixture of nostalgia and modernity in suburbia was commonplace and unremarkable.

Critics such as Lancaster thought that the Tudorbethan vision of the past was entirely inappropriate for modern life. In his cartoon of

5.3 Advertisement for Modern Homes & Estates Ltd, from *Evening Standard Guide to House Purchase, c.* 1930s

'Stockbroker's Tudor', Lancaster juxtaposed the said house with an electricity pylon, an aeroplane, a car (as streamlined as the plane) and a modern woman (Figure 5.4). In the accompanying caption Lancaster observed

> [t]he extraordinary fact that all over the country the latest and most scientific methods of mass production were ... utilised to turn out a stream of old oak beams, leaded window-panes and small discs of bottle-glass, all structural devices which our ancestors lost no time in abandoning as soon as an increase in wealth and knowledge enabled them to do so.[65]

Despite the condemnation of both traditionalists and Modernists, houses that combined the past with the present were readily available and wholly desirable in the interwar years.

Modernity and nostalgia came together in the Tudorbethan suburban semi in what Ian Davis tellingly calls a 'spirit of ambiguity', which he identifies in five areas:

> the desire for strong anchorage with the distant past in the buildings' style, whilst wanting (at least in the bathroom or kitchen) all the latest and progressive ideas in planning or labour-saving appliances; the need for a cosy, warm, inward-looking house with oak beams and brick fireplaces whilst simultaneously wanting an expansive outlook for light, air and sunlight; a concern to express the owner's individuality in his home whilst still recognising that it was part of a street or community; the ambition to own a house that gave an unmistakable appearance of affluence but at a minimum cost to the purchaser; finally, the wish to live in a practical house, that hinted at modernity.[66]

Yet these qualities were anything but ambiguous to many of the home-owners who lived in these houses and found pleasure in them. As Davis observes, for Modernists the opposing values of the Tudorbethan can only be ambiguous because they represent a middle way and not an out-and-out commitment. However, as Davis rightly points out: 'the balancing act performed in hanging on to the past whilst grasping for all the

5.4 Illustration of 'Stockbroker's Tudor' by Osbert Lancaster, from *Pillar to Post: English Architecture without Tears*, 1938

advantages of modern living' recurred within the Daily Mail Ideal Home Exhibition catalogues of the interwar years.[67] In the end, despite his passionate defence of the suburban semi, Davis himself is bound by these absolute values of Modernism, which he seems not to be able to conceptually overcome. For suburbanites, then, the seemingly contradictory values embodied in the interwar Tudorbethan semi were not ambiguous at all but a pragmatic, as well as a romantic, solution that satisfied the desire for an ideal home that was modern and comfortable.

The Tudorbethan style's popularity with the masses, particularly the new middle classes, made it an object of derision. As well as being associated with semis, it was also a popular style for bungalows. In 1929 a report on *The Thames Valley from Cricklewood to Staines* by the Council for the Preservation of Rural England complained that 'the bungalow with its sham-half timber, its tinsel and more ephemeral trimmings is rapidly creeping up the banks'.[68] Contemporary critics used the phrase 'bungaloid growth' to describe what was thought to be a pernicious spreading. The equation of the masses with unhealthy biological growths, bacteria or disease, has, as Carey notes, a longer history stemming back to the French biologist Louis Pasteur.[69]

An additional reason for the long-standing denigration of the Tudorbethan was its association with women. Arthur Edwards, in his highly influential study *The Design of Suburbia* (1981), echoed many critics of the interwar period by describing the Tudorbethan as 'a principal constituent of speculative suburbia's ugliness'.[70] He also pointed out that the Tudorbethan was 'in tune with suburbia's romantic spirit', which he ascribed to the rise in the status of women fostered by the Representation of the People Act in 1918.[71] Women were interested in the design of the home. Magazines such as *Ideal Home*, which catered to middle-class women, presented half-timbered detached houses set in woodland glades as the ideal. Women, Edwards suggested, were attracted by the combination of conservatism and minor novelty in the Tudorbethan. As I have noted above, what critics so despised about the Tudorbethan was precisely its combination of tradition and modernity. Yet it was the modern features – the latest materials, techniques and technologies that aided labour-saving – for which women clamoured. For many interwar critics and some subsequent ones, women were associated with both the 'sham' Modernistic and the 'sham' Tudor.

The unplanned individuality of the spec-built Tudorbethan house contrasted strongly with the plain neo-Georgian architecture of local authority estates. While semi-detached Tudorbethan houses were laid out in pairs of alternating design, emphasising their individuality and difference from one another, neo-Georgian houses were planned in a collective, unifying style to enhance the similarities of houses in a scheme. The neo-Georgian could be used to join terraces of houses in a single unified composition. When it was used for semi-detached houses it emphasised the centre of a pair and stressed their whole appearance, whereas the Tudorbethan emphasised the separateness and individuality of a pair, placing the front doors on the edge of the block.[72] Tudorbethan was, then, emphatically different from council housing. Thus, the two architectural styles were used to express and came to signify different values. The Tudorbethan expressed private individuality and the neo-Georgian, public collectivity and community.

For many builders, the Tudorbethan was just another style. For example, E. & L. Berg Ltd advertised Tudorbethan designs in the same brochure that included their Wells Coates-designed Modernist 'Sunspan' house that was displayed at the 1934 Ideal Home Exhibition.[73] The much-derided Tudorbethan semi offered much that the new homeowning classes desired. The interwar Ideal Home exhibitions were full of such houses in villages with poetic names such as the 'Hamlet of Heart's Desire' (1925), 'Village of the Open Doors' (1926), 'Village of "Welcome In"' (1929) and 'Old English Street' (1932). Tudorbethan may have been a term of abuse among rational planners, modern architects and intellectuals, but it fulfilled a vision of domestic contentment, reflexive nostalgia and a modern way of life for many suburbanites.

For such homeowners, there was nothing contradictory or even ambiguous about wanting modern living in a Tudorbethan house. For example, 'Sunbeam Town' at the 1928 Ideal Home Exhibition consisted of eight houses in varying styles, including R.A. Duncan's Modernist House of the Future. The latter was sandwiched between a 'simple Georgian house' and an 'up-to-date Tudor style Home'. 'Here', declared the catalogue, 'the very latest scientific discoveries in relation to the effect of sunshine on health are given practical domestic application.'[74] Two of the houses were Tudorbethan, a style that was usually thought to be dark because of its lattice windows. The AMA Potter's Bar 'Sun-Trap' house and Universal's 'Sun-Bath' house combined half-timbered external details with 'vita-glass' windows, which were located to catch sunlight from every available angle throughout the day. Thus the 'Sun-Trap' Tudor house was a 'sun-shine home without a single dark corner' and the 'Sun-Bath' house was described as an 'Up-to-Date Tudor-Style Home' (with its timbers arranged as a sunrise on the gable, a design more commonly associated with Moderne), both traditional and modern. The *Daily Mail* was able to call Sunbeam Town as a whole 'a complete exposition of modern housing', despite the seemingly disparate, even opposed, architectural styles of the houses.[75] This points to a definition of modern that embraced traditionalesque styles without contradiction. As Fallan says, such 'traditionalesque' design was 'probably more about *allusion* than *illusion*'.[76]

Antique, traditional and 'repro'

Throughout the interwar period the taste for antique, traditional and reproduction or 'repro' decoration and furniture thrived. Restored country cottages were often furnished by combining antiques in a 'charming and eclectic' style with cream distempered walls (Figure 5.5).[77] They featured prominently in interiors magazines from the 1920s. From the late nineteenth century, among some of the solidly middle and upper middle

5.5 Living room, Mill Cottage, Mill Corner, Northiam, East Sussex, 1921

classes there was a taste for early Victorian chintzes, Persian rugs and Georgian furniture or authentic vernacular furniture such as Windsor chairs, often purchased from country house sales.[78] Patina on furniture was valued as a sign of age and authenticity.[79] It was common for antiques from different periods to be combined together. As Lancaster pointed out, '[i]n … furnishing considerable deviations from strict period accuracy were permissible. The eighteenth-century four-posters, Regency samplers and Victorian chintzes all soon came to be regarded as Tudor by adoption.'[80] The possession of antiques and the idea of the passed down heirloom implied good breeding and good taste through cultural capital and connoisseurship and in cultures of collecting.

Many lower-middle-class and working-class householders such as Ronald and Miriam Kingham decorated in a style little changed since the mid-Victorian period. They often had 'dark varnished wallpaper, cast-off Victorian furniture and linoleum'.[81] Dark colours on textiles and walls was a pragmatic choice, having the added advantage of hiding the dirt produced by open coal fires. Despite dreams of an ideal home, undoubtedly many of those who became first-time homeowners had to make do with a mixture of donated and second-hand furniture. Indeed, there was a thriving trade in second-hand furniture and many of the large furniture retailers had second-hand departments.

One of the decisions facing purchasers of new homes such as the Kinghams and Freedmans regarded mouldings. Although mouldings were simplified, picture rails and Delft racks (high shelves to hold Delft plates and other wares) continued to be fitted in new houses by many builders well into the 1930s. The Kinghams' front and rear reception rooms had both picture rails and coving to the ceiling.[82]

The modernity of the technology of electricity was no bar to traditional designs. Wall-lights and chandeliers, with wooden fittings imitating candles and mock-parchment shades, were available that combined traditionalism with the convenience of electric wiring. Standard lamps and table lamps were made with barley twist stems in imitation of old candlesticks. Alabaster bowls or 'fly-catchers' suspended on three chains were popular for central electric pendants. Tradition and modernity was available in the form of the phono-lamp (Figure 1.7).

The focus of the sitting room remained the fireplace and there were numerous designs available. Some fireplaces made use of wood mantels; others gave the period appearance of an over-sized inglenook. The Kinghams' front room was heated by a red-tiled, arched, 'Devon' fireplace with a wooden mantelpiece. The fireplace of their rear reception room was cast iron, of an older style more commonly associated with the Edwardian period and the Art Nouveau movement. This may have been the choice of the Kinghams or it might simply have been something from a slightly earlier period to which the builder had access. Art Nouveau designs of tulips and lilies continued to be popular into the 1940s. Despite their modernity elsewhere in the house, the Freedmans also chose an Art Nouveau design for the coloured leaded lights on the front elevation of their house (fanlights at the top of the bay windows, the front door and the hall window).[83]

Many of the elements of Edwardian decoration continued after the First World War. Wallpaper manufacturers offered decorative friezes pasted beneath picture rails showing, for example, seascapes featuring Tudor galleons. More adventurous householders could choose Modernistic borders and corner pieces. However, it was more common for the neutral 'porridge'-coloured and textured wallpapers intended to be used with these decorative pieces to be used on their own (Figures 1.5 and 1.6). As part of the interest in the Tudor period, grained or 'scumbled' woodwork made to look like old English oak or painted chocolate brown was popular for doors and other woodwork. Panelling was popular for halls and reception rooms, effected in dark-stained ply or an imitation wallpaper. For example, Marks Freedman chose a complicated wallpaper arrangement with 'border styling' to imitate panelling for his front and rear reception rooms, although this was another of the schemes that he abandoned after receiving a quote for the costs.[84]

Traditional Jacobean-style trees-of-life designs, updated to 1930s tastes by new colour combinations, or even combining geometric Modernistic elements, were popular for wallpaper and soft furnishings such as upholstery, curtains and lampshades (Figure 1.7 and Plate 18). Liberty's produced reproductions of Old English needlework, hand-embroidered in India, such as 'Nell Gwynne's bedcover'.[85] Shepherdesses and crinoline ladies frequently appeared as embroidered decoration on textiles such as cushions and tablecloths. Floral chintzes were also popular.

Domestic flooring also combined the traditional with the modern and labour-saving. Carpet tended to be laid in squares, rather than fitted to the edge of the room; carpeting wall to wall was said to create more work as the edges could not easily be lifted for cleaning (Figure 4.5). Sylised floral Axminster designs were commonplace (Figure 1.6). Parquet was desirable but expensive. Marks Freedman asked his builder to lay cleaned, waxed and polished quarter-inch herringbone parquet, or alternatively American strip oak flooring, but once he received quotes for £11 17s and £10 9s 6d respectively he abandoned his plans, presumably due to expense.[86] He may have had to make do instead, as so many did, with stained floorboards to imitate dark oak. Linoleum was a popular choice for floors, usually laid in squares like carpet, sometimes even in designs that were imitations of oriental or Axminster carpets (Plate 6). Liberty's produced their own patent 'Tilo-leum' floor covering, giving 'the effect of an old-world (9-inch) red-tiled floor'. Their advertisement boasted that it was 'soft, warm and resilient to the tread, and extremely durable'.[87] It depicted a baronial hall with latticed windows and beams lit by candles mounted in an iron chandelier and in sconces on the wall (Figure 5.6). The room had heavy Jacobean furniture and a massive brick fireplace with 'cosy corners' on either side, whose mantelpiece held a selection of brassware. Liberty's promoted the idea that homeowners could be traditional as well as enjoying modern comforts.

Where new furniture was bought, it was usually thought safer to invest in something 'traditional' that would last. Consequently, there was a thriving market in traditional and reproduction decoration and furniture. Conventional design history, as Attfield argued, has 'tended to celebrate professional industrial designers and neglect trade designers … who catered for a clientele with traditional tastes'.[88] Thus there has been relatively little attention paid to the manufacturers and retailers of traditional furniture and furnishings that proliferated in the inter-war years. At the top end of the market, Liberty's produced 'genuine reproductions' of Old English styles that combined apparent authenticity and craftsmanship with modern materials and techniques. Spriggs advertised 'Oak Furniture made from Old Timber, which will blend with Old Furniture',[89] echoing the craze for integrating old seasoned timbers, allegedly salvaged from ships, in houses.[90]

A plethora of 'Old English' styles were available, including 'cottage-style' Windsor chairs, supposedly 'authentic' 'aged' reproductions of

TILO-LEUM, CARPETS AND UPHOLSTERY

TILO-LEUM (Liberty & Co's Patent).

(98) A floor covering which gives the effect of an old-world (9-inch) red-tiled floor.   Soft, warm and resilient to the tread, and extremely durable.   Now **5/11** a square yard.   Laying extra.

SAMPLE FORWARDED ON APPROVAL

ORIENTAL CARPETS and RUGS (Modern).

(94)   Made exclusively for Liberty & Co and include quite inexpensive examples, in which utility and durability are combined with artistic excellence.   Oriental carpets and rugs now compare quite favourably in cost with the machine-made products of European looms.

ORIENTAL CARPETS and RUGS (Antique).

(95)   The unique collection of antique carpets now on exhibition in Liberty & Co's Showrooms have been garnered from sources ranging from the Levant to the China Sea, and include some of the finest and rarest examples of the Oriental weavers of bygone days

UPHOLSTERY WORK

LIBERTY & CO'S Upholstery work is of the best quality only, and in quoting allowance is made for (1) strong and well-made frames, (2) finely tempered springs, (3) good quality horsehair, (4) best linen webbing, and (5) strong Hessian.   Calico is always used as a first covering, securing a longer life to whatever outer covering may be selected.

ESTIMATES POST FREE.

LIBERTY & CO LTD   REGENT STREET LONDON

16

5.6 Illustration of Liberty's Tilo-leum floor covering, from Liberty & Co. Ltd catalogue, *c.* 1920s

Tudor and Jacobean antiques and invented historical 'Jacobethan' styles. 'Jacobethan' and 'Old English' reproduction furniture, mass-produced by the latest techniques, was a popular choice for interwar houses, regardless of whether the house was built in a Tudorbethan or Moderne style, and further shows the appeal of a reflexive nostalgia for Merrie England.

At the bottom of the reproduction furniture hierarchy was, as Attfield has pointed out, '"repro" or "dark" (stained) furniture of indeterminate style'.[91] 'Jacobethan' or Old English reproduction furniture often featured barley twists and bulbous legs. Dining room suites with gate-leg or refectory tables were popular, with carver chairs and huge sideboards combined into 'massive' or 'handsome' suites.[92] For example, the 'Henry VIII' dining lounge, with bulbous legs, was advertised as bringing 'antique beauty into your home' (Plate 17).[93] Customers could often choose between turned or twisted legs on tables. Old English, wheel-back, ladder-back and other traditional styles of chairs found a ready market. Traditional dressers also remained in production. The heavily carved court cupboard with a raised back was an alternative to the sideboard. Much such furniture was made from dark oak, described as 'figured', 'weathered' or Jacobean, although the cheaper end tended to be stained Norwegian deal.

Feminine Queen Anne style furniture was thought more appropriate for bedrooms than the masculine Jacobethan styles found in the sitting room and dining room. Bow legs and bow centres to sideboards, reminiscent of Queen Anne and often in walnut, were also popular. While some claimed to be full 'repro', others merely nodded at the style with, for example, cabriolet legs combined with Modernistic carved decoration and handles. Tub chairs, produced in Modernistic simplified curved styles but also in Queen Anne styles, were sometimes placed in bedrooms.

Like speculative builders, most manufacturers and retailers were not fully paid-up Modernists. Many had a range of both traditional and modern furniture. For example, Story's of Kensington displayed a series of room sets in one of their catalogues: one scene had 'cottage-like' furniture for the dining room, including an 'oak spinning stool' and 'an attractively Carved oak Court-cupboard'; another in the 'style of the olden days' included a '[f]ine Cromwellian [*sic*] oak Arm-Chair'.[94] The more modern styles that Story's sold were reminiscent of the post-Arts and Crafts modernity exemplified by Gordon Russell's furniture – what Saler has described as 'Medieval Modernism' – rather than the Modern Movement.[95]

The taste for reproduction 'Old English' furniture and furnishings, though motivated in part by nostalgia, was not a desire to fake the ownership of antiques and pass things off as inherited family pieces. For some, the authentic patina of the surfaces of antiques was not only undesirable, it was positively abhorrent. It brought with it the stigma of dirt, making do and secondhand-ness. 'Used' furniture also raised a very real fear of vermin and pests such as bed bugs that many had experienced in rented housing. Furthermore, it was common for interiors not to stick consistently to one period style, even in the same room. For example, a 'modern' suite might be combined with a traditional display cabinet. For many, modern and traditional decoration and furniture could exist side by side. For example, residents of a New Malden home in the 'Suntrap' style with curved Crittall bay windows with decorative chevrons (Figure 3.6) made a mixture of choices in their interior. In their sitting room (Figure 5.7) a striking Modernistic three-piece suite with exaggerated curved lines on the armrests was upholstered in a fabric consisting of curved lines that echoed its form. Placed on these armrests were antimacassars in a Jacobean patterned fabric, seemingly at odds not just with the suite but the rest of the room. To Modernist critics such combinations were bad taste, but to many suburbanites they were comfortable and modern choices.

In *Lares et Penates*, Birnstingl was sympathetic to those with a taste for the genuine antique, provided it was from the correct period. He also

5.7 Sitting room in 1930s 'Suntrap' house, New Malden, Surrey, 1948

approved of some reproduction furniture, acknowledging 'its beauty, its durability, its excellent workmanship'. However, he cautioned against an 'over-developed historical sense that is the cause of the desire for period houses and period furniture', 'bought on account of associations which may be but unconsciously apprehended'.[96] For new homeowners in interwar suburbia, however, such associations were part of a reflexive nostalgia that animated and informed the purchase and decoration of their homes.

Critics like Birnstingl were especially hostile to a 'third type of furniture', which he claimed 'has the merits neither of the genuine or reproduced antiques, nor of the well-made modern pieces, it is the furniture which fills many genteel lower-middle-class homes; furniture which is at once pretentious and vulgar in design, shoddy in manufacture; in two words – utterly meretricious'.[97] Birnstingl's views typified those of official authorities of 'good design'. For example, in their series of glass lantern slides intended to educate the public about 'good design' in the

5.8 Slide of 'dining room suite of bad design', in Design and Industries Association Collection of Glass Lantern Slides, *c.* 1930s

1930s, the DIA included a photo of a 'dining room suite of bad design' (Figure 5.8). For the taste makers of the DIA, the Modernistic design of the furniture, with bulky geometric forms resting on fluted legs with unnecessarily applied surface decoration on top of a busy wood veneer, typified all that was wrong with mass-manufactured furniture and sub-urban taste. This 'third type of furniture' was not only condemned by critics and reforming organisations such as the DIA, but has also been overlooked in histories of domestic design because it does not fit easily into existing categories such as 'Modernism', 'antique', 'traditional' or 'reproduction'. Furthermore, it is not adequately categorised by the ret-rospective and invented term of 'Art Deco' or the contemporary terms of 'Jazz Modern', 'Moderne' or 'Modernistic'. It has also been excluded because there has been a reluctance to consider aspirational working- and lower-middle-class taste – often seen by contemporary observers as feminised – while at the same time extolling the virtues of working-class vernacular furniture or the connoisseurship and cultural capital of the middle- and upper-class taste for the antique.

What Birnstingl dismissed as 'utterly meretricious' in fact represented the emergence of a new, modern aesthetic within the interior of the inter-war home that has little to do with either utilitarian functionalism or

Arts and Crafts 'good design'. Some furniture was a hybrid of modern and Jacobethan. Barley twists and bulbous legs were combined with Modernistic detailing and described as 'modern'. Modern designs were just one more choice available alongside reproduction, cottage-style, Old English and Jacobethan furniture. While some claimed to be full 'repro', others merely nodded at the style with, for example, cabriolet legs combined with Modernistic carved decoration and handles. Consumers could often choose between 'modern' or 'antique' finishes on the same piece of furniture, or between plain (square), turned or twisted legs. This was facilitated by the use of 'standard parts' by larger manufacturers. Stock parts in a variety of styles such as Queen Anne, Jacobean, 'labour-saving' or 'modern' were combined with decorations such as geometric and stylised floral carvings. These formed both supposedly 'traditional' types of furniture such as sideboards and court dressers or new types such as the telephone table and the tea trolley, which responded to new, modern ways of daily life in the interwar home. Furniture such as the tea trolley, with its resolutely modern function, was available in stained wood and antique styles, usually represented by optional barley-twist legs, to blend in with the rest of the furniture. For the sitting room, the modern innovation of the three-piece suite was produced in deep, comfortable designs and upholstered in tapestry, leather or a synthetic alternative, or perhaps in woven fabric that married geometric shapes with stylised floral motifs. The 'third type of furniture', despite hostility from critics who thought it 'bad design', represented a very real response to the condition of suburban modernity and the processes of modernisation, which simultaneously looked backwards to the past while looking forward to the future.

The romance of the 'Old English' home

Not all architectural critics despised the taste for the 'Old English' home. The writer F.R. Yerbury, secretary of the Architectural Association and a frequent contributor to the Ideal Home Exhibition, saw distinct advantages in what he termed 'Old English' architecture. His background curiously echoed the ideals and aspirations found in suburbia. Born in 1885, Yerbury was the son of a Cricklewood clerk, who was himself the son of a London builder.[98] He joined the Architectural Association as an office boy in 1901, having left school at the age of 12. By 1911 he had worked his way up to acting secretary, becoming full secretary a year later (a post he held until 1937). In 1913 he moved to the exclusive Hampstead Garden Suburb.[99] In the pre-war years Yerbury participated enthusiastically in the AA's Camera and Sketching Club and by 1920 had published several books of photographs and commentary on architecture. In 1922 he led an AA trip to Holland, visiting old farms and cities, as well as modern housing. The latter became the subject of a collaborative article with Howard Robertson, principal of the AA.[100] This was the first of more than 150 joint articles published in the following eight years, illustrated by Yerbury's photographs.[101] Yerbury co-wrote *Old Domestic Architecture of Holland* in 1924; two years later, he published *Georgian Details of Domestic Architecture*.[102] In the same year he also started a series of books on modern architecture.[103] In the late 1920s both traditionalist and Modernist camps attacked Robertson and Yerbury's work.[104]

A desire for an authentically English style appears to have motivated Yerbury when he included an imagined 'Old English Kitchen' in his display of 'Old Kitchens of the Nations' at the Ideal Home Exhibition in 1926 (Figure 5.9). An article in the *Daily Mail* described this reconstruction of the English kitchen as having:

> such old-world charm and peacefulness that it will enchant visitors perhaps more than any. With its brick floor and chintz-decked mantelpiece, with pewter and china ornaments and brass, with its grandfather clock and bed-warmer, with its wide open fireplace with bread oven at one side – it breathes the very spirit of the Old English countryside as it was a hundred years ago.[105]

Yerbury seemed to suggest that his kitchen was imagined and represented the spirit of Old England rather than being an accurate

DAILY MAIL IDEAL HOME EXHIBITION, OLYMPIA, 1926.   ALFIERI PICTURE SERVICE
12 RED LION COURT, E.C. 4
THE ENGLISH KITCHEN

5.9 Postcard of 'Old English Kitchen', from 'Kitchens of the Nations' at the Daily Mail Ideal Home Exhibition, 1926

reconstruction, commenting that although it would be 'well known to visitors … there are not many remaining entirely unchanged from the past'.[106]

Yerbury thought that the Modern Movement was inappropriate for the British. Together with his collaborator Howard Robertson, he visited the Housing Exhibition in Stuttgart in 1927. The Deutscher Werkbund and the Stuttgart municipality organised the exhibition as an object lesson in working- and middle-class housing through the display of the most modern architectural ideas.[107] In a review of the exhibition, Robertson and Yerbury displayed a notion of England's long and civilised history to explain the suitability of traditional vernacular architecture, reflecting resonances of Arts and Crafts ideals. As they put it,

> A little more plumbing, heating, and light and air, a little consideration in replanning for the furtherance of the labour-saving ideal, are all that is required to make the English cottage type serve admirably for the working

or middle classes. The matter of economy, the question of speedy erection, are more debatable points; but so far it has not been found that any of the more radical departures in design and construction have justified the disadvantages attendant upon their introduction.[108]

Such an assertion is particularly significant here, since it could well serve as an accurate description of the ideals of interwar suburbia.

Like Yerbury and Robertson, J.M. Richards was also sympathetic to suburbia. His 1946 book, *The Castles on the Ground*, pointed out that suburban style conjured up an escapist vision of a more stable past that satisfied the longing for tradition and homeliness after the First World War and the economic uncertainties of the years that followed:

> echoing the country squire's own tradition-rooted architecture; there are the red roofs and chimneys – or a caricature of them, if you like – of manorial England, the smooth lawns and lattice windows belonging to the good old times when the immediate world was a self-sufficient place, where the world beyond the horizon could be ignored and a slump on the New York stock exchange did not result in the sudden dismissal of numberless breadwinners from their employment at Middlesbrough or Nottingham or West Drayton. It is all too clear why the outside world is barred as far as possible from intrusion into the suburban jungle.[109]

In his defence of suburbia, Richards suggested that speculative builders' Tudorbethan was a series of social symbols forming elaborate codes. The economic insecurity of those who had moved up the social scale, he thought, led them to desire a manorial architectural style of an imagined stable past.[110] A poster for the Woolwich Equitable Building Society depicted a Tudorbethan house, far removed from the horrors of the First World War and the reality of England's diminishing world status and declining Empire (Plate 5). The Tudorbethan vernacular allowed for the free play of familiar elements that were recombined and personalised. Suburban style was both negative and positive for Richards. It operated as a form of escapism, shutting out the horrors of modern life, giving 'a sense of belonging to a fairly sympathetic world', and was creative, 'an opportunity of making out of that world something personal'.[111] As Wright says, '[i]n its connection with everyday life the national past addresses the question of *historicity*, of cultural authenticity and security in the face of change'.[112]

For the architect Ernest Trobridge, an Englishman's home was quite literally a castle. At first glance, one of the buildings he designed appeared to be a suburban house in a vaguely 'cottage' style, with an enormous extension built on to its façade in the form of a double turreted castle, complete with mock drawbridge and battlements.[113] This was Whitecastle Mansions in Kingsbury, built in about 1935. It was not actually an individual dwelling but contained nine flats.[114] A picture of Whitecastle Mansions, labelled 'bad example', was included in the DIA's sequence of lantern slides warning against the horrors of 'bad design' (Figure 5.10). For the maker of this slide, such suburban self-expression was the opposite of

5.10 Slide of Ernest Trobridge's Whitecastle Mansions, labelled 'bad example', in Design and Industries Association Collection of Glass Lantern Slides, *c.* 1935

'good design'. Such manifestations of the Tudor were also condemned by influential members of the design profession such as Anthony Bertram and Noel Carrington. Mock Tudor was a particular *bête noire* of design reformers who wanted to revive craft industries and embrace the aesthetic possibilities of modern production. As Jonathan Woodham says, 'The prevailing adage for design in everyday life was "form follows meaning", rather than the modernist adage of "form follows function".'[115] As Woodham notes, designers were pragmatic; for example, architectural practices worked in a range of styles, historical and modern.

Despite their disdain for the bad taste of the lower middle classes, some critics recognised the profound emotional importance that homeowners found in domestic objects. In a defence of the romance of the 'Old English' home, Robertson and Yerbury railed against Modernist strictures of hygiene: 'Our pictures, furniture, photographs, curios, are so often things that perform their function of decoration very badly; but they have the virtue – to their owners – of recalling memories of things and places and persons.'[116] They stressed the importance of everyday objects and possessions. These 'household gods', they declared, though they have been 'cherished' and 'affectionately maintained', have had their death-knell sounded by 'modern notions of labour-saving as a reinforcement in the crusade against the microbe'.[117]

As part of the nostalgia for a Protestant notion of Old England as a seafaring expansionist nation, Delftware and its traditional imagery became very popular in suburban decor. Naïve images of windmills, clogs and Dutch children appeared not only on Delft tiles and other pottery, but also, in characteristic blue and white, on textiles and wallpaper (Plate 15). This was part of an interwar revival of interest in the seventeenth century, when Delft production first spread from Holland to England and when King William III ruled both countries. For example, Yerbury included an Old Dutch kitchen in his 1926 Ideal Home Exhibition display of 'Old Kitchens of the Nations' which had a striking similarity to his Old English one.

Mass production brought a whole host of 'Old English' ornaments and knick-knacks within the reach of consumers. This extended to all kinds of household fixtures, fittings and technologies. For the hall, barometers with names such as 'Jacobean', 'Cromwell', 'Puritan' and 'St. James' could be found in the pages of an Army and Navy stores mail order catalogue.[118] Wireless sets, which became an increasingly important focal point for the sitting room, could be disguised in Jacobethan cabinetry. 'Old English' ornaments such as reproduction horse brasses and other 'cottage brass' including ornamental wall plaques and jardinières were all the rage. A huge amount of reproduction brass work was on display at the annual British Industries Fair. Examples included hearth sets consisting of box-end seat curb, fire screen, companion stand and coal scuttle or cabinet. The fireplace was a particular display point for a range of functional and decorative objects. Paraphernalia for the hearth included firedogs, bellows, pokers, companion sets and coal scuttles. One popular design was the 'Bilston knight', a companion set in the shape of a knight, with matching firedogs, with a poker concealed under his helmet and the tongs, dustpan and brush hidden behind his hollow back.[119] Mass Observation's 1937 mantelpiece survey recorded a variety of 'Old English' objects such as Toby jugs. Many 'household gods' were styled as 'oriental' or 'exotic' and brought with them connotations of Britain's Empire, whether they were made at home or abroad.

The detritus of Empire: the elephant on the mantelpiece

The crafts produced by so-called 'peasant workers' in the Empire were highly prized in England, as the rows of ebony elephants, Benares work and the like that could be found in many interwar homes testify. As Jan Morris has remarked, there has long been a 'latent English taste for the spiced and the half-foreign which was a driving motive of imperialism'.[120] Yet art and design historians have paid little serious critical attention to the taste for the everyday exotic in the home. Fuelled by

Empire, this taste was demonstrated in furniture and decorative objects, possession of which implied both understanding and appreciation, as well as the stories and memories attached to souvenirs of places visited and lives lived.

Those who returned from the Empire brought with them possessions and proceeded to decorate their homes along the same lines as they had abroad, in a kind of Englishness twice removed; a nostalgia for nostalgia. George Orwell describes an example in his 1939 novel *Coming up for Air*. Here, the frustrated suburban narrator describes the home of his wife Hilda's family, part of 'a considerable Anglo-Indian colony in Ealing':

> It's almost impossible, when you get inside these people's houses, to remember that out in the street it's England and the twentieth century. As soon as you set foot inside the front door you're in India in the 'eighties. You know the kind of atmosphere. The carved teak furniture, the brass trays, the dusty tiger-skulls on the wall, the Trichinopoly of cigars, the red-hot pickles, the yellow photographs of chaps in sun-helmets, the Hindustani words that you're expected to know the meaning of, the everlasting anecdotes about tiger-shoots and what Smith said to Jones in Poona in '87. It's a sort of little world of their own they've created, like a kind of cyst … It was so full of spears, blow-pipes, brass ornaments, and the heads of wild animals that you could hardly move about in it.[121]

While Orwell's suburban colonials harboured restorative nostalgia for the pre-war Empire, new suburbanites could adopt a more reflexive nostalgia by buying exotic objects from shops in Britain. In the early 1920s, for example, Clifton Reynolds (who later found fame as the writer of the Glory Hill Farm books and was husband to Nancie Clifton Reynolds, the domestic advice writer and broadcaster) worked as a commercial traveller for a company that imported goods from Japan. He went around England hiring a series of 'stock rooms', some in buildings expressly for that purpose, others attached to hotels. He would set out his goods in the rooms and then invite likely retail shopkeepers to make appointments to choose stock. He described a typical display in Wolverhampton in the early 1920s:

There was a vast collection of showy oriental goods to make an attractive interior, including heavy pile carpets from India, brilliantly embroidered draperies from China, carved chairs and tables, countless vases and ornaments, brass trays, gongs, cloisonné ware and many really fine pieces of chinese [*sic*] porcelain. There was incense too, and when all was complete I set some alight in a simple burner to give an 'atmosphere' to the whole … Only opium was lacking.[122]

Mass production in Britain also brought a whole host of ornaments and knick-knacks within the reach of consumers, some of which were styled as 'oriental' or 'exotic' and carried connotations of Britain's Empire, despite being made at home. For example, Kinco brass ware, produced by the Kingston-on-Thames based British Metal Ltd, was advertised with graphics depicting Egyptian craftsmen alongside photos of their products. The company was keen to stress both the quality of its products – 'ware just as exquisite and lacking none of the artistry that marks the Hindu craftsman's achievements, has now been wrought by British workmen' – and their good value – 'similar articles imported from abroad, cost upwards of ten times the price asked for Kinco'. The range of 'beautiful and useful' designs started at the relatively modest cost of one shilling.[123]

The mantelpieces in Mass Observation's 1937 survey commonly displayed imperial objects including oriental vessels such as Chinese ginger jars (frequently in pairs) and Benares brass work in a range of sizes from small pin trays to large chargers. While some of the imperial detritus on mantelpieces was undoubtedly gifts or souvenirs from the Empire and colonies, other items were purchased at home in Britain from catalogues. The 1932–33 catalogue of the Army and Navy Co-operative Society (Figure 5.11) depicted a plethora of exotic objects made in the British Empire and further afield. For example, one page included a bamboo paper basket of unidentified origin; Japanese carved black wood stands for bowls, vases or ornaments; Japanese draught screens and fire screens (folding); Indian work baskets; Chinese scissors in sets of five with large

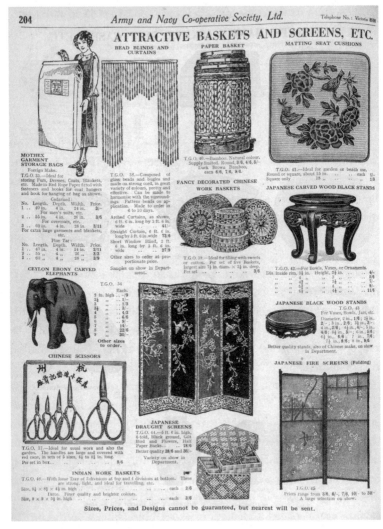

5.11 Illustration of 'attractive baskets and screens, etc.' featuring ebony elephants, from Army and Navy Co-operative Society Ltd catalogue, 1931–32

handles covered in red cane; fancy decorated Chinese work baskets in sets of five, 'ideal for filling with sweets or cotton'; and ebony elephants from Ceylon available in a range of ten sizes, with other sizes to order.[124]

Elephants, made of ivory, ebony, teak or brass, were one of the most popular objects and the most commonly found animal in Mass Observation's 1937 mantelpiece survey. A view from a mantelpiece can be seen on the front cover of a 1920s encyclopaedia on the constituents of the modern English home (Plate 19). This image brings together several elements of suburban Empire: an ebony elephant, an 'Oriental' vase and a Tudorbethan house. What was the elephant's particular appeal as an everyday exotic object in the home at a time when there was ambivalence about the future of the British Empire?

Elephants had long been found in Victorian and Edwardian houses as both animal remains and representations. Ivory tusks were trophies of big game hunters; elephants' feet were fashioned into umbrella stands, liqueur cabinets and other vessels. Elephants featured frequently in popular memoirs and imperial adventures, such as Kipling's *Just So Stories*, first published in 1902, which was part of the childhood of many interwar suburbanites. Elephants were also associated with zoos and circuses, such as Jumbo the elephant who resided in London Zoo from 1865 before being bought by P.T. Barnum for his circus. Stories of elephants escaping from the circus also circulated; one such example was fictionalised by Arnold Bennett in his 1908 *Old Wives' Tales*. The unruly elephant in the story was shot and became 'a victim to the craze of souvenirs', with its flesh made into umbrella stands and other domestic objects in English homes. As Kurt Koenigsberger notes, Bennett's elephant 'takes up residence as an alien yet oddly familiar presence'.[125]

Elephants could also be found in various forms in the new suburbia of the 1920s. Ornaments of elephants were reminders of the imperial networks that many families had, washing up in the home as part of the detritus of Empire. Carved elephants were convenient to send as gifts from the Empire and colonies to family and friends, or to be brought back to Britain by former settlers. Along with dogs, elephants were the most popular animals to be found in Mass Observation's 1937 mantelpiece survey. One respondent reported: 'On the central section, left hand side, standing rather close together, are two ebony elephants, a present from a friend in Ceylon.'[126] Another reported on 'A schoolmaster's house in Brownhills, age 50, where was found 2 large ebony elephants (good ones, bought by son from Burma).'[127]

Aside from Empire, just why were elephant ornaments such appealing household gods? For example, a 1922 photo of a British suburban interior shows several placed on top of a display cabinet (Figure 1.3). The elephant was traditionally a symbol of strength, intelligence, wisdom, loyalty, wealth and good luck in Chinese and Indian cultures. Ancient Chinese beliefs that elephants should always be placed facing the door to bring good luck were adopted by some British households. Representations of elephants have been found in many cultures, from the earliest times when people made images, including on continents where they have never lived. Dan Wylie has suggested that with the exception of cats, dogs and horses, 'no other single mammal has been so prominent in artistic representations in the animal world'.[128]

Ornamental elephants were also subject to change. An illustration in a catalogue of Claygate Old English fireplaces of 1937 depicted seven elephants of various sizes on a mantelpiece, one in ebony and six in teak, illustrating a new fashion in elephant ornaments (Plate 20). The previous year, the women's magazine *Britannia and Eve* offered a pair of teak elephants to its readers: 'The decorative value of elephants has long been recognized, but fashions, even in elephants, change, instead of the ivory and ebony ones to which we have grown accustomed, there is now a vogue for teak ones of Burmese origin.'[129] Elephants also appeared in other media such as ceramics and Bakelite, sometimes in stylised Modernistic designs, but they retained their imperial resonances. By the mid-1930s, the symbolism of the elephant had, for some, shifted irrevocably. In George Orwell's 1936 essay 'Shooting an Elephant', the elephant's slow and painful death became a metaphor for all he saw wrong with British imperialism and the subjugation of colonial subjects. Yet the elephant on the mantelpiece remained a powerful household god that could embody family stories and memories as a souvenir of places visited and lives lived. It could also be made in England and purchased from a catalogue or off the shelf. While today ornamental elephants are more likely to be regarded as symbols of an endangered species hunted to near extinction, in interwar Britain they were a potent icon of imperial nostalgia, domestic tradition and family identity.

Conclusion

The Tudorbethan semi was a potent manifestation of a specific response to the experience of modernity in interwar Britain. Nostalgia was an intrinsic component of the suburban vision of modernity that interwar suburbia offered. However, it was mostly a reflexive nostalgia in which homeowners actively engaged with styles and objects in order to mark their own identities and meanings in suburban Britain.

The idea of 'home' was important in the construction of a distinctly British national and imperial identity that has been overlooked by many architectural and design historians. 'Home' in an imperial context embraced the microscopic, in the form of the individual dwelling, and the macroscopic, as the 'mother country', looking outwards to the wider shores of the Empire. The further-flung colonies and dominions influenced the British ideal home, as sources for raw materials and exotic objects as well as places from which the ideal home was imagined and on to which the ideal home was mapped.

The mixture of antique styles and modern materials that made up the Tudorbethan semi was condemned by critics as inappropriate in modern dwellings for modern inhabitants. Many were especially hostile to speculatively built houses. Contemporary architects and critics saw the Tudorbethan house as ersatz and backward-looking; the antithesis of Modernism. A few critics, such as Yerbury and Robertson, recognised the appeal of the Old English style, yet they were the exception, and much academic scholarship has continued the contemporary regard for Tudorbethan as 'bad design'. The Tudorbethan was an architectural style that allowed its inhabitants to dwell in the past, while looking forwards to the future. Thus, the suburban interwar homeowner travelled between Tudor times and modern times. The Tudorbethan semi was unmistakably English, but it was filled with the spoils and labour of Empire. It was traditional, but it was built and equipped with the latest technology. It was timeless, yet it was a solution for modern life. It stood for a glorious past when England was a dominant world power, but it was also feminine and domestic, shut off from the outside world.

It did not necessarily follow that a Tudorbethan house would have a Tudorbethan interior. Smith Bros, the builder of the Kinghams' house, declared in their advertising leaflet (Figure 2.1): 'These well-designed houses represent the last word in Modern Planning. The pleasing Medieval elevation lends striking contrast to the exceptionally Light, Spacious and Convenient Interior.'[130] It was common for householders to combine traditional and modern elements in one decorative scheme in the same room. Suburbanites tended to look backwards to a romanticised hybrid Old English or Jacobethan tradition in the dining room, the sitting room or parlour, and also forwards to Hollywood Moderne glamour, most often in the bedroom. Some furniture combined elements of both tradition and the Modernistic. While some of the furniture that filled the Tudorbethan semi may have been nostalgically 'Jacobethan' in its styling, it was modern in its purpose. Critics bemoaned the fact that prospective interwar homeowners were constricted by what builders and retailers of furniture and furnishings made available. They sought to rectify this by educating the public in 'good design', which meant either 'medieval Modernism' derived from the Arts and Crafts movement or the Modern Movement, in the hope that this might cause a demand that builders and retailers would have to supply. It was desirable for the kitchen and bathroom to contain the most 'modern' fittings and appliances available in the guise of labour-saving.

Despite the condemnation of both traditionalists and Modernists, Tudorbethan houses that combined the past with the present were readily available and wholly desirable in the interwar years. As Gloag maintained in 1944, an Englishman's house was still his castle: 'It is certainly not a "machine for living in": it is something more human and civilised and comfortable – it is a home.'[131]

6

Afterword: modernising the interwar ideal home

I have told four individual stories of interwar home ownership and home-making in this book that reveal different aspects of emotional investment in domestic design. Turning to the subsequent histories of these houses reveals the afterlife of the interwar home and also gives an opportunity to comment further on the themes of this book. I will consider in particular how the houses I have discussed have been modernised and adapted and how the lives of their occupants have changed. To what extent are they still 'ideal homes'?

The home front: Respondent 082

The day reports of Mass Observation Respondent 082, a Marlow house-wife, provide a vivid picture of the 'ideal home' she created for herself, her husband and her daughter. As I discussed in Chapter 4, theirs was a private, home-centred life. Her days were filled with housework, organised to give her time for reading. She found both her own working-class relatives and her husband's snobbish, middle-class family difficult. Family, friends and neighbours were judged according to her own rigorous standards of respectability, which encompassed everything from the nature of their reading matter to the state of the washing hung on their clothes lines.

Respondent 082's final series of day reports, made in September 1938, documented her fears about the outbreak of war and the advance preparations made by the authorities and individual householders. Her account focused on the impact that this had on the privacy and sanctity of her home. However, she retained some optimism, writing 'In spite of everything, my hubby and myself think there will be no war as far as England is concerned.' She continued: 'On Sunday 25th a man called from the A.R.P. with gas masks. Eileen opened the door to him. She went quite white when he told her what he had called about. I asked him in, and asked Eileen to try on a gas mask but she wouldn't, so I tried one on first and was able to persuade her to do so.'[1] The fear of gas attacks was very real and people were urged to carry gas masks at all times and to practise wearing them, leading to incongruously alien appearances in homely suburban settings (Figure 6.1). On 27 September Respondent 082 talked to a neighbour (a housewife, aged 36)[2] who was painting her gate, and who told her that:

> her husband is at the moment cementing cracks under the window, pre-paratory to making a downstairs room gas proof. I suggest that an upstairs room would be better because my hubby says gas lies low. I tell her that we have a large piece of lino ready, to cover the whole of window of one room. The idea is to place it in position in an emergency, and seal the edges.[3]

So despite Respondent 082's assertion that she did not think there would be a war, the household had clearly been making preparations by invent-ing their own ad hoc design solutions.

The other talking point was the possibility of taking in evacuee children and family members were war to break out. The man fitting gas masks told her that Marlow was considered to be a safe area and that house-holds would be expected to take in children evacuated from London.[4] The thought of taking in family members seems to have caused Respondent 082 more anxieties than the possibility of evacuee children. On 30 September she received a letter from one of her sisters who lived in Croydon, telling

6.1 A father instructing his sons in the proper way to wear a gas mask at their London home, 1 January 1937

her that her youngest child was to be evacuated to Wiltshire. Her sister asked if she and the rest of the family (four altogether) could come and stay with her in Marlow. She recorded her reaction:

> I had been expecting this letter. I do not want them. They are a family we do not get on very well with for more than a few hours. I show the letter to hubby and he says "If the house is going to be full of quarrelling relations I'm getting a tent and clearing out". I say, "I'd come with you" but it doesn't help to solve the problem of how to answer the letter.[5]

There is a clear sense that the sanctity of the home will be disturbed. She replied, explaining that the people of Marlow had already been warned that they would have to take refugees, but that if war did break out, 'And THEY FIND THEMSELVES IN IMMINENT DANGER' (emphasis in original), they could come and stay until they made other arrangements.[6] She also wrote to her mother in London telling her that she was expecting London schoolchildren and if war broke out and her mother was evacuated she would visit her. She did not invite her mother to stay as she knew her mother would not be parted from her father, and 'I wouldn't have that damned swine staying here.' No mention was made of her husband's family.

Respondent 082's conversations with her neighbours reveal that they were exercised by the thought of having evacuee children staying in their homes, with many of them trying to think up excuses for why they would not be able to accommodate them. But for Respondent 082, potential evacuees came as a relief, because this meant that she would not have room for difficult, and vulgar, family members. Later, another official visited to inspect the house and told her that she was considered to have room for a mother and child. This caused her some anxieties as she felt that the noise of a young child would disrupt her husband's sleep after he finished a shift. Her last report for Mass Observation ended by saying

> I have spoken to four people representing 4 different households and the impression I have is one of mild resentment at having to throw open their

houses to strangers. Then there are my own reactions. At first I felt I would take in refugees but did not want them. Analysing this I came to the conclusion that I would welcome them *if they were of my own choosing*. I mean if I could pick them out of a crowd.[7]

The ideal home was under attack during the Second World War, literally and metaphorically.

The war had a dramatic effect on housing. Rent control was again applied to all new rented property at the outbreak of the war, and was not repealed until the late 1960s. Neglect and aerial bombing had a dramatic effect on housing stock; 450,000 homes were destroyed by bombs and over three million were listed by the War Damage Commission as suffering from damage as a result of enemy action. New housebuilding virtually ceased. One solution to this chronic shortage of housing was emergency factory-made houses or 'prefabs' (Figure 6.2). By 1947, 170,000 state-financed prefabs had been completed. This programme built on some of the experiments with efficient building techniques and standardised parts developed in the 1920s and 1930s. Some of those who were bombed out of inner-city areas with poor-quality old housing loved their prefabs for their modernity, appreciating especially their fitted kitchens and bathrooms.[8]

The war also ushered in a huge expansion of local authority housing. One million local authority dwellings were built between 1945 and 1951 by the post-war Labour government, which effectively doubled the amount of public sector housing. Until the late 1960s housebuilding by the private sector was matched or exceeded by local authorities and new town corporations. Consequently, the proportion of houses rented from local authorities or new town corporations more than doubled after the war from 12 per cent in 1947 to 29 per cent by 1983.[9]

People were forced to make modifications to their homes and evacuate them. Time was spent in bomb shelters of various kinds, ranging from those improvised from furniture – hiding under the kitchen table – to cellars and basements, Anderson shelters constructed in back gardens,

6.2 A sitting room in a prefab, 7 Hopewell Road, Kingston-upon-Hull, East Yorkshire, 1945

communal shelters in tunnels such as the London Underground and even cave systems. All these brought with them the challenge of being 'at home' in such spaces. Decisions were made about what worldly possessions should be saved. For evacuees, there was the challenge of having to adapt to living in other people's homes.

Many, of course, lost their homes in the enemy bombing campaign. Subsequently some had to adapt to forms of communal living. British Restaurants, set up to help those living in compromised homes or rehoused communally, together with the restrictions and deprivations of the wartime diet, brought new challenges of efficiency for the women who staffed them.[10] Many had to 'make do and mend', and were encouraged in their efforts by government campaigns. The government's

'Utility' furniture scheme, available via coupons to those who had suffered bomb damage, brought 'good design' as endorsed by the Council of Industrial Design, largely in the form of Medieval Modernism, to the masses.[11]

Making do and mending and the Utility furniture scheme continued for many years after the war. For many in the years following the war, interior décor was unchanged. The V&A's 'Britain Can Make It' exhibition in 1946 was dubbed 'Britain Can't Have It' by the press.[12] The election of the Labour government, the founding of the welfare state and a renewed state building campaign of another raft of 'homes fit for heroes' brought with it new ideas about design. Scandinavian Modernism and optimism in a new 'atomic age' influenced the development of the 'Contemporary Style' in design.[13] Le Corbusier's 'machines for living in' inspired tower blocks. This was exemplified in the Homes and Gardens pavilion at the 1951 Festival of Britain, which made the modernity of the interwar years appear old-fashioned. For many householders, the Contemporary Style, like the Modernistic before it, was confined to the purchase of small items of furniture such as kidney-shaped occasional tables with splayed legs or 'atomic' patterned textiles, rather than wholesale redecoration and new furniture.[14] The spirit of making do persisted and most suburban dwellers, like the Colletts in Wolvercote, retained their perfectly serviceable interwar furniture and decoration. Traditional tastes in décor and furnishing from the interwar years continued into the post-war period. This is illustrated vividly in a 1950 photograph of a woman knitting by the fireplace while a man's slippers warm in front of it (Figure 6.3). The fireplace is interwar Modernistic in form but made of traditional bricks. On the mantelpiece are teak elephants and above it traditional pistols and a sunburst mirror. The wingchair in which she sits is upholstered in typical interwar Jacobethan fabric. This mixture of traditional and modern, as I have indicated in this book, was commonplace in the interwar home, and this particular suburban taste survived well into the second half of the twentieth century. Even in the 1980s, many

6.3 A woman knitting in front of the fire, *c.* 1950

did not go along with the exhortation of the interiors retailer IKEA to 'chuck out your chintz', and traditional tastes continued, combined with 'all mod cons'.

Housewifery and housework: Cecilia, Tillie, Miriam and Respondent 082

The first chapter of this book described Cecilia Collett's kitchen at 17 Rosamund Road, Wolvercote, as I first encountered it when I bought the house in 1995 (Plates 1 and 2). Cecilia's kitchen was seemingly unchanged from when the house was built in 1934. With its Belfast sink flanked on either side by enamel-topped tables and its space for a free-standing gas cooker and a dresser, and its larder in the hall accessed via the dining room, sixty years later it was far from an 'ideal home'. There was no evidence of plumbing for a modern, front-loading washing machine. Perhaps she had an old-fashioned twin tub? Her washing was hung on an old-fashioned washing line, running nearly the length of the garden, rather than a modern rotary line. And there was only one electric socket in the kitchen, suggesting that she did without a freezer, tumble dryer or microwave, let alone other small appliances, for which there was barely room anyhow. The design and material culture of the house suggested a housewifely life still lived according to the domestic standards of the 1930s.

I hope that the lives of Tillie Freedman, Miriam Kingham and Respondent 082 became easier with the advent of fitted kitchens and domestic appliances. However, as cautioned in Chapter 4, this did not necessarily mean that they spent less time doing housework; rather, they did it to higher standards. I would like to think that Respondent 082 no longer had to give over the whole of every Monday to washing. Perhaps she could wash little and often in the week? She might have had some time to squeeze in some reading as an automatic washing machine took on some of the hard labour of washday and a tumble drier meant that she did not have to make frequent trips out to the garden to bring in the washing when it rained. I also suspect that Respondent 082 would have wanted a fitted kitchen and would have embraced the new technologies of convenience and frozen foods facilitated by the freezer and the microwave. I hope that she might have also acquired a dishwasher to spare her from some of the worst of her much-hated dirty dishes. I also hope that her marriage became more 'companionate'. There is no evidence in her reports that Respondent 082's 'hubby' helped with any domestic work, apart from digging vegetables from the garden for dinner. Perhaps in some of these households the couple did the dishes together, with one washing and the other drying? A 2004 study concurred with Vanek's 1971 work that claimed that women's time spent on housework had barely changed since 1926, and rejected Gershuny and Robinson's later claims otherwise.[15] Bittman, Rice and Wajcman argue that domestic technology continues not to reduce women's unpaid labour, and in some cases increases it, concluding that 'the domestic division of labour by gender remains remarkably resistant to technological innovation'.[16] Plus ça change!

Cecilia Collett was widowed at a relatively young age, which made her a homeowner. In the 1950s few women had their own bank accounts and most had to rely on allowances from their husbands (often known as 'housekeeping' money) as their only source of income. Married women's earnings were added to their husband's and taxed at his higher rate, as were the savings of non-working women. Investments, pensions and mortgages were generally unavailable to women and were left to men to sort out. Women were not able to take out a mortgage or apply for credit without the approval of their husband or another male relative. One of the biggest shifts for women of the post-war generation was the opportunity to become homeowners in their own right. As part of the general shift towards home ownership since the 1920s, women have become independent homeowners as well as homemakers.

Things began to change when women began to enter paid work in increasing numbers in the 1960s and consequently began to take more control of their own finances. Feminists campaigned for the Sex Discrimination Act, which gave women full financial rights for the first time in 1975. It not only promised women equal pay (although this was often a right in theory rather than practice), but meant that women could not be refused goods, facilities or services on grounds of gender. Despite this new legislation, change came about slowly. Since then, with more working women, mortgages taken out in joint names and assessed on joint income have become the norm. This was aided by the introduction of independent taxation for married women in 1990.

I also wonder if Respondent 082, Miriam Kingham or Tillie Freedman might have taken on paid work outside the home. This seems most likely, perhaps, for Tillie, who was childless. What was it like for Respondent 082's daughter as she grew up? Both Cecilia and Tillie had sons who went on to marry. What was it like for their wives? Did they juggle paid work with household duties and motherhood? Most women now expect to have careers, but many find it hard to balance work and home life once they have children. It is paradoxical that women's aspirations and expectations have gone up at a time when work has become harder and more demanding. When working women take career breaks or shift to part-time work they often experience extreme financial pressures. There is an irony that the Equal Pay Act (1970) led to a rise in house prices. With average house purchases based on dual incomes, it can be difficult to adjust to the partial or complete loss of one salary. Furthermore, whereas homeowners in the boom years of the 1930s might have been expected to pay about twice their annual salary for a family home, the national average of £256,000 for a new house in February 2015[17] roughly corresponded to over nine times the average salary of £27,600.[18]

Nevertheless, women who take a career break or shift to part-time work often find to their surprise that there are pleasures to be had in homemaking (and even housework!) and discover a hitherto unknown life in suburbia. Any woman who has ever attended a coffee group of that mainstay of middle-class career-women-turned-mothers, the National

Childbirth Trust, can attest that suburbia offers women positive opportunities to assert specifically feminine identities and culture. Women are only too aware of such contradictions; they are skilful, knowledgeable and even subversive consumers.

There are also different types of households in Britain that are more visible now. The birth rate has fallen and for many women, being childless is a positive choice. Divorce is on the increase. Single parents and 'blended' families following divorce are more common. Not only are people marrying later or not at all, but they are also living longer. The 'baby boom' generation are becoming of pensionable age. Civil partnership and gay marriage have made same-sex households more visible. The 'ideal home' is no longer occupied by the heterosexual family of two adults and two children.

'An Englishman's home is his castle': the Freedmans

In the early twenty-first century, a National Trust survey that sought to investigate the preferences of 1,000 adults for historical styles through houses, characters and costumes discovered that, in the Trust's words, 'An Englishman's home is not actually a castle, but a Tudor mansion' complete with latticed windows and dark beams.[19] For Sarah Staniforth, Historic Properties Director at the National Trust, this result was no surprise: 'I believe the style's enduring appeal lies in its versatility of scale and approachability', she said. 'It works well with larger houses … as well as smaller houses we can all imagine living in.' She pointed out that the past has an uncanny way of firing our imaginations: 'Historic houses provide a sense of continuity and contact with the past', she said. 'Good architecture lifts our spirits and inspires us.'[20]

Although respondents to the National Trust's survey were happy to dwell in the past, they wanted to live in the present. When asked what historical period they would prefer to live in, the majority opted for the present day or the twentieth century. This desire to live in the past but

6.4 1 Burleigh Gardens, Enfield, north London, 2017

with all the 'mod cons' of the present was formed in the interwar years and symbolised by the Tudorbethan semi. This is why, much to the dismay of the architectural establishment, speculative builders and housebuyers alike still heavily favour this architectural style, fitted with all the latest 'mod cons', which has become one of the dominant vernaculars.[21]

Many of the houses of interwar suburbia have now been modernised. For example, the exterior of Marks and Tillie Freedman's north London house is much changed from the original (Figure 6.4). It now has a large, single-storey extension. The original wooden window frames have been replaced with brown uPVC windows. Their original stained glass panels have been removed, and they have been re-glazed with an Old England metal glazing bar effect. A porch with Georgian-style classical columns has been added to the front of the house. The front garden has been replaced with a brick-paved drive with parking for three cars. Security has been enhanced by a burglar alarm. For the current owners, modernisation seems to have consisted of a further historicising of the house, albeit carried out in modern materials. In July 2016 Zoopla estimated the house to be worth £714,00, nearly double its value when it last sold in December 2004.[22] This makes it highly unlikely to be affordable to a young couple like the Freedmans at the start of their married life with only one income today.

Original features: the Kinghams

An estate agent's brochure from February 2013 reveals that Ronald and Miriam Kingham's house in Edmonton has, like the Freedmans', subsequently been modernised. The original layout of two reception rooms and a small kitchen remains downstairs, with the addition of an extension across the back of the house adding a conservatory off the dining room and a laundry room off the kitchen. A large outbuilding (17 ft 10 in. × 14 ft 5 in. (5.4 × 4.4 m)) has been erected in the garden, which the estate agent described as a games room, photographed in their brochure complete with snooker table and electronic one-armed bandit machine. The front garden has been paved over for car parking. The wooden windows have been replaced with uPVC frames with double-glazing. While some neighbouring houses have had all traces of their Tudor details erased, the façade of 23 Bromley Road has been painted in white with its fake beams marked out in black paint. Details of the interior in the brochure reveal that some of the house's original details have also been retained. The original fireplaces, coving and picture rails have been retained, the latter stripped down to their wood in the sitting room. One of the walls in the bathroom has had its plaster stripped to reveal its original bricks. Its presentation in the brochure suggests a home staged for selling: decorated in neutral tones, sympathetically modernised and retaining some original features to add character and distinctiveness.

As the house has changed hands over the last twenty years, its price has echoed the peaks of the housing market: £68,000 in August 1996;

£235,000 in August 2005; £290,000 in May 2012; £299,995 in February 2013. In July 2016 its value was estimated at £445,000.[23] Its frequent changing of hands suggests an element of property speculation, typical of the current London market.

17 Rosamund Road: preservation and modernisation

I will end where I started. My husband and I got to know intimately every nook and cranny of the Colletts' 17 Rosamund Road in Wolvercote between 1995 and 2000. We agonised over what elements of their original decoration scheme we should keep and which bits of furniture we should hang on to. We tried to sympathetically modernise the house on our very tight budget without losing its character, installing central heating and new plumbing with the help of a relative who was a plumber. We also rewired the house ourselves, spending the Christmas holidays with all the floorboards up, lying on our stomachs drilling holes through the joists for the new wiring, overseen by a friend who was a retired electrician. We hired a rather terrifying hammer drill to take out rectangles of brick and plaster to recess electric sockets in each room. As we excavated the house it revealed active woodworm and, horror of horrors, dry rot. I vented my frustrations with my postdoctoral research with a huge mallet on the plaster on the bathroom walls, which our mortgage company insisted had to be removed and treated with modern chemicals. I stubbornly refused to replace the rusting, metal Crittall windows with double-glazed uPVC like my neighbours (and we could not have afforded to anyway), preferring to restore them by rubbing the metal down with a wire brush and giving them a coat of Hammerite rust-repellent paint.

We also resisted a fitted kitchen, keeping the Belfast sink with an enamelled table either side (Plate 2). We added a kitchen cabinet, which we brought with us with us from our rented London flat. It was made from aluminium, produced in the Second World War under the government's

Utility furniture scheme.[24] It consisted of a free-standing dresser with a cupboard at the bottom and shelves at the top, with storage drawers and compartments hidden behind doors and a pull-out work surface at waist height for tasks such as rolling out pastry.[25] It irritated the design history purist in me because its original cream enamelled surface had been covered with modern green paint by a previous owner. I also fretted that it was not the correct period for the house. We later replaced it with a more historically correct 1930s wooden and metal cabinet by Easiwork.[26]

We already owned a 1920s enamelled gas cooker, purchased from a small ad in a local newspaper, and this took pride of place in the kitchen. I regularly gave the hob a coat of Zebo Black Grate Polish, delighting in its retro, interwar black and yellow packaging. I cleaned the kitchen's quarry tiles on my hands and knees with a scrubbing brush and maintained them with a coat of old-fashioned Cardinal Red Tile Polish. I visited Cath Kidston's original London shop, which, before she became a household name with a global empire, sold a mixture of vintage textiles and homewares alongside a few of her own designs. There I bought some kitsch, yellow, 1950s curtains covered with rows of stylised chefs and vegetables for the kitchen. When I got to know my very elderly widowed neighbour Harry up the road, I realised that our small, lean-to kitchen was a later addition; planning records reveal that it was added – as a scullery – in 1948.[27] Harry cooked and lived in the rear reception room – which we used as a dining room but which he called a living room – with his front room kept for best as a parlour. This different spatial arrangement and nomenclature spoke volumes about the modern aspirations of the Colletts.

The larder proved useless as it was too sunny and too far away from the kitchen, so we knocked it through to the cupboard under the stairs and installed a toilet and a small corner sink sourced from a salvage yard. This meant we could remove the rather disgusting toilet from the bathroom. We could not afford to move the bathroom upstairs as many of our neighbours had done and we did not want to sacrifice one of the bedrooms to make the space. Moving the toilet out of the original bathroom gave us room to fit a salvaged, wall-hung sink in its place. We retained the original cast iron bath that stood on simple legs, complete with its globe taps. We managed to find just enough undamaged Modernistic patterned lino in another room of the house to lay on the bathroom floor and restore with linseed oil. We opened up more of the space under the stairs and plumbed the washing machine in there, hiding it behind new double doors, designed to echo the proportions of the other internal doors. We also replaced the window in the dining room with a salvaged Crittall door and a small window to open up the view so we could step out directly into the back garden.

We worked on the house in every spare moment and finally moved in properly on New Year's Day 1996. Decorating was quite easy as most of the house had only a single layer of paint hidden behind the grime and cobwebs. Our budget could not stretch to wallpaper so we repainted, researching 'authentic' period colours. We were also careful to use period finishes such as distemper. We sourced additional alabaster 'flycatcher' lightshade bowls at car boot sales for a few pounds each. Their special fittings with three hooks proved hard to find but we persisted and found some reproduction ones in a smart shop in Chelsea that were eyewateringly expensive but, as far as I was concerned, essential. We hung heavy, faded, velvet curtains that I had bought at Birmingham's rag market to keep out draughts. I decorated the front room in cream paint that I mixed myself with distemper and pigments. We already had an off-white, Habitat two-seater sofa in a Modernistic style, which matched well with one of the house's original armchairs. A geometric, walnut-veneered tallboy that I had bought some years previously at an auction for £35 proved useful for hiding our small television and videos. We got the original fireplace working and I was delighted to find a kitsch, 'Bilston knight' fireside companion set at a car boot fair.

We retained the original dining room sideboard and sofa, adding our own table with folding flaps and four gold-sprayed, metal-framed,

Modernistic café chairs with green leatherette upholstery, another of my Birmingham market finds. I chose paint for the walls to match the burnt orange stylised flowers on an Alfred Meakin 1930s tea service that we had been given as a wedding present. Upstairs, we replaced the tiny sagging bed in the master bedroom with our larger modern one that could accommodate my husband's height, chosen because of its curved wooden headboard with vaguely Modernistic lines. My 1930s oak dressing table with black, ziggurat designs on the doors and chrome and red Bakelite handles took pride of place. We also brought with us his and hers bird's-eye maple Modernistic wardrobes, given to us by a neighbour when we rented in London, which fitted in the two larger bedrooms. We turned the second bedroom into a joint study, painting it in red flat oil paint. The tiny third bedroom, once we had got rid of the airing cupboard and its hot water tank, just about accommodated a 1950s 'put-u-up' sofa bed with Sputnik-styled upholstery for guests, sourced from a house clearance man with whom we did some swaps.

Our friends joked that I had curated the interior and should offer the house to the National Trust. My grandparents visited and my Nan was totally bemused as to why we wanted all that old-fashioned furniture that she remembered from her childhood. For her, the pinnacle of modernity was her post-war prefab with a fitted kitchen and fibreglass curtains. A close second was her corporation house in Stevenage new town, filled with modern, Scandinavian-style Ercol teak furniture, for which my grandfather saved up, as he did not approve of hire purchase and never had a credit card. My grandparents found the modernity of my interwar home very out-of-date.

My sister persuaded us to take in a stray cat and a few months later we got a male kitten to satisfy my intense broodiness, which made the house feel more like a home. Six months' later I fell pregnant with my first child and we turned the third bedroom into a nursery, decorating it with sale bargain Laura Ashley wallpaper with tiny pastel stars to match a 1950s Perspex lampshade that looked like a planet.

We agonised over covering up the dreary pebbledash rendering on the exterior of the house, as it was original, but we eventually painted the outside cream and the Crittall windows in black. I tackled the overgrown front garden, patiently sieving out bindweed roots and turned it into a romantic English cottage garden with perennials donated by my aunt and uncle, supplemented by annuals. I pored over seed catalogues and taught myself the names of all the plants that took my fancy. When I was commissioned to write about Constance Spry for the *Oxford Dictionary of National Biography* I spent my fee on plants in her honour, including the beautifully scented pink tea rose that bore her name. In honour of the birth of our son, a friend bought us the delicate, off-white climbing rose Madame Alfred de Carriere, which I had admired in the garden at Sissinghurst, and we planted it to climb up the front of the house. James set to work on the back garden, removing the brambles and digging a vegetable patch, but sorely regretted planting Jerusalem artichokes, which invaded the new lawn.

We immersed ourselves in homemaking. I even used some of the domestic advice manuals that I had acquired for my PhD research for real, taking perverse pleasure in the domesticity that my version of feminism had previously sought to reject. I taught myself how to cook a roast dinner in the tiny kitchen and then eke out the leftover meat, mincing it in a hand-cranked grinder clamped to the pull-down flap of the kitchen cabinet, for thrifty meals over the next few days. I often felt a strange kinship with the women depicted in the many interwar domestic novels, homemaking magazines and Ideal Home Exhibition catalogues that I had read in the course of my research, who struggled to get by on a modest income, learning the arts of homemaking by trial and error. Domesticity was in turns pleasurable, pride-provoking, emotionally satisfying, exhausting, frustrating and tedious.

Slowly we began to change the house from my original, curated, authentic vision of an interwar house as we came up against impracticalities. My attempts at baking became increasingly frustrating as I lacked the mind-set to work in an orderly way on the compact kitchen cabinet. Eventually I caved in and demanded a fitted kitchen. On our very modest budget we purchased a remaindered 'Shaker'-style kitchen from IKEA with pale grey gloss doors. I rejected the long 'Shaker' handles in favour of chunkier 'retro' ones purchased from a hardware shop. We finished the kitchen with a basic, matt white work surface, all we could afford. We never did get around to tiling the splashbacks, and we retained the quarry-tiled floor. Our Hotpoint fridge, at least twenty years old, went on the blink when I was pregnant and James entered a competition on the Internet – accessed by dialling up, since this was 1996 – for a coloured, combined fridge-freezer, a great novelty but also, I noted approvingly, a feature of American kitchens of the 1950s. To his surprise he won and chose his prize in racing green.

As our son became mobile we took the door off the kitchen and replaced it with a stair gate so that he could play in the adjoining dining room in full view. I began to long for a large, combined kitchen/living room rather than a small kitchen. The downstairs bathroom was great during the day but a pain at night, and we wished we had the money for a loft extension to give us some more space so that we could move the bathroom upstairs. Our wooden floors with loose carpets and rugs proved draughty for a crawling baby and my grandparents lent us the money for fitted carpet for the sitting room, hall and stairs. Heat escaped through gaps in the warped metal Crittall window frames, and their thin original glass gave little insulation. When the temperature fell to below freezing, the inside of the windowpanes became covered in a sheet of ice. I fantasised about winning the lottery so I could replace them with new Crittall double-glazed units (uPVC would have been a step too far).

Despite all these disadvantages we were happy in our little house. I worked as an associate lecturer for the Open University so I was at home for most of the time. We were blessed with two hot summers and I regularly put my son down for a nap in his pram under the apple tree we had planted at the bottom of the garden while I marked essays on the patio. Then the reality struck that my husband's departmental lectureship would soon be ending. We were struggling financially with me only working part-time, and I was increasingly frustrated by not having a proper academic post. James looked for a job and felt obliged to take the first one he was offered, which was in Belfast. The Northern Ireland peace process began to look unstable between him being offered the job and us moving, so we decided that we would hold on to number 17 for the time being to give us an escape route.

The house did not make an ideal rental. We knew that we could get more rent with new windows, fitted carpets throughout the house, knocking through the reception rooms and relocating the bathroom. But we did not have the capital and I had invested too much in my vision of the house. We initially let the house to friends; one of their sets of parents visited and were horrified by our 1920s gas cooker, which they insisted on having condemned as unsafe. From a distance, I chose an unfitted gas cooker with an eye-level grill, as close as I could get to a period one. Eventually when I was pregnant with my second child, we decided that we had to sell because we were too emotionally attached to the house. We figured that we would never settle in Belfast if we still longed for our ideal home in Oxford. In retrospect it was a foolish financial decision, as even though we sold the house for nearly three times what we had paid for it only five years previously, its value subsequently rocketed.

We have since owned four other houses but have not invested the same time or emotion in them. As we moved to a 1950s detached house, a large Victorian terrace, an Edwardian semi and a Georgian terrace with a medieval past, I gradually shed the Modernistic – I still cannot quite bring myself to say Art Deco – furniture and furnishings of Rosamund Road. This is not to say that I decorated and fully furnished each subsequent house in correct period style. I developed more eclectic tastes. Like many of my generation, I developed a passion for what is now commonly known as 'Mid-Century Modern' furniture, a term as invented as Art Deco that is used to cover everything from the American designers

Charles and Ray Eames, Scandinavian furniture, high-quality Ercol furniture and moderately priced G-Plan, also encompassing Americana and 'atomic' style, roughly covering the period 1945 to the late 1970s.[28] This, of course, is consciously 'retro' and knowingly 'modern'. In the fifteen years or so that I have collected this style prices have trebled, and it has also influenced design on the high street.

The invention of Mid-Century Modern has gone alongside the proliferation of a diverse range of 'vintage' subcultures. For some, vintage is a question of re-enactment, trying to stay as faithful as possible to the clothing and tastes of a particular period. Live events such as Goodwood Revival or the Chap Olympics offer opportunities to perform vintage identities. For some, this is extended to their homes.[29] I have a bulging file of examples of people who live a vintage lifestyle. What I was doing all those years ago in Oxford does not seem quite so eccentric now.

Some women, me included, have performed the idea of the housewife with a knowing, camp wink. The television chef Nigella Lawson's *How to Be a Domestic Goddess* has a lot to answer for.[30] The BBC's enormously popular *Back in Time for Dinner* series revealed the arduousness and frustration of the lives of the housewives of the past. However, the identity of the professional housewife in its interwar sense has all but disappeared. As I was in the final throes of writing this book, I listened to a debate on BBC Radio 4 in which the president of the British Housewives' League talked about changing the organisation's name. The term 'housewife' seems to have gone out of popular use, replaced today by the idea of the 'stay-at-home mum' propagated by online forum Mumsnet. Some heterosexual couples return to traditional gender roles after children. Many women have a double burden of paid work and running a household. Few can afford to stay at home even if they want to. The housewife continues to exist in the media but, at the time of writing, even Unilever were acknowledging that they should change the stereotyped and out-dated image of the housewife in their advertisements.[31]

But what of 17 Rosamund Road today? As far as I can ascertain, the woman to whom we sold the house in 2001 still owns it. On the outside, she has retained our colour scheme of cream-painted render and, somewhat surprisingly given the proliferation of uPVC in the rest of the road, black Crittall windows. An outside porch has been added that retains the original front door and side window. The cottage garden that I nurtured at the front of the house has been further enhanced with the addition of a winding path. Listed for rental in March 2015, the details reveal some significant modernisation in the interior of the house. Indeed, was I to enter it now I do not think I would recognise it as the house I left in 1999. According to the details, 'The property comprises of 3 bedrooms, 2.5 bathrooms, 2 reception rooms and a light open kitchen. The house also has a beautiful garden and parking.'[32] Planning applications reveal that the small rear kitchen that I knew was demolished and replaced with a much larger single-storey extension running across the full width of the house. The bathroom has been moved upstairs to the small bedroom and a loft conversion has been undertaken to create a third bedroom with an en suite bathroom lit by side and rear dormer windows.[33]

As for the decoration of the interior, nothing remains of my carefully researched restoration. In an unsuccessful attempt to sell it in 2011, it was described as 'Think Artisan Interiors meets Chelsea Flower Show rooted in the ever popular village of Wolvercote.'[34] According to the 2015 rental details, 'The property has been tastefully decorated by the owner as it has been her home.' The interior space is completely different to when I left it. The reception rooms have been knocked through to create one large room, which opens through double-glazed doors into the extended kitchen/dining room. The latter has large double doors with glazing bars echoing the Crittall windows at the rear, leading out on to a patio. The window in the rear bedroom has been replaced by double doors leading out on to a balcony overlooking the garden.

Photographs reveal the interior décor and furniture to be an updated version of the interwar, middle-class style that was popular for renovated country cottages, comprising pale walls with brightly coloured feature walls, antique rugs placed on fitted coir matting, a mixture of traditional and modern furniture, with a few 'exotic' pieces redolent of foreign travel. This is all very typical of a certain type of north Oxford interior.

As I finish this book, I am in the throes of another house move. Ironically, despite it being fifteen years since we sold 17 Rosamund Road, and now having two, full-time, senior academic salaries, my husband and I could not afford to purchase our first house in Wolvercote at its current valuation.[35] Indeed housebuilding is at an all-time low and home ownership is in terminal decline. Britain's second woman Prime Minister, Theresa May, has invoked Margaret Thatcher's persona of a housewife-like chancellor of the domestic economy: we have to live within our means. Post the vote for Brexit in June 2016 there seems to have been a return to the idea of 'Little England'. Some pro-Leave champions frequently invoked the Empire as the pinnacle of Britain's past greatness. In 1978, at the height of the government's 'right to buy' scheme for council house tenants, Martin Pawley claimed that 'the story of the twentieth century house begins with housing and ends with homes'.[36] There is a very different story in the twenty-first century. Peaking at 71 per cent in 2003, home ownership currently stands at 64 per cent, with sharp declines for younger people, many of who, like my teenage children, dubbed 'generation rent', are never likely to become homeowners.[37] The number of private rented tenants has also overtaken those in social housing for the first time.[38] Post-Brexit there is evidence that house prices have begun to fall in some parts of the country such as London. Crises with refugees across the world mean that for many the idea of home is fraught with anxieties and uncertainties. The lure of the 'ideal home' as constructed in interwar England remains a strong cultural aspiration, but politically and economically it seems more tenuous and out of reach.

Notes

Notes to Introduction

1 https://www.bbc.co.uk/programmes/b09l64y9/episodes/guide.
2 See https://www.nationalarchives.gov.uk/help-with-your-research/researc h-guides/census-records/
3 https://www.nationalarchives.gov.uk/help-with-your-research/ research-guides/1939-register/
4 http://www.massobs.org.uk
5 https://www.bl.uk/collection-guides/uk-electoral-registers
6 https://www.your-move.co.uk and https://www.zoopla.co.uk
7 https://www.nationalarchives.gov.uk/help-with-your-research/ research-guides/people-business-trades/
8 https://moda.mdx.ac.uk
9 https://c20society.org.uk

Notes to Chapter 1

1 Chancellors, '17 Rosamund Road, Wolvercote, Oxford', not dated [1995]. All subsequent descriptions of the house (in italics) are taken from this source.
2 For this type of fireplace, see Museum of Domestic Design and Architecture, Middlesex University, London (hereafter MoDA), BADDA 332, leaflet by Candy and Company Ltd, *Devon fires: Here's to cosy rooms!*, c. 1935–40.
3 John Betjeman coined the term 'Jacobethan' in *Ghastly Good Taste or a Depressing Story of the Rise and Fall of English Architecture* (London: Anthony Blond, 1970).

4 Chancellors, '17 Rosamund Road'.

5 D.S. Ryan, 'The Daily Mail Ideal Home Exhibition and suburban modernity, 1908–51', PhD dissertation, University of East London, 1995.

6 N. Humble, *The Feminine Middlebrow Novel, 1920s to 1950s: Class, Domesticity and Bohemianism* (Oxford: Oxford University Press, 2001).

7 E. Moriarty, 'Wolvercote House', Flickr, www.flickr.com/photos/37166458@N06/3941549306/ (accessed 12 June 2015).

8 P. Scott, *The Making of the Modern British Home: The Suburban Semi and Family Life Between the Wars* (Oxford: Oxford University Press, 2013).

9 G. Speight, 'Who bought the inter-war semi? The socio-economic characteristics of new-house buyers in the 1930s', *University of Oxford Discussion Papers in Economic and Social History*, 38 (December 2001), 17.

10 Collett family tree, http://trees.ancestry.co.uk/tree/58673431/family (accessed 29 November 2016).

11 A. Spokes Symons, *The Changing Faces of Wolvercote with Wytham and Godstow* (Witney: Robert Boyd Publications, 1997), 46.

12 See Class: RG13; Piece: 1386; Folio: 46; Page: 31, *Ancestry.com.1901 England Census* [database online]. Provo, UT, USA: Ancestry.com Operations Inc., 2005; Class: RG12; Piece: 1169; Folio: 134; Page: 15; GSU roll: 6096279, Ancestry.com. *1891 England Census* [database online]. Provo, UT, USA: Ancestry.com Operations Inc., 2005; Class: RG11; Piece: 1504; Folio: 168; Page: 46; GSU roll: 1341363, Ancestry.com and The Church of Jesus Christ of Latter-day Saints. *1881 England* Census [database online]. Provo, UT, USA: Ancestry.com Operations Inc., 2004; Oxfordshire Family History Society; Oxford, Oxfordshire, England; *Anglican Parish Registers*; Reference Number: PAR212/1/R3/3, Ancestry.com. *Oxfordshire, England, Church of England Marriages and Banns, 1754–1930* [database online]. Lehi, UT, USA: Ancestry.com Operations Inc., 2016; Class: RG14; Piece: 8154; Schedule Number: 157, Ancestry.com. *1911 England Census* [database online]. Provo, UT, USA: Ancestry.com Operations Inc., 2011 (all accessed 13 March 2017).

13 P. Scott, 'Did owner-occupation lead to smaller families for interwar working-class households', *Economic History Review*, 61.1 (2008), 99–124.

14 A second edition was published as MoDA, *Little Palaces: House and Home in the Inter-War Suburbs* (London: Middlesex University Press, 2003).

15 K. Arber, *Thirtiestyle: Home Decoration and Furnishings from the 1930s* (London: Middlesex University Press, 2015); J. Gardner, *Houses of the Art Deco Years* (Felixstowe: Braiswick, 2004); Scott, *The Making of the Modern British Home*; F. Jensen, *The English Semi-Detached House: How and Why the Semi Became Britain's Most Popular House-Type* (Huntingdon: Ovolo, 2007); I.A. Rock, *The 1930s House Manual: Care and Repair for All Popular*

House Types (Yeovil: Haynes Publishing, 2005); G. Stevenson, *The 1930s Home* (Oxford: Shire Publications, 2009); M. Swenarton, *Building the New Jerusalem: Architecture, Housing and Politics 1900–1930* (Watford: IHS BRE Press, 2008); T. Yorke, *The 1930s House Explained* (Newbury: Countryside Books, 2006); T. Yorke, *Art Deco House Styles* (Newbury: Countryside Books, 2011). Other more general books on the British home that have included substantial sections on the interwar period include H. Barrett and J. Phillips, *Suburban Style: The British Home, 1840–1960* (Boston, MA: Little Brown, 1993 [1987]); D. Cohen, *Household Gods: The British and their Possessions* (New Haven, CT: Yale University Press, 2009); P. Lewis, *Everyman's Castle: The Story of Our Cottages, Country Houses, Terraces, Flats, Semis and Bungalows* (London: Frances Lincoln, 2014); A. Ravetz with R. Rurkington, *The Place of Home: English Domestic Environments, 1914–2000* (London: Taylor and Francis, 2011 [1995]).

16 See also Scott, 'Did owner-occupation lead to smaller families'; P. Scott, 'Mr Drage, Mr Everyman, and the creation of a mass market for domestic furniture in interwar Britain', *Economic History Review*, 62.4 (2009), 802–27; P. Scott, 'Selling owner-occupation to the working-classes in 1930s Britain', discussion paper, University of Reading Business School, 2004; P. Scott, 'Visible and invisible walls: suburbanization and the social filtering of working-class communities in interwar Britain', discussion paper, University of Reading Business School, 2004.

17 Ryan, 'The Daily Mail Ideal Home Exhibition'; D. Sugg Ryan, 'Living in a "half-baked pageant": the Tudorbethan semi and suburban modernity in Britain, 1918–39', *Home Cultures*, 8.3 (2011), 217–44; D.S. Ryan, '"All the world and her husband": the Daily Mail Ideal Home Exhibition, 1908–39', in M. Andrews and M.M. Talbot (eds), *All the World and Her Husband: Women in Twentieth-Century Consumer Culture* (London: Cassell, 2000), 10–22.

18 J. Attfield, *Wild Things: The Material Culture of Everyday Life* (Oxford: Berg, 2000), 190.

19 J. Attfield, 'FORM/female FOLLOWS FUNCTION/male: feminist critiques of design', in J.A. Walker (ed.), *Design History and the History of Design* (London: Pluto Press, 1989), 199–225.

20 K. Fallan, 'One must offer "something for everyone": designing crockery for consumer consent in 1950s' Norway', *Journal of Design History*, 22.2 (2009), 133.

21 J. Attfield, 'The role of design in the relationship between furniture manufacture and its retailing 1939–1965 with initial reference to the furniture firm of J. Clarke', PhD dissertation, University of Brighton, 1992; J.M.

Woodham, 'Twentieth-century Tudor design in Britain: an ideological battleground', in T.C. String and M.G. Bull (eds), *Tudorism: Historical Imagination and the Appropriation of the Sixteenth Century* (Oxford: Oxford University Press, 2011), 129–53; Fallan, 'One must offer "something for everyone"'.

22 M. Turner, 'Decoration', in MoDA, *Little Palaces: House and Home in the Inter-war Suburbs* (London: Middlesex University Press, 2003), 31–42.

23 C. Reed, *Bloomsbury Rooms: Modernism, Subculture, and Domesticity* (New Haven, CT: Yale University Press for The Bard Graduate Center for Studies in the Decorative Arts, Design, and Culture, 2004).

24 M.T. Saler, *The Avant-Garde in Interwar England: Medieval Modernism and the London Underground* (Oxford: Oxford University Press, 1999).

25 P. Greenhalgh, 'The English compromise: modern design and national consciousness, 1879–1940', in W. Kaplan (ed.), *Designing Modernity: The Arts of Reform and Persuasion 1885–1945* (London: Thames and Hudson, 1995), 111–42.

26 A. Powers, 'Was there a George VI style?', *Apollo*, 160.10 (2004), 72–7.

27 K. Wilson, *Livable Modernism: Interior Decorating and Design During the Great Depression* (New Haven, CT: Yale University Press in association with Yale University Art Gallery, 2004).

28 A. Light, *Forever England: Femininity, Literature and Conservatism between the Wars* (London: Routledge, 1991); M. Sullivan and S. Blanch, 'Introduction: the middlebrow – within or without modernism', *Modernist Cultures*, 6.1 (2011), 1–17.

29 B. Elliott, 'Modern, moderne, modernistic: Le Corbusier, Thomas Wallis and the problem of Art Deco', in P.L. Caughie (ed.), *Disciplining Modernism* (Basingstoke: Palgrave Macmillan, 2009), 132.

30 See J. Attfield and P. Kirkham (eds), *A View from the Interior: Feminism, Women and Design* (London: The Women's Press, 1988); P. Sparke, *As Long as it's Pink: The Sexual Politics of Taste* (London: Pandora, 1995); P. Kirkham (ed.), *The Gendered Object* (Manchester: Manchester University Press, 1996); A.J. Clarke, *Tupperware: The Promise of Plastic in 1950s America* (Washington, DC: Smithsonian Institution Press, 1999).

31 See M. Csikszentmihalyi and E. Rochberg-Halton, *The Meaning of Things* (Cambridge: Cambridge University Press, 1981); D. Miller, 'Appropriating the state on the council estate', in T. Putnam and C. Newton (eds), *Household Choices* (London: Futures, 1990), 43–55.

32 P. Bourdieu, *Distinction: A Social Critique of the Judgement of Taste* (London: Routledge and Kegan Paul, 1984); D. Miller, *Material Culture and Mass Consumption* (Oxford: Basil Blackwell, 1987).

33 J. Hoskins, *Biographical Objects: How Things Tell the Stories of People's Lives* (London: Routledge, 1998).

34 Bourdieu, *Distinction*. See also D. Miller, *The Comfort of Things* (London: Polity, 2009).

35 See, for example, H. Ashton, *Bricks and Mortar* (London: Persephone Books, 2004); L. Cooper, *The New House* (London: Persephone Books, 2004); D. Mackail, *Greenery Street* (London: Persephone Books, 2002); S. Waters, *The Little Stranger* (London: Virago, 2010); G. Patterson, *Number 5* (Harmondsworth: Penguin, 2004).

36 See also B. Bryson, *At Home: A Short History of Private Life* (London: Black Swan, 2011); W. Rybczynski, *Home: A Short History of an Idea* (Harmondsworth: Penguin, 1987).

37 A. Smith and J. Thomson, *Street Life in London* (Edinburgh: MuseumsEtc, 2014); H. Spender, *Worktown: Photographs of Bolton and Blackpool, Taken for Mass Observation 1937/38* (Brighton: Gardner Centre Gallery, 1977)

38 B. Elliott, 'Art Deco worlds in a tomb: reanimating Egypt in modern(ist) visual culture', *South Central Review*, 25.1 (2008), 114–35.

39 C. Edwards, *Turning Houses into Homes: A History of the Retailing and Consumption of Domestic Furnishings* (Aldershot: Ashgate, 2005).

40 H. Atkinson, *The Festival of Britain: A Land and Its People* (London: I.B. Tauris, 2012); J.M. Woodham and P. Maguire (eds), *Design and Cultural Politics in Postwar Britain: The "Britain Can Make It" Exhibition of 1946* (Leicester: Leicester University Press, 1998).

41 F. Hackney, '"Use your hands for happiness": home craft and make-do-and-mend in British women's magazines in the 1920s and 1930s', *The Journal of Design History*, 19.1 (2006) 23–38; J. Hollows, 'Science and spells: cooking, lifestyle and domestic femininities in British *Good Housekeeping* in the inter-war period', in S. Bell and J. Hollows (eds), *Historicizing Lifestyle* (Aldershot: Ashgate), 21–40.

42 Design and Industries Association Collection of Glass Lantern Slides, 'Housing', not dated, AAD3/4–1978.

43 O. Lancaster, *Homes Sweet Homes* (London: John Murray, 1953 [1939]), 72.

44 B. Latour, *Reassembling the Social: An Introduction to Actor-Network-Theory* (Oxford: Oxford University Press, 2005).

45 For reasons of space, the garden is excluded from this study. See M. Hollow, 'Suburban ideals on England's interwar council estates', *Journal of the Garden History Society*, 39.2 (2011), 203–17; J. Roberts, 'The gardens of Dunroamin: history and cultural values with specific reference to the gardens of the inter-war semi', *International Journal of Heritage Studies*, 1.4 (1996), 229–37; R. Preston, 'Our chief hobby: the design and culture

of English suburban gardens, 1920–1940', MA dissertation, V&A/RCA, 1994.

46 M. Swenarton, *Homes Fit for Heroes: The Politics and Architecture of Early State Housing in Britain* (London: Heinemann Educational, 2002).

47 Scott, *The Making of the Modern British Home*; L. Whitworth, 'Men, women, shops and "little shiny homes": the consuming of Coventry, 1930–1939', PhD dissertation, University of Warwick, 1997.

48 J. Giles, *The Parlour and the Suburb: Domestic Identities, Class, Femininity and Modernity* (Oxford: Berg, 2004); Humble, *Feminine Middlebrow Novel*; J. Hollows, *Domestic Cultures* (Maidenhead: Open University Press, 2008).

49 See especially A.A. Jackson, *The Middle Classes 1900–1950* (Nairn: David St John Thomas, 1991); D.L. North, 'Middle-class suburban lifestyles and culture in England, 1919–1939', PhD dissertation, University of Oxford, 1988.

50 Light, *Forever England*, 211.

51 D. Gittins, *Fair Sex: Family Size and Structure in England, 1900–1939* (London: Hutchinson, 1982); Scott, 'Did owner-occupation lead to smaller families'.

52 L. Davidoff, J. L'Esperence and H. Newby 'Landscape with figures: home and community in English society', in J. Mitchell and A. Oakley (eds), *The Rights and Wrongs of Women* (Harmondsworth: Penguin, 1976), 139–75.

53 L. Davidoff and C. Hall, *Family Fortunes: Men and Women of the English Middle Class 1780–1850* (London: Routledge, 1992 [1987]), 358. See also Rybczynski, *Home*.

54 *Daily Mail Ideal Home Exhibition Catalogue 1912* (London: Associated Newspapers, 1912), 4.

55 A. Davin, 'Imperialism and motherhood', *History Workshop Journal*, 5 (1978), 9–65.

56 I coined the term 'suburban modernity' in Ryan, 'The Daily Mail Ideal Home Exhibition'. Since then it has been adopted by others, including David Gilbert, Judy Giles, Mica Nava, Rebecca Preston, Joanne Hollows and Michael Law. See M. Law, *The Experience of Suburban Modernity: How Private Transport Changed Interwar London* (Manchester: Manchester University Press, 2014); M. Nava, 'Modernity tamed? Women shoppers and the rationalization of consumption in the inter-war period', in M. Andrews and M.M. Talbot (eds), *All the World and Her Husband: Women in Twentieth-Century Consumer Culture* (London: Cassell, 2000), 46–64; D. Gilbert and R. Preston, '"Stop being so English": suburban modernity and national identity in the twentieth century', in D. Gilbert, D. Matless and B. Short (eds), *Geographies of British Modernity* (Oxford: Blackwell, 2003), 187–203; J. Giles, '"Something that little bit better": suburban modernity,

prudential marriage and self-improvement', in Giles, *The Parlour and the Suburb*, 29–64; D. Gilbert, 'The Edwardian Olympics: suburban modernity and the White City games', in M. O'Neill and M. Hatt (eds), *The Edwardian Sense: Art, Design and Performance in Britain, 1901–1910* (New Haven, CT: Yale University Press for The Yale Center for British Art and The Paul Mellon Centre for Studies in British Art, 2010), 73–97.

Notes to Chapter 2

1 MoDA, BADDA 4315.5, R. Kingham, National Building Society mortgage deed, 10 October 1932.

2 P. Scott, *The Making of the Modern British Home: The Suburban Semi and Family Life between the Wars* (Oxford: Oxford University Press, 2013), 101–2; A.A. Jackson, *The Middle Classes 1900–1950* (Nairn: David St John Thomas, 1991), 30–1.

3 P. Scott, 'Did owner-occupation lead to smaller families for interwar working-class households?', discussion paper, University of Reading Business School, 2004; P. Scott, 'Selling owner-occupation to the working-classes in 1930s Britain', discussion paper, University of Reading Business School, 2004; P. Scott, 'Visible and invisible walls: suburbanization and the social filtering of working-class communities in interwar Britain', discussion paper, University of Reading Business School, 2004; G. Speight, 'Who bought the interwar semi? The socio-economic characteristics of new-house buyers in the 1930s', *University of Oxford Discussion Papers in Economic and Social History*, 38 (December 2001), 1–35.

4 M. Swenarton and S. Taylor, 'The scale and nature of the growth of owner-occupation in Britain between the wars', *Economic History Review*, 38.3 (1985), 373–92; D. Bayliss, 'Revisiting the cottage council estates: England, 1919–39', *Planning Perspectives*, 16 (2001), 169–200.

5 Ronald Frederick Kingham family tree, http://trees.ancestry.co.uk/tree/31489591/person/19623688365 (accessed 13 March 2017); Kingham family tree, https://www.ancestry.co.uk/family-tree/person/tree/31489591/person/19623688365/story; https://www.ancestry.co.uk/family-tree/person/tree/31489591/person/19623202364/story; https://www.ancestry.co.uk/family-tree/person/tree/31489591/person/19623333354/story (accessed 13 March 2017). Information also from Class: RG14; Piece: 7374; Schedule Number: 351, Ancestry.com, *1911 England Census* [database online]. Provo, UT, USA: Ancestry.com Operations Inc., 2011; Class: RG11; Piece: 1423; Folio: 75; Page: 17; GSU roll: 1341346, Ancestry.com and The Church of Jesus Christ of Latter-day Saints, *1881 England Census* [database online].

Provo, UT, USA: Ancestry.com Operations Inc., 2004; Class: RG14; Piece: 7362; Schedule Number: 366, Ancestry.com, *1911 England Census* [database online]. Provo, UT, USA: Ancestry.com Operations Inc., 2011; Class: RG14; Piece: 1377 and Class: RG13; Piece: 280; Folio: 93; Page: 40, Ancestry.com. *1901 England Census* [database online]. Provo, UT, USA: Ancestry.com Operations Inc., 2005 (all accessed 13 March 2017).

6 C. Horwood, *Keeping Up Appearances: Fashion and Class Between the Wars* (Stroud: Sutton Publishing, 2005), 41–3.

7 P. Vaughan, *Something in Linoleum: A Thirties Education* (London: Sinclair-Stevenson, 1994), 51.

8 W.H. Fraser, *The Coming of the Mass Market* (London: Macmillan, 1981), 1–26; P. Scott, 'Mr Drage, Mr Everyman, and the creation of a mass market for domestic furniture in interwar Britain', *Economic History Review*, 62.4 (2009), 802–27; P. Scott, 'The twilight world of interwar British hire purchase', *Past and Present*, 177.1 (2002), 195–225; Jackson, *Middle Classes*, 27.

9 N. Branson, *Britain in the Nineteen Twenties* (London: Weidenfeld and Nicolson, 1975), 92–3.

10 This was a common theme in novels about clerks. See especially G. Grossmith and W. Grossmith, *The Diary of a Nobody* (Stroud: Alan Sutton, 1991 [1892]); H.G. Wells, *Kipps* (London: Dent, 1993 [1905]).

11 Speight, 'Who bought the interwar semi?', 1. See also Scott, *Making of the Modern British Home*.

12 Speight, 'Who bought the interwar semi?', 2.

13 Ibid., 3.

14 G. Braybon and P. Summerfield, *Out of the Cage: Women's Experiences in Two World Wars* (London: Pandora, 1987).

15 D. Beddoe, *Back to Home and Duty: Women Between the Wars, 1918–1939* (London: Pandora, 1989); J. Lewis, 'In search of a real equality: women between the wars', in F. Gloversmith (ed.), *Class, Culture and Social Change: A New View of the 1930s* (Brighton, Harvester, 1980).

16 M. Glucksmann, *Women Assemble: Women Workers and the New Industries in Inter-War Britain* (London: Routledge, 1990).

17 B. Melman, *Women and the Popular Imagination in the 20s: Flappers and Nymphs* (London: Macmillan, 1988), 15–37; S. Alexander, 'Becoming a woman in London in the 1920s and 1930s', in S. Alexander, *Becoming a Woman and Other Essays in 19th and 20th Century Feminist History* (London: Virago, 1994), 203–24.

18 F. Hackney, '"They opened up a whole new world": feminine modernity, the feminine imagination and women's magazines, 1919–1939', PhD dissertation, Goldsmith's College, University of London, 2010.

19 L. Whitworth, 'Men, women, shops and "little shiny homes": the consuming of Coventry, 1930–1939', PhD dissertation, University of Warwick, 1997, 156.

20 J. Giles, *The Parlour and the Suburb: Domestic Identities, Class, Femininity and Modernity* (Oxford: Berg, 2004), 29–64; Horwood, *Keeping up Appearances*, 57–69.

21 J. Harris, *Private Lives, Public Spirit: A Social History of Britain 1870–1914* (Oxford: Oxford University Press, 1993), 96–122.

22 *Daily Mail*, 23 October 1919. Quoted in T. Jeffrey and K. McClelland, 'A world fit to live in: the *Daily Mail* and the middle classes, 1918–1939', in J. Curran, A. Smith and P. Wingate (eds), *Impacts and Influences: Essays on Media Power* (London: Methuen, 1987), 42.

23 Ibid.

24 See C.S. Peel, *The New Home: Treating of the Arrangement, Decoration and Furnishing of a House of Medium Size to be Maintained by Moderate Income* (Westminster: Archibald Constable, 1898); C.S. Peel, *The Labour Saving House* (London: John Lane, The Bodley Head, 1917); C.S. Peel, *Ten Shillings a Head per Week for House Books* (Westminster: Archibald Constable, 1902); C.S. Peel, *Marriage on Small Means* (London: Constable, 1914); C.S. Peel, *How to Keep House* (Westminster: Archibald Constable 1902).

25 C.S. Peel, *Life's Enchanted Cup: An Autobiography (1872–1933)* (London: John Lane, The Bodley Head, 1933), 230.

26 C.S. Peel, *A Hundred Wonderful Years: Social and Domestic Life of a Century, 1820–1920* (London: John Lane, The Bodley Head, 1926), 155.

27 Ibid., 161.

28 Ibid.

29 *Daily Mail*, 25 July 1919, 5.

30 *Daily Mail*, 16 September 1919, 4.

31 Melman, *Women and the Popular Imagination*, 15–37.

32 George Orwell, *Coming Up for Air* (Harmondsworth: Penguin, 2001), 136–7.

33 *Daily Mail*, 22 September 1919, 4.

34 A. Light, *Forever England: Femininity, Literature and Conservatism between the Wars* (London: Routledge, 1991), 12–13.

35 J. Giles, *Women, Identity and Private Life in Britain, 1900–50* (Basingstoke: Macmillan, 1995), 66.

36 Horwood, *Keeping up Appearances*, 61.

37 Glucksmann, *Women Assemble*, 240–1.

38 G. Speight, 'Building society behaviour and the mortgage lending market

in the interwar period: risk-taking by mutual institutions and the interwar housebuilding boom', DPhil dissertation, University of Oxford, 2001.

39 Giles, *The Parlour and the Suburb*, 42–3.

40 MoDA, BADDA 4313.11, R. and M. Kingham, mortgage deed with Liverpool Friendly Society, 9 July 1947.

41 N. Branson and M. Heinemann, *Britain in the Nineteen Thirties* (St Albans: Panther, 1973), 166.

42 Light, *Forever England*, 8–10.

43 Ibid., 211.

44 Jackson, *Middle Classes*, 154.

45 Ibid., 156.

46 J. Burnett, *A Social History of Housing, 1815–1985* (London: Routledge, 1986), 252; C. Loch Mowat, *Britain between the Wars, 1918–1940* (London: Methuen, 1955), 226–31.

47 M. Swenarton, *Homes Fit for Heroes: The Politics and Architecture of Early State Housing in Britain* (London: Heinemann Educational Books, 1981).

48 C. Reiss, *R.L. Reiss – A Memoir*, http://cashewnut.me.uk/WGCbooks/web-WGC-books-1965-1.php (accessed 27 July 2015).

49 Ibid.

50 Burnett, *Social History of Housing*, 252; Mowat, *Britain between the Wars*, 226–31.

51 M. Spring Rice, *Working-Class Wives: Their Health and Conditions* (Harmondsworth: Penguin, 1939).

52 P. Johnson, *The Freedoms of Suburbia* (London: Frances Lincoln, 2009), 78.

53 D. Hardy and C. Ward, *Arcadia for All: The Legacy of a Makeshift Landscape* (London: Five Leaves Publications, 2003); C. Ward, *Cotters and Squatters: Housing's Hidden History* (London: Five Leaves Publications, 2002).

54 D. Hardy, *Utopian England: Community Experiments 1900–1945* (London: Routledge, 2000).

55 R. Bruegemann, *Sprawl: A Compact History* (Chicago: University of Chicago Press, 2006), 117.

56 A. Glendenning, *Demons of Domesticity: Women and the English Gas Industry, 1889–1939* (Aldershot: Ashgate, 2004), 219–28.

57 MoDA, BADDA 4313.1, H. Smith Bros, Huxley Garden Estate promotional leaflet, 1932.

58 Ann Spokes Symonds, 'The Cutteslowe Walls', http://www.bbc.co.uk/oxford/content/articles/2009/03/26/cutteslowe_feature.shtml. (accessed 31 July 2013).

59 Speight, 'Who bought the interwar semi?', 4.

60 Scott, *Making of the Modern British Home*, 224–8; P. Craig, 'The house

that Jerry built: building societies, the state and the politics of owner-occupation', *Housing Studies*, 1 (1986), 87–108.

61 Ancestry.com, *London, England, Electoral Registers, 1832–1965* [database online]. Provo, UT, USA: Ancestry.com Operations Inc., 2010 (accessed 13 March 2017).

62 Scott, 'Selling owner-occupation', 2.

63 M. Pember Reeves, *Round About a Pound a Week* (London: Virago, 1979).

64 Scott, 'Selling owner-occupation', 3.

65 M. Turner, 'Decoration', in MoDA, *Little Palaces: House and Home in the Inter-war Suburbs* (London: Middlesex Polytechnic, 2003), 31.

66 Jackson, *Middle Classes*, 173.

67 Scott's Life Histories database, documenting interwar home ownership, has a mean price of £600 with a standard deviation of £173 and a median of £575. Scott, *Making of the Modern British Home*, 8.

68 Speight, 'Who bought the interwar semi?', 16.

69 Burnett, *Social History of Housing*, 253.

70 Branson, *Britain in the Nineteen Twenties*, 93–4; Scott, *Making of the Modern British Home*, 2.

71 M. Pugh, *'We Danced All Night': A Social History of Britain Between the Wars* (London: The Bodley Head, 2008), 66.

72 MoDA, BADDA 4313.1, H. Smith Bros, Huxley Garden Estate promotional leaflet, 1932.

73 MoDA, BADDA 2003.24, M. Freedman, transcript of East Barnet Valley Urban District Council application form, 24 July 1934.

74 MoDA, BADDA 4313.9, letter from National Building Society to R. Kingham, 27 November 1935.

75 J.R. Gold and M.M. Gold '"A place of delightful prospects": promotional imagery and the selling of suburbia', in Leo Zoon (ed.), *Place Images in Media: Portrayal, Experience and Meaning* (Lanham, MD: Rowman and Littlefield, 1990).

76 *Daily Mail Ideal Home Exhibition Catalogue 1926* (London: Associated Newspapers, 1926), 15.

77 *Daily Mail Ideal Home Exhibition Catalogue 1930* (London: Associated Newspapers, 1930), 23.

78 *Daily Mail Ideal Home Exhibition Catalogue 1933* (London: Associated Newspapers, 1933), 12.

79 Scott, *Making of the Modern British Home*, 154

80 MoDA, BADDA 4271, *The North London Exhibition: 1933 Souvenir* (London: George Reed and Sons, 1933).

81 B. MacFarlane, 'Homes fit for heroines: housing in the twenties', in Matrix (ed.), *Making Space: Women and the Man Made Environment* (London: Pluto Press, 1984).

82 T. Logan, *The Victorian Parlour: A Cultural Study* (Cambridge: Cambridge University Press, 2001); S.A. Worden, 'Furniture for the living room: an investigation into the interaction between society, industry and design in Britain from 1919 to 1939', PhD dissertation, Brighton Polytechnic, 1980.

83 J. Attfield, 'The empty cocktail cabinet: display in the mid-century British domestic interior', in J. Attfield, *Bringing Modernity Home: Writings on Popular Design and Material Culture* (Manchester: Manchester University Press, 2007), 62–70.

84 Mass Observation Archive, University of Sussex, *Directive to New Observers*, June 1937, 1.

85 R. Hurdley, *Home, Materiality, Memory and Belonging: Keeping Culture* (New York: Palgrave Macmillan, 2013).

86 R. Lewis and A. Maude, *The English Middle Classes* (Harmondsworth: Penguin, 1953), 13.

87 J. Carey, 'The suburbs and the clerks', in J. Carey, *The Intellectuals and the Masses: Pride and Prejudice among the Literary Intelligentsia, 1880–1939* (London: Faber and Faber, 1992), 46–70.

88 Alexander, 'Becoming a woman'; Giles, *The Parlour and the Suburb*; J. Hollows, *Domestic Cultures* (Maidenhead: Open University Press, 2008); R. Felski, *Doing Time: Feminist Theory and Postmodern Culture* (New York: New York University Press, 2000).

89 J. Giles and T. Middleton, *Writing Englishness: An Introductory Sourcebook* (London: Routledge, 1995), 249.

90 A. Huyssen, 'Mass culture as woman: modernism's other', in T. Modleski (ed.), *Studies in Entertainment: Critical Approaches to Mass Culture* (Bloomington, IN: Indiana University Press, 1986), 44–62.

91 It comprised over 150 speculative essays, published between 1923 and 1931. For a full bibliography, see Airminded – To-day and To-morrow, http://airminded.org/bibliography/to-day-and-to-morrow/ (accessed 15 June 2016).

92 H.J. Birnstingl, *Lares et Penates or The Home of the Future* (London: Kegan Paul, 1928), 21–2.

93 Carey, *The Intellectuals and the Masses*, 53.

94 J. Holder, '"Design in everyday things": promoting modernism in Britain, 1912–1944', in P. Greenhalgh (ed.), *Modernism in Design* (London: Reaktion, 1990), 123–44.

95 Light, *Forever England*, 36.

96 J.M. Richards, *The Castles on the Ground* (London: Architectural Press, 1946).

97 *Metro-Land*, written and presented by Sir John Betjeman; produced by Edward Mirzoeff, BBC Enterprises, 1984. See also J. Betjeman, *Ghastly Good Taste: Or, a Depressing Story of the Rise and Fall of English Architecture* (London: Anthony Blond, 1970 [1933]), especially his genealogical tree on the 'growth of good taste' showing 'the deep pit of speculative building', 108–9.

98 C. Steedman, *Landscape for a Good Woman: A Story of Two Lives* (London: Virago, 1986), 7–8.

99 V. Walkerdine, 'Dreams from an ordinary childhood', in V. Walkerdine, *Schoolgirl Fictions* (London: Verso, 1990), 62.

100 For example, R. Hoggart, *The Uses of Literacy: Aspects of Working-Class Life, With Special Reference to Publications and Entertainments* (London: Chatto and Windus, 1957).

101 J. Stevenson and C. Cook, *The Slump: Society and Politics During the Depression* (London: Jonathan Cape, 1977).

Notes to Chapter 3

1 O. Lancaster, *Homes Sweet Homes* (rev. edn, London: John Murray, 1953 [1939]), 9.

2 Ibid., 76.

3 Ibid.

4 Ibid., 72.

5 Ibid.

6 For example, M. Berman, *All That is Solid Melts into Air: The Experience of Modernity* (London: Verso, 1983).

7 C. Baudelaire, *The Painter of Modern Life and Other Essays*, ed. and trans. J. Mayne (London: Phaidon, 1964). Examples of the adoption of Baudelaire's definition of modernity can be found in T.J. Clark *The Painting of Modern Life: Paris in the Art of Manet and his Followers* (London: Thames and Hudson, 1984); G. Pollock, 'Modernity and the spaces of femininity', in G. Pollock, *Vision and Difference: Art and the Women's Movement 1970–85* (London: Pandora, 1988), 50–90; F. Frascina, N. Blake, B. Fer, T. Garb and C. Harrison, *Modernity and Modernism: French Painting in the Nineteenth Century* (New Haven, CT: Yale University Press, 1993); J. Wolff, 'The invisible flâneuse: women and the literature of modernity', *Theory, Culture and Society*, 2.3 (1985), 37–48.

8 J. Harris, *Private Lives, Public Spirit: A Social History of Britain, 1870–1914* (Oxford: Oxford University Press, 1993), 36.

9 Berman, *All That is Solid Melts into Air*, 21.

10 J.B. Priestley, *English Journey* (London: Heinemann, 1984 [1934]), 375.

11 B. Elliott, 'Art Deco worlds in a tomb: reanimating Egypt in modern(ist) visual culture', *South Central Review*, 25.1 (2008), 114–35.

12 A. Clendenning, *Demons of Domesticity: Women and the English Gas Industry, 1889–1939* (Aldershot: Ashgate, 2004); L. Hannah, *Electricity before Nationalization: A Study of the Development of the Electricity Supply Industry in Britain to 1948* (London: Macmillan, 1979).

13 A. Light, *Forever England: Femininity, Literature and Conservatism between the Wars* (London: Routledge, 1991), 10.

14 Ibid.

15 N. Humble, *The Feminine Middlebrow Novel, 1920s to 1950s: Class, Domesticity and Bohemianism* (Oxford: Oxford University Press, 2001); M. Sullivan and S. Blanch, 'Introduction: the middlebrow – within or without modernism', *Modernist Cultures*, 6.1 (2011), 1–17.

16 W. Benjamin, 'The flâneur', in *Charles Baudelaire: A Lyric Poet in the Era of High Capitalism* (London, NLB, 1973), 36.

17 Pollock, 'Modernity and the spaces of femininity'; Wolff, 'The invisible flâneuse'; R. Felski, *The Gender of Modernity* (Cambridge, MA: Harvard University Press: 1995).

18 A. Vickery, 'Shaking the separate spheres', *Times Literary Supplement*, 12 March 1993, 6–7; E. Wilson, *The Sphinx in the City: Urban Life, the Control of Disorder, and Women* (London: Virago, 1991).

19 M. Morris, 'Things to do with shopping centres', in S. Sheridan (ed.), *Grafts: Feminist Cultural Criticism* (London: Verso, 1988), 221. See also E.D. Rappaport, *Shopping for Pleasure: Women in the Making of London's West End* (Princeton, NJ: Princeton University Press, 2000); R.H. Williams, *Dream Worlds: Mass Consumption in Late Nineteenth-Century France* (Berkeley, CA: University of California Press, 1982).

20 J. Giles, *The Parlour and the Suburb: Domestic Identities, Class, Femininity and Modernity* (Oxford: Berg, 2004); J. Hollows, *Domestic Cultures* (Maidenhead: Open University Press, 2008).

21 Morris, 'Things to do with shopping centres', 202.

22 Harris, *Private Lives, Public Spirit*, 36.

23 Ibid., 34.

24 B. Schwarz, 'Englishness and the paradox of modernity', *New Formations*, 1.1 (1987), 153.

25 J.M. Richards, *The Castles on the Ground* (London: Architectural Press, 1946), 42.

26 See P. Greenhalgh, 'The struggles within French furniture, 1900–1930',

in P. Greenhalgh (ed.), *Modernism in Design* (London: Reaktion, 1990), 54–82.

27 D. Miller, 'Modernism and suburbia as material ideology', in D. Miller and C. Tilley (eds), *Ideology, Power and Prehistory* (Cambridge: Cambridge University Press, 1984), 40.

28 B. Elliott, 'Modern, moderne, modernistic: Le Corbusier, Thomas Wallis and the problem of Art Deco', in P.L. Caughie (ed), *Disciplining Modernism* (Basingstoke: Palgrave Macmillan, 2009), 128–46.

29 J. Gould, 'Gazetteer of modern houses in the United Kingdom and the Republic of Ireland', *The Modern House Revisited – Twentieth Century Architecture 2, The Journal of the Twentieth Century Society*, 2 (1996), 112–26; A. Powers, *Modern: The Modern Movement in Britain* (London and New York: Merrell, 2005); S. Smiles (ed.), *Going Modern and Being British: Art, Architecture and Design in Devon, c.1910–60* (Bristol: Intellect, 1998); F.R.S. Yorke, *The Modern House in England* (London: Architectural Press, 1937).

30 I. Bentley, 'Arcadia becomes Dunroamin: suburban growth and the roots of opposition', in P. Oliver, I. Davis and I. Bentley, *Dunroamin: The Suburban Semi and Its Enemies* (London: Pimlico, 1994), 74. See also A.A. Jackson, *Semi-Detached London: Suburban Development, Life and Transport, 1900–39* (Didcot: Wild Swan, 1991), 105–8; H. Barrett and J. Phillips, *Suburban Style: The British Home, 1840–1960* (London: Little Brown, 1993), 130–4.

31 Smiles (ed.), *Going Modern*; Jackson, *Semi-Detached London*; F. Jensen, *Modernist Semis and Terraces in England* (Aldershot: Ashgate, 2012).

32 Bentley 'Arcadia becomes Dunroamin', 75. This point is also made in Miller, 'Modernism and suburbia'.

33 E. Waugh, *Decline and Fall* (London: Penguin Books, Kindle Edition, 2012-05–31), Kindle Locations 2369–2372.

34 I. Davis, 'One of the greatest evils: Dunroamin and the Modern Movement', in P. Oliver, I. Davis and I. Bentley, *Dunroamin: The Suburban Semi and Its Enemies* (London: Pimlico, 1994), 27–53.

35 H. Robertson and F.R. Yerbury, 'The housing exhibition at Stuttgart', in A. Higgott, *Travels in Modern Architecture, 1925–1930* (London: Architectural Association, 1989), 45. First published in three parts in *The Architect and Building News*, 11, 18 and 25 November 1927.

36 Ibid., 45.

37 Ibid.

38 H. Robertson and F.R. Yerbury, 'Modernism for moderate means: some small town houses in Paris', in A. Higgott, *Travels in Modern Architecture, 1925–1930* (London: Architectural Association, 1989), 84–7. First published in *The Architect and Building News*, 6 September 1929.

39 Ibid.

40 H. Robertson and F.R. Yerbury, 'The quest of the ideal', in A. Higgott, *Travels in Modern Architecture, 1925–1930* (London: Architectural Association, 1989), 16. First published in *The Architect and Building News*, 10 May 1929.

41 Powers, *Modern*, 16.

42 J. Gloag, *The Englishman's Castle: A History of Houses, Large and Small, in Town and Country, from AD 100 to the Present Day* (London: Eyre and Spottiswoode, 1944), 161–2.

43 Ibid., 163.

44 E. Darling, *Re-forming Britain: Narratives of Modernity before Reconstruction* (London: Routledge, 2007).

45 *Daily Mail Ideal Home Exhibition Catalogue 1928* (London: Associated Newspapers, 1928), 115.

46 *Illustrated London News*, 18 February 1928, 258.

47 *Daily Mail Ideal Home Exhibition Catalogue 1928* (London: Associated Newspapers, 1928), 115–17.

48 Ibid., 115–17.

49 Ibid.

50 E. Darling, 'Finella, Mansfield Forbes, Raymond McGrath, and modernist architecture in Britain', *Journal of British Studies*, 50.1 (2011), 125–55.

51 *Illustrated London News*, 18 February 1928, 259.

52 C. De Stasio, 'Arnold Bennett and the late Victorian "woman"', *Victorian Periodicals Review*, 28.1 (1995), 40–53.

53 J. Carey, *The Intellectuals and the Masses: Pride and Prejudice among the Literary Intelligentsia, 1880–1939* (London: Faber and Faber, 1992), 152–81.

54 A. Bennett 'The House of the Future: Foreword', *Ideal Home Exhibition Catalogue 1928*, 111–13.

55 S. Cantacuzino, *Wells Coates: A Monograph* (London: Gordon Fraser, 1978), 21.

56 Ibid.

57 B. Hillier, 'Foreword: Art Deco revisited', in B. Hillier and S. Escritt, *Art Deco Style* (London: Phaidon, 2003), 8.

58 B. Hillier, 'Art Deco: a total style?', in B. Hillier and S. Escritt, *Art Deco Style* (London: Phaidon, 2003), 21.

59 See E.E. Guffey, '*Moderne* times', in E.E. Guffey, *Retro: The Culture of Revival* (London: Reaktion, 2006), 66–97.

60 Hillier, 'Art Deco: a total style?', 24.

61 C. Benton, T. Benton and G. Wood (eds), *Art Deco 1910–1939* (London: V&A Publications, 2003).

62 Ibid., 23.

63 Elliott, 'Modern, moderne, modernistic'.

64 P. Greenhalgh, 'The English compromise: modern design and national consciousness, 1879–1940', in W. Kaplan (ed.), *Designing Modernity: The arts of Reform and Persuasion 1885–1945* (London: Thames and Hudson, 1995), 131.

65 D. Hebdige, 'Towards a cartography of taste', in D. Hebdige, *Hiding in the Light: On Images and Things* (London: Routledge, 1988), 45–76.

66 Ibid.

67 B. Rice and T. Evans, *The English Sunrise* (London: Matthews Miller Dunbar, 1977), 29.

68 Jackson, *Semi-Detached London*, 107.

69 'P.B.', 'Ideal Home Exhibition, Olympia', *Journal of the Royal Society of Arts*, 14 April 1934, 598.

70 A. Bertram, *Design* (Harmondsworth: Penguin, 1942), 56.

71 See J. Holder, '"Design in everyday things": promoting modernism in Britain, 1912–1944', in P. Greenhalgh (ed.), *Modernism in Design* (London: Reaktion, 1990), 136.

72 Ibid., 137.

73 *Modern Home*, February 1929, 15.

74 D.S. Ryan, *The Ideal Home through the 20th Century* (London: Hazar, 1997), 55, 57.

75 I. Anscombe, *A Woman's Touch: Women in Design from 1860 to the Present Day* (Harmondsworth, Penguin, 1985), 172. See also M. Battersby, *The Decorative Thirties* (London: Studio Vista, 1976), 54–9.

76 K. Arber, *Thirties Style: Home Decoration and Furnishings from the 1930s* (London: Middlesex University Press, 2003), 43.

77 'Square clocks are now in fashion', *Modern Home*, 1.2 (1928), 75.

78 J. Gloag, 'Introduction', in J. Gloag (ed.), *Design in Modern Life* (London: George Allen and Unwin, 1934), 13.

79 F. Pick, 'The meaning and purpose of design', in J. Gloag (ed.), *Design in Modern Life* (London: George Allen and Unwin, 1934), 133–4.

80 Ibid.

81 Holder, 'Design in everyday things'.

82 H.J. Birnstingl, *Lares et Penates or The Home of the Future* (London: Kegan Paul, 1928), 24.

83 Quoted in A.M. Edwards, *The Design of Suburbia: A Critical Study of Environmental History* (London: Pembridge Press, 1981), 30.

84 R. Cork, *Vorticism and Abstract Art in the First Machine Age* (London: Gordon Fraser, 1976), 94.

85 C. Edwards, '*Multum in parvo*: "a place for everything and everything in its place". Modernism, space-saving bedroom furniture and the Compactom wardrobe', *Journal of Design History*, 27.1 (2014), 17–37.

86 *Modern Home*, April 1929, 4.

87 MoDA, BADDA 509, Frederick Lawrence Ltd, *Inspirations for Modern Homes*, n.d., 13.

88 MoDA, BADDA 267, Arding & Hobbs Ltd, *Beautiful Homes* (1937), 32.

89 MoDA, BADDA 509, Frederick Lawrence Ltd, *Inspirations for Modern Homes*, n.d., 53.

90 C. Edwards, 'The context and conservation of patent metamorphic furniture 1780–1920', in *The Object in Context: Crossing National Boundaries* (Munich: International Institute for Conservation of Historic and Artistic Works, 2006), 275–89; C. Taylor, 'The Regency period library metamorphic chair', MA dissertation, University of Central Lancashire 2009.

91 Cutting glued to photograph of grandfather clock cocktail cabinet, 3 April 1934, Daily Mail Photograph Library.

92 A. Bertram, *The House: A Summary of the Art and Science of Domestic Architecture* (London: Adam and Charles Black, 1945), 45.

93 J. Attfield, *Bringing Modernity Home: Writings on Popular Design and Material Culture* (Manchester: Manchester University Press, 2007), 65.

94 Ibid., 67.

95 Cutting glued to photograph of oak settee, 4 March 1929, Daily Mail Picture Library.

96 O. Lancaster, *Pillar to Post: English Architecture without Tears* (London: John Murray, 1948 [1938]), 62.

97 Birnstingl, *Lares et Penates*; G. Hooper, 'English modern: John Gloag and the challenge of design', *Journal of Design History*, 28.4 (2015), 368–84. doi:10.1093/jdh/epv018.

98 Birnstingl, *Lares et Penates*, 38. The title can be loosely translated as 'household gods'.

99 Ibid., 29.

100 Ibid., 38–9.

101 M.T. Saler, *The Avant-Garde in Interwar England: Medieval Modernism and the London Underground* (Oxford: Oxford University Press, 2001).

102 Greenhalgh, 'English compromise', 136.

103 *Daily Mail*, 12 January 1920, 8.

104 A. Davin, 'Imperialism and motherhood', *History Workshop Journal*, 5 (1978), 9–65.

105 H. Dover, *Home Front Furniture: British Utility Design, 1941–1951* (Aldershot: Scolar, 1991).

106 Birnstingl, *Lares et Penates*, 75.

107 F. Jensen, *The English Semi-Detached House: How and Why the Semi Became Britain's Most Popular House-Type* (Huntingdon: Ovolo, 2007), 178–9.

108 A. Powers, *Modern*, 15–16.

109 N. Pevsner, *An Enquiry into Industrial Art in England* (Cambridge: Cambridge University Press, 1937). See also N. Pevsner, *Pioneers of Modern Design: From William Morris to Walter Gropius* (Harmondsworth: Penguin, 1960).

110 See A. Forty, *Objects of Desire: Design and Society, 1750–1980* (London: Thames and Hudson, 1986); N. Hamilton (ed.), *Design and Industry: The Effects of Industrialisation and Technological Change on Design* (London, Design Council, 1980); N. Hamilton (ed.), *From Spitfire to Microchip: Studies in the History of Design from 1945* (London: Design Council, 1985); J. Heskett, *Industrial Design* (London: Thames and Hudson, 1980); F. MacCarthy, *A History of British Design 1830–1970* (London: George Allen and Unwin, 1979); P. Sparke, *Consultant Design: The History and Practice of the Designer in Industry* (London: Pembridge Press, 1983); P. Sparke, *An Introduction to Design and Culture in the Twentieth Century* (London: Routledge, 1986); R. Stewart, *Design and British Industry* (London: John Murray, 1987); J.M. Woodham, *The Industrial Designer and the Public* (London: Pembridge Press, 1983). Later examples include Holder, 'Design in everyday things'; D. Jeremiah, *Architecture and Design for the Family in Britain, 1900–1970* (Manchester: Manchester University Press, 2000); A. Powers, *Britain* (London: Reaktion, 2007).

111 *Modern Home*, February 1929, 29.

112 Ibid., 44.

113 Ibid., 46

114 B. Penner, *Bathroom* (London: Reaktion, 2014).

115 Birnstingl, *Lares et Penates*, 67.

116 Ibid., 76–7.

117 D. Cohen, *Household Gods: The British and their Possessions* (New Haven, CT: Yale University Press, 2009), 195.

118 S.R. Campion, *Sunlight on the Foothills* (London: Rich and Cowan, 1941), 160.

119 Ibid., 161.

120 F. Hackney, '"Use your hands for happiness": home craft and make-do-and-mend in British women's magazines in the 1920s and 1930s', *Journal of Design History*, 19.1 (2006), 23–38

121 *Modern Home*, April 1929, 59.

122 *Modern Home*, February 1929, 92.

123 *Modern Home*, June 1929, 92.

124 *Modern Home*, April 1929, 92.

125 Roger Smithells, 'A Victorian room transformed', *Good Housekeeping*, April 1935, 38–9. The term 'nigger' was used in the interwar years to describe a dark brown colour.

126 MoDA, BADDA 188, Catesby's, *How to modernize your home at little cost* (c. 1930s), front cover.

127 Ibid., 2.

128 MoDA, BADDA 2003, Marks and Tillie Freedman, correspondence, 1 Burleigh Gardens, Southgate, 1934.

129 MoDA, BADDA 2003.24, M. Freedman, transcript of East Barnet Valley Urban District Council application form, 24 July 1934.

130 MoDA, BADDA 2003.6, receipt from H. Seymour Couchman & Sons, 18 June 1934.

131 MoDA, BADDA 2003.24, Freedman, mortgage application. See also M. Pugh, *'We Danced All Night': A Social History of Britain Between the Wars* (London: The Bodley Head, 2008), 66.

132 MoDA, BADDA 2003.61, letter from V. Joyce, clerk of East Barnet Urban District Council, to M. Freedman, 18 September 1934.

133 MoDA, BADDA 2003.3, letter from V. Joyce to M. Freedman, 14 June 1934.

134 Tillie was six years Marks's junior. Born in 1907, her birth was registered in the district of St George in the East. See Marks Freedman family tree, http://trees.ancestry.co.uk/tree/53339610/family (accessed 3 September 2016). Information also from Class: RG13; Piece: 289; Folio: 166; Page: 39, Ancestry.com, *1901 England Census* [database online]. Provo, UT, USA: Ancestry.com Operations Inc., 2005; Class: RG14; Piece: 1438, Ancestry. com, *1911 England Census* [database online]. Provo, UT, USA: Ancestry. com Operations, Inc., 2011; Ancestry.com, *England and Wales, Civil Registration Marriage Index, 1916–2005* [database online]. Provo, UT, USA: Ancestry.com Operations, Inc., 2010; Ancestry.com, *London, England, Electoral Registers, 1832–1965* [database online]. Provo, UT, USA: Ancestry. com Operations, Inc., 2010, http://search.ancestry.co.uk/cgi-bin/sse.dll?i ndiv=1&dbid=8753&h=53332645&ssrc=pt&tid=53339610&pid=134931906 54&usePUB=true; http://interactive.ancestry.co.uk/1795/40020_190585– 00214/110204942?backurl=https://www.ancestry.co.uk/family-tree/ person/tree/53339610/person/13493190654/facts/citation/40169079046/ edit/record (all accessed 13 March 2017).

135 http://www.zoopla.co.uk/property/1-burleigh-gardens/london/n14– 5ah/15207807 (accessed 22 July 2016).

136 MoDA, BADDA 2003.7, letter from H. Seymour Couchman & Sons to Marks Freedman, 21 June 1934.

137 MoDA, BADDA 2003.50, letter from A.T. Rowley (London) Ltd to M. Freedman, 16 August 1934.

138 MoDA, BADDA 2003.52, copy of account no. 1760, 17 August 1934.

139 MoDA, BADDA 2003.20, letter from A.T. Rowley (London) Ltd to M. Freedman, 19 July 1934.

140 https://www.flickr.com/photos/8866197@N07/1124897120 (accessed 13 March 2017).

141 MoDA, BADDA 2003.45, letter from A.T. Rowley (London) Ltd to M. Freedman, 13 August 1934.

142 P. Mapes, 'Household management', in MoDA, *Little Palaces: House and Home in the Inter-war Suburbs* (London: Middlesex University Press, 2003), 52.

143 MoDA, BADDA 2003.16, letter from M. Freedman to A.T. Rowley (London) Ltd, 2 July 1934.

144 Pevsner, *Enquiry into Industrial Art*, 22.

145 Ibid., 24.

146 MoDA, BADDA 2003.41, letter from M. Freedman to Messrs A.T. Rowley (London) Ltd, 10 August 1934.

147 MoDA, BADDA 2003.73, letter from M. Freedman to A.T. Rowley (London) Ltd, 30 Sept 1934.

148 For a discussion of 'good design' as a historically defined movement, see J. Attfield, 'The empty cocktail cabinet', in J. Attfield, *Bringing Modernity Home: Writings on Popular Design and Material Culture* (Manchester: Manchester University Press, 2007), 62–70.

Notes to Chapter 4

1 Daily Express, *The Housewife's Book* (London: The London Express Newspaper, n.d. [*c.* 1935]), front cover.

2 M. Morris, 'Things to do with shopping centres', in S. Sheridan (ed.), *Grafts: Feminist Cultural Criticism* (London: Verso, 1988), 202.

3 J. Giles, *The Parlour and the Suburb: Domestic Identities, Class, Femininity and Modernity* (Oxford: Berg, 2004); J. Hollows, *Domestic Cultures* (Maidenhead: Open University Press, 2008).

4 Mass Observation Archive (hereafter MOA), Day Survey Writer 82 (hereafter DS82), Day Survey for June 1937.

5 Ibid., June 1938, emphasis in original.

6 Ibid.

7   Ibid., August 1937.

8   Ibid.

9   Ibid., June 1937.

10 Ibid., August 1937.

11 Ibid., 12 October 1937.

12 Ibid., August 1937.

13 Ibid., June 1937.

14 Daily Express, *The Housewife's Book*, 18.

15 MOA, DS82, June 1937.

16 R. Samuel, 'North and South: a year in a mining village', *London Review of Books*, 17.12 (22 June 1995), 3–6.

17 MOA, DS82, September 1937.

18 Ibid.

19 See Giles, *Parlour and the Suburb*. See also F. Hackney, '"Use your hands for happiness": home craft and make-do-and-mend in British women's magazines in the 1920s and 1930s', *Journal of Design History*, 19.1 (2006), 23–38; C. Langhamer, 'The meanings of home in postwar Britain', *Journal of Contemporary History*, 40.2 (2005), 341–62.

20 MOA, DS82, June 1937.

21 Daily Express, *The Housewife's Book*, 20.

22 MOA, DS82, September 1937.

23 Mass Observation, *An Inquiry into People's Homes* (London: Murray, 1943), 6–7.

24 Ibid., xi.

25 See, for example, E. Miles [H. Killick], *The Ideal Home and Its Problems* (London: Methuen, 1911). See also L. Delap, *Knowing their Place: Domestic Service in Twentieth-Century Britain* (Oxford: Oxford University Press, 2011); A. Light, *Mrs Woolf and the Servants: The Hidden Heart of Domestic Service* (Harmondsworth: Penguin, 2007); S. Todd, 'Domestic service and class relations in Britain 1900–1950', *Past and Present*, 203 (2009), 181–204.

26 S. Todd, *The People: The Rise and Fall of the Working Class, 1910–2010* (London: Hodder and Stoughton, Kindle Edition, 2014–04–10), Kindle locations 422–3.

27 D. Beddoe, *Back to Home and Duty: Women between the Wars, 1918–1939* (London: Pandora, 1989).

28 Todd, *The People*, Kindle location 574.

29 M. Glucksmann, *Women Assemble: Women Workers and the New Industries in Inter-War Britain* (London: Routledge, 1990), 229.

30 J. Lewis, *Women in England, 1870–1950: Sexual Divisions and Social Change* (Brighton: Wheatsheaf, 1984), 190–1.

31 Beddoe, *Back to Home and Duty*, 86.

32 J. Lewis, 'In search of a real equality: women between the wars', in F. Gloversmith (ed.), *Class, Culture and Social Change* (Brighton: Harvester, 1980), 211.

33 Todd, *The People*, Kindle locations 292–3.

34 Ibid., Kindle locations 810–11.

35 C. Horwood, *Keeping Up Appearances: Fashion and Class between the Wars* (Stroud: Sutton Publishing, 2005), 58.

36 Todd, *The People*, Kindle locations 779–81.

37 Ibid., Kindle locations 836–7.

38 N. Beauman, *A Very Great Profession: The Woman's Novel 1914–39* (London: Virago, 1983), 107.

39 Light, *Mrs Woolf and the Servants*, 169.

40 Todd, *The People*, Kindle locations 1232–3.

41 Delap, *Knowing their Place*, 78.

42 Glucksmann, *Women Assemble*, 246.

43 S. Bowden and A. Offer, 'The technological revolution that never was: gender, class, and the diffusion of household appliances in inter-war England', in V. de Grazia and E. Furlough (eds), *The Sex of Things: Gender and Consumption in Historical Perspective* (London: University of California Press, 1996), 244–74.

44 Anon., *Women and Housing: Labour Saving in the Home. Report of a Conference of Women's Organisations Held at the Daily Mail Ideal Home Exhibition, Olympia, London, on February 10th, 1920* (London: Garden Cities and Town Planning Association, 1920), 12.

45 Ibid.

46 *Daily Mail*, 16 August 1919, 5.

47 A. Forty, *Objects of Desire: Design and Society 1750–1980* (London: Thames and Hudson, 1986), 217.

48 J. Lanchester, *Making Time: Lillian Moller Gilbreth – A Life Beyond "Cheaper by the Dozen"* (Boston, MA: Northeastern University Press, 2004), 250.

49 B. MacFarlane, 'Homes fit for heroines: housing in the twenties', in Matrix (ed.), *Making Space: Women and the Man-Made Environment* (London: Pluto Press, 1984).

50 A. Ravetz, 'A view from the interior', in J. Attfield and P. Kirkham (eds), *A View from the Interior* (London: Virago, 1989), 194.

51 MacFarlane, 'Homes fit for heroines', 28.

52 B. Campbell, *The Iron Ladies: Why Do Women Vote Tory?* (London: Virago, 1987), 34–69. See also B. Schwarz, 'The language of constitutionalism:

Baldwinite Conservatism', in T. Bennett et al. (eds), *Formations of Nation and People* (London: Routledge and Kegan Paul, 1984), 152–70.

53 M. Andrews, *The Acceptable Face of Feminism: The Women's Institute as a Social Movement* (London: Lawrence and Wishart, 1997).

54 Anon., *Women and Housing.*

55 A. Clendenning, *Demons of Domesticity: Women and the English Gas Industry, 1889–1939* (Aldershot: Ashgate, 2004); S. Worden 'Powerful women: electricity in the home, 1919–40', in J. Attfield and P. Kirkham (eds), *A View from the Interior* (London: Virago, 1989), 128–47.

56 Worden, 'Powerful women'.

57 D. Dean, *The Thirties: Recalling the English Architectural Scene* (London: Trefoil Books, 1983), 61–3.

58 G. Darley, 'The power house', in T. Rivers, D. Cruickshank, G. Darley and M. Pawley, *The Name of the Room: A History of the British House and Home* (London: BBC Books, 1992), 133. See also E.A. Darling, 'Elizabeth Denby, housing consultant: social reform and cultural politics in the inter-war period', PhD dissertation, University College London, 1999; J. Woodham, 'Women, design and the state: a case study of Elizabeth Denby and the Council for Art and Industry', in J. Seddon and S. Worden (eds), *Women Designing: Redefining Design in Britain between the Wars* (Brighton: University of Brighton, 1994), 41–5.

59 C. Reynolds, *Autobiography* (London: The Bodley Head, 1947), 136. See also D. Sugg Ryan, 'Reynolds, Nancie Clifton [*real name* Agnes Margaret Warden Hardie; *married name* Reynolds] (1903–1931), domestic advice writer and broadcaster', *Oxford Dictionary of National Biography* (Oxford: Oxford University Press, Sept 2015), http://www.oxforddnb.com/view/article/105938 (accessed 4 September 2016).

60 *Daily Mail*, 15 April 1929.

61 *Radio Times*, 2 September 1927.

62 Broadcast on 3 October 1927.

63 Broadcast on 31 December 1928; published in *The Listener*, 16 January 1929.

64 *Daily Mail Ideal Home Exhibition Catalogue 1922* (London: Daily Mail, 1922), 8.

65 Such magazines did not, however, achieve truly mass circulation until the 1950s. See F. Hackney, '"They opened up a whole new world": feminine modernity, the feminine imagination and women's magazines, 1919–1939', PhD dissertation, Goldsmith's College, University of London, 2010; M. Ferguson, *Forever Feminine* (London: Heinemann, 1983); C. White, *Women's Magazines, 1693–1968* (London: Michael Joseph, 1970).

66 Mass Observation, *An Inquiry into People's Homes*, xiii.

67 D. Mackail, *Greenery Street* (London: Persephone Books, 2002 [1925)]), 191–2.

68 N. Clifton Reynolds, *Easier Housework by Better Equipment* (London: Country Life, 1929), 47, 57.

69 Daily Express, *The Housewife's Book*, 27.

70 *Daily Mail Ideal Labour-Saving Home*, preface (London: Associated Newspapers, 1920).

71 Ibid., 64.

72 Reynolds, *Easier Housework*, 199.

73 Ibid., 1

74 E. Heathcote, *The Meaning of Home* (London: Frances Lincoln, 2012), 58.

75 N. Humble, *The Feminine Middlebrow Novel 1920s to 1950s: Class, Domesticity and Bohemianism* (Oxford: Oxford University Press, 2001), 124.

76 MOA, DS82, September 1937.

77 C. Zmroczek, 'The weekly wash', in S. Oldfield (ed.), *The Working-Day World: Women's Lives and Culture(s) in Britain 1914–1945* (London: Taylor and Francis, 1994), 7.

78 Ibid., 11.

79 MoDA, BADDA 4313.1, H. Smith Bros, Huxley Garden Estate promotional leaflet, 1932.

80 Mass Observation, *An Inquiry into People's Homes*, 110–11.

81 Daily Express, *The Housewife's Book*, 111.

82 P. Mapes, 'Household management', in MoDA, *Little Palaces: House and Home in the Inter-war Suburbs* (London: Middlesex University Press, 2003), 49.

83 Zmroczek, 'The weekly wash', 11.

84 Mass Observation, *An Inquiry into People's Homes*, xiii.

85 Zmroczek, 'The weekly wash', 12.

86 MOA, DS82, June 1937.

87 Ibid.

88 See L. Hannah, *Electricity before Nationalization: A Study of the Development of the Electricity Supply Industry in Britain to 1948* (London: Macmillan, 1979).

89 Zmroczek, 'The weekly wash', 15.

90 MOA, DS82, September 1937.

91 Forty, *Objects of Desire*, 189.

92 Zmroczek, 'The weekly wash', 14–15.

93 Bowden and Offer, 'The technical revolution', 246.

94 Ibid., 268.

95 Ibid., 269.

96 Ibid.; G. Lees-Maffei, 'Studying advice: historiography, methodology, commentary, bibliography', *The Journal of Design History*, 16.1 (2003), 1–14.

97 G. Porter, 'Putting your house in order: representations of women and domestic life', in R. Lumley (ed.), *The Museum Time-Machine: Putting Culture on Display* (London: Routledge, 1988), 102–7.

98 Todd, *The People*, Kindle locations 820–1.

99 Bowden and Offer, 'The technical revolution', 265–6

100 Ibid., 266.

101 *Journal of the Royal Society of Arts*, 14 April 1933, 525.

102 D. Hebdige, 'Towards a cartography of taste', in D. Hebdige, *Hiding in the Light* (London: Routledge, 1988), 45–76; T. de Rijk, 'Pioneers and barbarians: the design and marketing of electrical household goods as Dutch Americana, 1930–45', *Journal of Design History*, 22.2 (2009), 115–32, doi: 10.1093/jdh/epp012

103 H.J. Birnstingl, *Lares et Penates or The Home of the Future* (London: Kegan Paul, 1928), 46–7.

104 See R. Schwartz Cowan, *More Work for Mother: The Ironies of Household Technology from the Open Hearth to the Microwave* (London: Free Association, 1989); C. Davidson, *A Women's Work is Never Done: A History of Housework in the British Isles, 1650–1950* (London: Chatto and Windus, 1982); C. Hardyment, *From Mangle to Microwave: The Mechanisation of Household Work* (Cambridge: Polity, 1988).

105 See J. Attfield, *Wild Things: The Material Culture of Everyday Life* (Oxford: Berg, 2000); A. Clarke, 'Taste wars and design dilemmas: aesthetic practice in the home', in C. Painter (ed.), *Contemporary Art and the Home* (Oxford: Berg, 2002), 131–51; Hollows, *Domestic Cultures*; D. Miller (ed.), *Home Possessions: Material Culture Behind Closed Doors* (Oxford: Berg, 2001).

106 *Daily Mail Ideal Home Exhibition Catalogue 1929* (London: Daily Mail, 1929), 195.

107 Ibid.

108 MOA, DS82, June 1937.

109 Ibid., September 1937.

110 Ibid., June 1937.

111 D. Riley, *Am I That Name? Feminism and the Category of 'Women' in History* (London: Macmillan, 1988).

112 Mapes, 'Household management', 50.

113 P. Oliver, 'A lighthouse on the mantelpiece: symbolism in the home', in P. Oliver, I. Davis and I. Bentley, *Dunroamin: The Suburban Semi and Its Enemies* (London: Pimlico, 1994), 179–81.

114 Ibid., 181.

115 J. Hoskins, *Biographical Objects: How Things Tell the Stories of People's Lives* (London: Routledge, 1998).

116 A. Vickery, 'Women and the world of goods: a Lancaster consumer and her possessions, 1751–81', in J. Brewer and R. Porter (eds), *Consumption and the World of Goods* (London: Routledge, 1993), 274–304.

117 Mass Observation, *An Inquiry into People's Homes*, xl.

118 Birnstingl, *Lares et Penates*, 57.

119 For an example, see A. Powers, 'Efficiency: from modernity to modernism', in A. Powers, *Britain* (London: Reaktion, 2007), 13–51.

120 Birnstingl, *Lares et Penates*, 41.

121 Ibid., 35.

122 Ibid., 96.

123 Powers, *Britain*, 29–30.

124 Ibid.

125 Birnstingl, *Lares et Penates*, 85.

126 P. Sparke, *An Introduction to Design and Culture in the Twentieth Century* (London: Routledge, 1986), 63–4.

127 *Daily Mail Ideal Labour-Saving Home*, preface.

128 Ibid., 43.

129 Ibid., 44.

130 Ibid., 46.

131 Birnstingl, *Lares et Penates*, 63.

132 Ibid., 28–9.

133 Ibid., 50.

134 Mass Observation, *An Inquiry into People's Homes*, 84.

135 Ibid., xi.

136 Ibid., 55.

137 Ibid.

138 Ibid., 84

139 S. Muthesius, *The English Terraced House* (New Haven, CT: Yale University Press, 1990),46.

140 Anthony Pepe & Co., 'Bromley Road, London', pdf brochure, 1 February 2013, 7.

141 Mapes, 'Household management', 46.

142 Anthony Pepe & Co., Bromley Road, 7.

143 Anon., *Women and Housing*, 8.

144 C.D. Rackham, 'Banishing the basement bogey', *Good Housekeeping*, VI.6 (February 1925), 54, 166.

145 MOA, DS82, September 1937.

146 MoDA, BADDA 4313.1, H. Smith Bros, Huxley Garden Estate promotional leaflet, 1932.

147 Reynolds, *Easier Housework* 219–20.

148 MoDA, BADDA 4313.1, H. Smith Bros, Huxley Garden Estate promotional leaflet, 1932.

149 Mass Observation, *An Inquiry into People's Homes*, xvii.

150 Reynolds, *Easier Housework*, 93.

151 Ibid., 224.

152 Ibid., 233–4.

153 J. Freeman, *The Making of the Modern Kitchen: A Cultural History* (Oxford: Berg, 2004), 42.

154 Reynolds, *Easier Housework*, 123.

155 MoDA, BADDA 4313.1, H. Smith Bros, Huxley Garden Estate promotional leaflet, 1932.

156 N.R. Hillier, *The Hoosier Cabinet in Kitchen History* (Bloomington, IN: Indiana University Press, 2009).

157 S. Willey, '"Housework made Easiwork": Easiwork Limited: The ideal modern kitchen 1919–1939', BA History of Art dissertation, Edinburgh University, 1989.

158 Reynolds, *Autobiography*, 157.

159 Reynolds, *Easier Housework*, 101–4.

160 Ibid., 227.

161 Ibid., 104.

162 S. Rothery, *The Shops of Ireland* (London: Francis Lincoln, 2009), 48; N. Warburton, *Ernö Goldfinger: The Life of an Architect* (London: Routledge, 2004), 76–7.

163 Willey, '"Housework made Easiwork"'.

164 D.G. Tanner, 'The House That Jill Built', in *Daily Mail Ideal Home Exhibition Catalogue 1930* (London: Associated Newspapers, 1930), 117.

165 Ibid.

166 'The House That Jill Built', *Modern Home*, June 1930, 101.

167 'Introduction', *Ideal Home Exhibition Catalogue 1930*, 18.

168 'The House That Jill Built', *Modern Home*, 40.

169 Ibid.

170 Tanner, 'The House That Jill Built', 117.

171 *Daily Mail*, 19 March 1930, 9.

172 Tanner, 'The House That Jill Built', 117.

173 Ibid., 118.

174 'The House That Jill Built', *Modern Home*, 40.

175 Ibid., 101.

176   Ibid.

177   Ibid., 41.

178   Tanner, 'The House That Jill Built', 120.

179   L.B. Atkinson, 'Women and electricity', *The Electrical Age*, July 1930, 6. Quoted in J.M. Woodham, *The Industrial Designer and the Public* (London: Pembridge Press, 1983), 48.

180   For an account of such experiments, see Schwartz Cowan, *More Work for Mother*, 102–50.

181   *Daily Mail Ideal Home Exhibition Catalogue 1936* (London: Associated Newspapers, 1936), 150.

182   See L. Davidoff and C. Hall, *Family Fortunes: Men and Women of the English Middle Class 1780–1850* (London: Routledge, 1992). For a critique, see A. Vickery, 'Shaking the separate spheres', *Times Literary Supplement*, 12 March 1993, 6–7. For a different approach, see J. Kelly, *Women, History and Theory* (Chicago: University of Chicago Press, 1984).

183   W. Heath Robinson, *My Line of Life* (London: Blackie, 1938), 178.

184   Ibid., 179.

Notes to Chapter 5

1   J. Gloag, *Design in Modern Life* (London: George Allen and Unwin 1946), 19–20.

2   In 1933 Gloag, together with Geoffrey Boumphrey and Edward Halliday, chaired a series of talks on BBC radio entitled 'Design in Modern Life'. Gloag edited the resulting book of essays that was published the following year.

3   J. Gloag, *The Englishman's Castle: A History of Houses, Large and Small, in Town and Country, from AD 100 to the Present Day* (London: Eyre and Spottiswoode, 1944), 161–2.

4   A. Bertram, *The House: A Summary of the Art and Science of Domestic Architecture* (London: Adam and Charles Black, 1945 [1935]), 15–16.

5   photoCLEC, 'Photographs, Colonial Legacy and Museums in Contemporary European Culture', http://photoclec.dmu.ac.uk/content/visual-nostalgia (accessed 17 June 2016).

6   S. Boym, *The Future of Nostalgia* (New York: Basic Books, 2001), 41–55.

7   A. Bertram, *Design* (Harmondsworth: Penguin, 1942), 58.

8   T.C. String and M.G. Bull, 'Introduction', in T.C. String and M.G. Bull (eds), *Tudorism: Historical Imagination and the Appropriation of the Sixteenth Century* (Oxford: Oxford University Press, 2011), 12.

9   A. Ballantyne and A. Law, *Tudoresque: In Pursuit of the Ideal Home*

(London: Reaktion, 2011); A. Howkins, 'The discovery of rural England', in R. Colls and P. Dodd (eds), *Englishness: Politics and Culture 1880–1920* (London: Routledge, 1986), 62–88; P. Mandler, *The Fall and Rise of the Stately Home* (New Haven, CT: Yale University Press, 1997); P. Readman, 'The place of the past in English culture c.1890–1914', *Past and Present*, 186.1 (2005), 147–200.

10 P. Wright, *On Living in an Old Country: The National Past in Contemporary Britain* (Oxford: Oxford University Press, 2009 [1985]), 21.

11 R. Samuel, *Theatres of Memory: Past and Present in Contemporary Culture*, vol. 1 (London: Verso, 1994), 22.

12 Howkins, 'Discovery of rural England', 70.

13 Ibid., 70–1.

14 P. Mandler, 'Revisiting the olden time: popular Tudorism in the time of Victoria', in T.C. String and M.G. Bull (eds), *Tudorism: Historical Imagination and the Appropriation of the Sixteenth Century* (Oxford: Oxford University Press, 2011), 21

15 Readman, 'Place of the past', 166–8.

16 P. Brooker and P. Widdowson, 'A literature for England', in R. Colls and P. Dodd (eds), *Englishness: Politics and Culture 1880–1920* (London: Routledge, 1986), 116–17.

17 J. Taylor, *A Dream of England: Landscape, Photography and the Tourist's Imagination* (Manchester: Manchester University Press, 1994), 64–89.

18 D. Sugg Ryan, '"Pageantitis": visualising Frank Lascelles' 1907 Oxford Historical Pageant', *Visual Culture in Britain*, 8.2 (2007), 63–82; D. Sugg Ryan, 'Spectacle, the public and the crowd: pageants and exhibitions in 1908', in M. O'Neill and M. Hatt (eds), *The Edwardian Sense: Art, Design and Spectacle in Britain, 1901–1910* (New Haven, CT: Yale University Press, 2010), 43–71.

19 B. Melman, *The Culture of History: English Uses of the Past, 1800–1953* (Oxford: Oxford University Press, 2006); see especially, 'Buy Tudor: the historical film and history as a mass commodity', 185–213.

20 L. Halliwell, *Halliwell's Filmgoer's Companion* (6th edn) (New York: Hill and Wang, 1977), 107.

21 Readman, 'Place of the past', 164.

22 G. Stamp, 'Neo-Tudor and its enemies', *Architectural History*, 39 (2006), 9.

23 Ibid., 16.

24 Howkins, 'Discovery of rural England', 63; D. Matless, *Landscape and Englishness* (London: Reaktion, 1998).

25 Samuel, *Theatres of Memory*, 22.

26 M. Girouard, *Sweetness and Light: The Queen Anne Movement, 1860–1900* (New Haven, CT: Yale University Press, 1984).

27 S. Muthesius, *The English Terraced House* (New Haven, CT: Yale University Press, 1990), 176.

28 Ballantyne and Law, *Tudoresque*, 73.

29 Howkins, 'Discovery of rural England', 73.

30 Ballantyne and Law, *Tudoresque*, 225.

31 Matless, *Landscape and Englishness*.

32 S. Daniels, *Fields of Vision: Landscape Imagery and National Identity in England and the United States* (London: Polity, 1994), 217–19.

33 See Ballantyne and Law, *Tudoresque*; A.D. King, *The Bungalow: The Production of a Global Culture* (London: Routledge and Kegan Paul, 1984); R.D. Jones, *Interiors of Empire: Objects, Space and Identity Within the Indian Subcontinent c.1800–1947* (Manchester: Manchester University Press, 2007).

34 J. Harris, *Private Lives, Public Spirit: A Social History of Britain 1870–1914* (Oxford: Oxford University Press, 1993), 6. See also P. Oliver, 'The galleon on the front door: imagery of the house and garden', in P. Oliver, I. Davis and I. Bentley, *Dunroamin: The Suburban Semi and Its Enemies* (London: Pimlico, 1994), 155–72.

35 P. Gilroy, *The Black Atlantic, Modernity and Double Consciousness* (London: Verso, 1993), 4.

36 Harris, *Private Lives, Public Spirit*, 3.

37 Ibid., 4.

38 P. Kennedy, *The Rise and Fall of the Great Powers: Economic Change and Military Conflict from 1500–2000* (London: Fontana, 1989), 290; B. Porter, *The Lion's Share: A Short History of British Imperialism, 1850–1983* (London: Longman, 1984).

39 P. Greenhalgh, *Ephemeral Vistas: The Expositions Universelles, Great Exhibitions and World's Fairs 1851–1939* (Manchester: Manchester University Press, 1988), 58–9.

40 M. Grant Cook and F. Fox, *The British Empire Exhibition 1924: Official Guide* (London: Fleetway Press, 1924), 9–10.

41 M. Bell, '"The pestilence that walketh in darkness": imperial health, gender and images of South Africa c.1880–1910', *Transactions of the Institute of British Geographers*, New Series, 18 (1993), 327–41; S. Constantine (ed.), *Emigrants and Empire* (Manchester: Manchester University Press, 1990). For the surplus women debate in the 1920s, see B. Melman, *Women and the Popular Imagination in the Twenties: Flappers and Nymphs* (London: Macmillan, 1988).

42 The most popular destinations were Canada, Australia, New Zealand and South Africa. Although emigration declined, thereafter the government assisted a total of 369,000 people between 1922 and 1929. These figures were balanced, however, by those who returned to Britain. See C. Loch Mowat, *Britain between the Wars, 1918–1940* (London: Methuen, 1955), 226.

43 Bell, "'The pestilence that walketh in darkness'", 339.

44 J.M. MacKenzie, *Propaganda and Empire: The Manipulation of British Public Opinion, 1880–1960* (Manchester: Manchester University Press, 1985).

45 N. Branson and M. Heinemann, *Britain in the Nineteen Thirties* (St Albans: Panther, 1973), 13. See also J.M. Woodham, 'Design and Empire: British design in the 1920s', *Art History*, 3.2 (1980), 232; Loch Mowat, *Britain between the Wars*, 366–72; MacKenzie, *Propaganda and Empire*, 93.

46 Loch Mowat, *Britain between the Wars*, 265–6.

47 Woodham 'Design and Empire'; S. Constantine "'Bringing the Empire alive": the Empire Marketing Board and imperial propaganda, 1926–33', in J.M. MacKenzie (ed.), *Imperialism and Popular Culture* (Manchester: Manchester University Press, 1986), 192–231.

48 R.N. Price, 'Society, status and jingoism: the social roots of lower middle class patriotism, 1870–1900', in J. Crossick (ed.), *The Lower Middle-Class in Britain, 1870–1914* (London: Croom Helm, 1977), 89–112.

49 T. Kuchta, *Semi-Detached Empire: Suburbia and the Colonization of Britain, 1880 to the Present* (Charlottesville, VA: University of Virginia Press, 2010).

50 photoCLEC, 'Photographs, Colonial Legacy and Museums in Contemporary European Culture', http://photoclec.dmu.ac.uk/content/visual-nostalgia (accessed 17 June 2016)

51 J. Gloag and L. Mansfield, *The House We Ought to Live In* (London: Duckworth, 1923), 115.

52 A. McClintock, *Imperial Leather: Race, Gender and Sexuality in the Colonial Contest* (New York and London: Routledge, 1995).

53 I. Davis, 'A celebration of ambiguity: the synthesis of contrasting values', in P. Oliver, I. Davis and I. Bentley, *Dunroamin: The Suburban Semi and Its Enemies* (London: Pimlico, 1994), 96.

54 Stamp, 'Neo-Tudor'.

55 J. Betjeman, *Ghastly Good Taste or a Depressing Story of the Rise and Fall of English Architecture* (London: Anthony Blond, 1970 [1933]), 108.

56 J.R. Gold and M.M. Gold, "'A place of delightful prospects": promotional imagery and the selling of suburbia', in L. Zoon (ed.), *Place Images in*

    Media: Portrayal, Experience and Meaning (Savage, MD: Rowman and Littlefield, 1990), 171.

57 Davis, 'A celebration of ambiguity', 96.

58 O. Lancaster, *Pillar to Post: English Architecture without Tears* (London: John Murray, 2nd edn, 1956 [1938]).

59 Ibid., 68.

60 I. Bentley, 'Arcadia becomes Dunroamin: suburban growth and the roots of opposition', in P. Oliver, I. Davis and I. Bentley, *Dunroamin: The Suburban Semi and Its Enemies* (London: Pimlico, 1994), 66.

61 *Daily Mail Bungalow Book: Reproductions of the Best Designs Entered in the Daily Mail Architects Competition for Labour-Saving Bungalows, 1922* (London: Associated Newspapers, 1922), xxxi.

62 MoDA, BADDA 117, John I. Williams and Sons (Oxted, Surrey), *In Tudor Times* (1923), 3.

63 *Daily Mail Ideal Houses Book: Reproductions of the Best Designs Entered in the Daily Mail Architects Competition, 1927* (London: Associated Newspapers, 1927), 59, xxxviii.

64 MoDA, BADDA 692, *Evening Standard, Guide to House Purchase* [c. 1930s], 20.

65 Lancaster, *Pillar to Post*, 62.

66 Davis, 'Celebration of ambiguity', 79.

67 Ibid., 80.

68 King, *Bungalow*, 185.

69 J. Carey, *The Intellectuals and the Masses: Pride and Prejudice among the Literary Intelligentsia, 1880–1939* (London: Faber and Faber, 1992), 25–6.

70 A.M. Edwards, *The Design of Suburbia: A Critical Study of Environmental History* (London: Pembridge Press, 1981), 130.

71 Ibid.

72 I. Bentley, 'Individualism or community?' in P. Oliver, I. Davis and I. Bentley, *Dunroamin: The Suburban Semi and Its Enemies* (London: Pimlico, 1994), 117.

73 MoDA, BADDA 457, E & L Berg & Co. Ltd, *The New Estates Magazine*, vol. 1. no. 3, n.d.

74 *Daily Mail Ideal Home Exhibition Catalogue 1928* (London: Associated Newspapers, 1928), 5.

75 *Daily Mail*, 18 February 1928, 8.

76 K. Fallan, 'One must offer "something for everyone": designing crockery for consumer consent in 1950s' Norway', *Journal of Design History*, 22.2 (2009), 142.

77 M. Turner, 'Decoration', in MoDA, *Little Palaces: House and Home in the Inter-war Suburbs* (London: Middlesex University Press, 2003), 32.

78 Ibid., 31–2; D. Cohen, *Household Gods: The British and their Possessions* (New Haven, CT: Yale University Press, 2009).

79 G. McCracken, *Culture and Consumption: New Approaches to the Symbolic Character of Consumer Goods and Activities* (Bloomington, IN: Indiana University Press, 1988), 31–43.

80 O. Lancaster, *Homes Sweet Homes* (rev. edn, London: John Murray, 1953 [1939]), 70.

81 Turner, 'Decoration', 33.

82 Anthony Pepe & Co., 'Bromley Road, London', pdf brochure, 1 February 2013, 3.

83 MoDA, BADDA 2003.23, designs for coloured leaded lights.

84 MoDA, BADDA, 2003.70, letter from A.T. Rowley (London) Ltd to M. Freedman, 24 September 1934. Annotated 'no panelling required'.

85 MoDA, BADDA 378, Liberty & Co. Ltd, *Liberty Fabrics for Dresses and Furnishing 1933* (1933), 24.

86 MoDA, BADDA 2003.11, letter from H. Seymour Couchman & Sons to M. Freedman, 27 June 1934.

87 MoDA, BADDA 378, Liberty, *Liberty Fabrics*, 16.

88 J. Attfield, *Bringing Modernity Home: Writings on Popular Design and Material Culture* (Manchester: Manchester University Press, 2007), 5.

89 MoDA, BADDA 453, William Spriggs & Co. Ltd., *Inexpensive Furniture*, n.d., 5.

90 Stamp, 'Neo-Tudor', 14.

91 J. Attfield, *Wild Things: The Material Culture of Everyday Life* (Oxford: Berg, 2000), 110.

92 MoDA, BADDA 509, Frederick Lawrence Ltd, *Inspirations for Modern Homes*, n.d., 18.

93 Geffrye Museum, *Bolsom's Furniture Catalogue, c.* 1935.

94 MoDA, BADDA 452, Story's Kensington, *The Furnishing of a Home*, January 1936, 6–7.

95 M.T. Saler, *The Avant-Garde in Interwar England: Medieval Modernism and the London Underground* (Oxford: Oxford University Press, 1999).

96 H.J. Birnstingl, *Lares et Penates or The Home of the Future* (London: Kegan Paul, 1928), 72.

97 Ibid., 75.

98 Yerbury was later to gloss over his humble suburban background and claim kinship with a grander branch of the Yerbury family.

99 A. Higgott, 'Frank Yerbury and the search for the new', in A. Higgott and

I. Jeffrey, *Frank Yerbury: Itinerant Cameraman* (London: Architectural Association 1987), 7; A. Higgott, 'Introduction', in A. Higgott, *Travels in Modern Architecture, 1925–1930* (London: Architectural Association, 1989), 10.

100 Higgott, 'Frank Yerbury and the search for the new', 7.

101 Ibid., 8.

102 F.R. Yerbury, D.F. Slothouwer and E.R. Jarrett, *Old Domestic Architecture of Holland* (London: Architectural Press, 1924); F.R. Yerbury, *Georgian Details of Domestic Architecture* (London: Ernest Benn 1926).

103 Higgott, *Travels*, 12.

104 Ibid., 14–15.

105 *Daily Mail*, 22 February 1926, 7.

106 *Daily Mail Ideal Home Exhibition Catalogue 1926* (London: Associated Newspapers, 1926), 196.

107 H. Robertson and F.R. Yerbury, 'The Housing Exhibition at Stuttgart', in Higgott, *Travels*, 45. First published in three parts in *The Architect and Building News*, 11, 18 and 25 November 1927.

108 Ibid.

109 J.M. Richards, *The Castles on the Ground* (London: Architectural Press, 1946), 30–1.

110 Ibid., 29–30.

111 Ibid., 32.

112 Wright, *On Living in an Old Country*, 26.

113 Archive of Art and Design, V&A Museum, London (hereafter AAD), AAD3/4–1978, Design and Industries Association Collection of Glass Lantern Slides, 'Housing', not dated.

114 P. Grant, 'From cottages to castles. A walk around Trobridge's Kingsbury' (London: Brent Archives), www.brent.gov.uk/media/387525/From%20 Cottages%20to%20Castles,%202012%20edition.pdf (accessed 21 June 2016); P. Grant, 'Ernest Trowbridge: Kingsbury's extraordinary architect' (London: Brent Archives), http://brent.gov.uk/media/387517/Ernest%20 Trobridge%20-%20Kingsburys%20Extraordinary%20Architect.pdf (accessed 21 June 2016)

115 J.M. Woodham, 'Twentieth century Tudor design in Britain: an ideological battleground', in T.C. String and M.G. Bull (eds), *Tudorism: Historical Imagination and the Appropriation of the Sixteenth Century* (Oxford: Oxford University Press, 2011), 129.

116 Higgott, *Travels*, 43.

117 Ibid.

118 MoDA, BADDA 770, Army and Navy Co-operative Society Ltd, *Catalogue 1931–2*, 1931, 1001.

119 'The quest for Bilston knights', www.blackcountrymemories.org.uk/knights/knights.htm (accessed 12 June 2015).

120 J. Morris, *Heaven's Command: An Imperial Progress* (Harmondsworth: Penguin, 1979 [1973]), 383.

121 G. Orwell, *Coming up for Air* (Harmondsworth: Penguin, 2001), 156–7.

122 C. Reynolds, *Autobiography* (London: The Bodley Head, 1947), 117.

123 *Good Housekeeping*, May 1925, 203.

124 MoDA, BADDA 770, Army and Navy Co-operative Society Ltd, *Catalogue 1931–2*, 204.

125 Ibid., 141.

126 Respondent 023, June 1937, mantelpiece reports, women A-G, Mass Observation archive, University of Sussex.

127 Respondent 063, June 1937, mantelpiece reports, women A-G, Mass Observation archive, University of Sussex.

128 D. Wylie, *Elephant* (London: Reaktion), 62.

129 'Good Buys of the month', *Britannia and Eve*, 12.3 (1936), 8.

130 MoDA, BADDA 4313.1, H. Smith Bros, Huxley Garden Estate promotional leaflet 1932.

131 Gloag, *Englishman's Castle*, 163.

Notes to Chapter 6

1 MOA, DS82, September 1938.

2 Ibid.

3 Ibid.

4 Ibid.

5 Ibid.

6 Ibid.

7 Ibid, emphasis in original.

8 B. Vale, *Prefabs: The Temporary Housing Programme* (London: Taylor and Francis, 1995).

9 J. Burnett, *A Social History of Housing, 1815–1985* (2nd edn, London: Routledge, 1986).

10 P.J. Atkins, 'Communal feeding in war time: British restaurants, 1940–1947', in I. Zweiniger-Bargielowska, R. Duffett and A. Drouard (eds), *Food and War in Twentieth Century Europe* (Farnham: Ashgate, 2011), 139–53.

11 H. Dover, *Home Front Furniture: British Utility Design, 1941–1951* (Aldershot: Scolar, 1991).

12 J.M. Woodham and P. Maguire (eds), *Design and Cultural Politics in*

Postwar Britain: The "Britain Can Make It" Exhibition of 1946 (Leicester: Leicester University Press, 1998).

13 L. Jackson, *Contemporary: Architecture and Interiors of the 1950s* (London: Phaidon, 1998).

14 S. Macdonald and J. Porter, *Putting on the Style: Setting up Home in the 1950s* (London: Geffrye Museum, 1990).

15 M. Bittman, J.M. Rice and J. Wajcman, 'Appliances and their impact: the ownership of domestic technology and time spent on household work', *The British Journal of Sociology*, 55.3 (2004), 401–23.

16 Ibid.

17 Office for National Statistics, House Price Index, February 2015, www.ons.gov.uk/economy/inflationandpriceindices/bulletins/housepriceindex/2015–04–14 (accessed 4 September 2016).

18 Office for National Statistics, Annual Survey of Hours and Earnings, 2015 Provisional Results, www.ons.gov.uk/employmentandlabourmarket/peopleinwork/earningsandworkinghours/bulletins/annualsurveyofhoursandearnings/2015provisionalresults (accessed 4 September 2015).

19 'Castles scorned for beams', *The National Trust*, 106 (Autumn 2005), 4.

20 www.24hourmuseum.org.uk/nwh_gfx_en/ART28930.html (accessed 22 August 2005).

21 G. Stamp, 'Neo-Tudor and its enemies', *Architectural History*, 39 (2006), 31.

22 www.zoopla.co.uk/property/1-burleigh-gardens/london/n14–5ah/15207807 (accessed 22 July 2016).

23 www.zoopla.co.uk/property/23-bromley-road/london/n18–1lf/15277000 (accessed 22 July 2016).

24 Dover, *Home Front Furniture*.

25 J. Freeman, *The Making of the Modern Kitchen: A Cultural History* (Oxford: Berg, 2003), 42–3.

26 S. Willey, '"Housework made Easiwork": Easiwork Limited: the ideal modern kitchen 1919–1939, BA (Hons) History of Art dissertation, Edinburgh University, 1989.

27 http://public.oxford.gov.uk/online-applications/applicationDetails.do?previousCaseType=Property&previousKeyVal=000POKMFLI000&activeTab=summary&previousCaseUprn=100120835376&previousCaseNumber=001HX1MFBU000&keyVal=4900327A_H (accessed 19 August 2016).

28 D. Bradbury, *Mid-Century Modern Complete* (London: Thames and Hudson, 2014); B. Quinn, *Mid-Century Modern: Interiors, Furniture, Design, Details* (London: Conran Octopus Interiors, 2004).

29 S.E. Baker, *Retro Style: Class, Gender and Design in the Home* (London: Bloomsbury, 2013).

30 J. Hollows, 'Feeling like a domestic goddess: postfeminism and cooking', *European Journal of Cultural Studies*, 6.2 (2003), 179–202.

31 https://www.theguardian.com/media/2016/jun/22/unilever-sexist-stereotypes-ads-sunsilk-dove-lynx (accessed 14 March 2017).

32 www.zoopla.co.uk/to-rent/details/36346401#sOxkHLZJiWvv4T20.99 (accessed 22 July 2016).

33 http://public.oxford.gov.uk/online-applications/propertyDetails.do?activeTab=relatedCases&keyVal=000POKMFLI000 (accessed 19 August 2016).

34 www.zoopla.co.uk/property-history/17-rosamund-road/wolvercote/oxford/ox2–8nu/22603414 (accessed 19 August 2016).

35 www.zoopla.co.uk/property/17-rosamund-road/wolvercote/oxford/ox2–8nu/17563936 (accessed 22 July 2016).

36 M. Pawley, *Home Ownership* (London: Architectural Press, 1978).

37 www.theguardian.com/society/2016/aug/02/home-ownership-in-england-at-lowest-level-in-30-years-as-housing-crisis-grows (accessed 4 September 2016).

38 www.theguardian.com/money/2014/feb/26/homeownership-england-lowest-level-25-years (accessed 4 September 2016).

Select bibliography

Primary sources

Archive and manuscript collections

Archive of Art and Design, Victoria and Albert Museum, London
'*Daily Mail* Ideal Home Exhibitions, Angex Ltd Exhibitions and International
    Exhibitions: Catalogues and Photograph Albums', AAD 9–1990
Design and Industries Association Collection of Glass Lantern Slides, 'Housing',
    not dated, AAD3/4–1978
Daily Mail, London
Daily Mail and indexes, cuttings files, photographs

Geffrye Museum, London
Bolsom's Furniture Catalogue, c. 1935

London Metropolitan Archives, London
Earls Court and Olympia Exhibition catalogues, cuttings files and photographs

Media 10 Ltd
Daily Mail Ideal Home Exhibition Catalogues, 1908–; T. Hopewell-Ash 'Daily
    Mail Ideal Home Exhibition at Olympia: A Record of Features Complied by
    T. Hopewell-Ash', *c.* 1982; Ideal Home Exhibition Photograph Albums; Cecil
    Lewis 'Report on the Ideal Home Exhibition', 1957

Mass Observation, University of Sussex
Mass Observation, *Directive to New Observers*, June 1937
Mass Observation, *Mantelpieces,* August 1948, file report, 3030
Mass Observation, *Report on Mantelpieces*, 1937

Museum of Domestic Design and Architecture, Middlesex University
Arding & Hobbs Ltd, *Beautiful Homes*, 1937, BADDA 267
Army and Navy Co-operative Society Ltd, *Catalogue*, 1931–32, BADDA 770
Be Modern at St Margaret's: Brochure for St Margaret's Estate, Edgware, Roger Malcolm Ltd, *c.* 1935, BADDA 315
Candy and Company Ltd, 'Devon fires: Here's to cosy rooms!', *c.* 1935–40, BADDA 332
Catesbys, *Colourful Cork Lino*, 1938, BADDA 181
Catesbys, 'How to modernize your home at little cost', *c.* 1930s, BADDA 188
E&L Berg & Co. Ltd, *The New Estates Magazine*, vol. 1, no. 3., n.d., BADDA 457
Evening Standard Guide to House Purchase, n.d., BADDA 692
Frederick Lawrence Ltd, *Inspirations for Modern Homes*, n.d., BADDA 509
John I. Williams and Sons (Oxted, Surrey), *In Tudor Times*, 1923, MoDA BADDA 117
Liberty & Co. Ltd, *Liberty Fabrics for Dresses and Furnishing 1933*, 1933, MoDA, BADDA 378
Marks and Tillie Freedman, correspondence, 1 Burleigh Gardens, Southgate, 1934, BADDA 2003
New Ideal Homesteads, *c.* 1930s, BADDA 460
Ronald and Miriam Kingham, correspondence, 23 Bromley Road, Edmonton, 1932–36, BADDA 4313
Story's Kensington, *The Furnishing of a Home*, January 1936, BADDA 452
William Spriggs & Co. Ltd, *Inexpensive Furniture*, n.d., BADDA 453

National Art Library, Victoria and Albert Museum, London
Ms English (typewritten), 'British Industrial Art in Relation to the Home, Dorland Hall, 1933'

Printed primary sources

Advice and design manuals and reports
Abercrombie, A. (ed.), *The Book of the Modern House* (London: Hodder and Stoughton, 1937)
Bertram, A., *Design* (Harmondsworth: Penguin, 1942)
Bertram, A., *Design in Daily Life* (London: Methuen, 1937)

Bertram, A., *The House: A Summary of the Art and Science of Domestic Architecture* (London: Adam and Charles Black, 1945 [1935])

Betjeman, J., *Ghastly Good Taste or a Depressing Story of the Rise and Fall of English Architecture* (London: Anthony Blond, 1970 [1933])

Birnstingl, H.J., *Lares et Penates or The Home of the Future* (London: Kegan Paul, 1928)

Black, C., *A New Way of Housekeeping* (London: Collins, 1918)

Boumphrey, G., *Your House and Mine* (London: George Allen and Unwin, 1938)

Clifton Reynolds, N., *Easier Housework by Better Equipment* (London: Country Life, 1929)

Council for Art and Industry, *Design and the Designer in Industry* (London: HMSO, 1937)

Council for Art and Industry, *Education for the Consumer* (London: HMSO, 1935)

Council for Art and Industry, *The Working Class Home: Its Furnishing and Equipment, Report* (London: HMSO, 1937)

Daily Express, *The Housewife's Book* (London: The London Express Newspaper, n.d. [*c.* 1935])

Daily Mail Bungalow Book: Reproductions of the Best Designs Entered in the Daily Mail Architects Competition for Labour-Saving Bungalows, 1922 (London: Associated Newspapers, 1922)

Daily Mail Ideal Houses Book: Reproductions of the Best Designs Entered in the Daily Mail Architects Competition, 1927 (London: Associated Newspapers, 1927)

Daily Mail Ideal Labour-Saving Home (London: Associated Newspapers, 1920)

Daily Mail Ideal (Workers) Homes: Reproductions of the Best Plans Entered in the Daily Mail's £2,000 Architects' Competition, 1919, vols. 1–3 [Northern Industrial Area; Midland Industrial Area; Southern and Midland Counties, Rural Area] (London: Associated Newspapers, 1919)

Frederick, C., *The New Housekeeping: Efficiency Studies in Home Management* (Garden City, NY: Doubleday, Page, *c.* 1913)

Frederick, C., *Scientific Management in the Home: Household Engineering* (Chicago: American School of Home Economics, 1919)

Frederick, C., *Selling Mrs. Consumer* (New York, Business Bourse, 1929)

Fry, R., *Vision and Design* (Harmondsworth: Pelican, 1940 [1920])

Gilman, C.P., *The Home: Its Work and Influence* (New York: McClure Phillips, 1903)

Gloag, J., *Simple Furnishing and Arrangement* (London: Duckworth, 1921)

Gloag, J., *Time Taste and Furniture* (London: Grant Richards, 1925)

Gloag, J. (ed.), *Design in Modern Life* (London: George Allen and Unwin, 1934)

Gloag, J., and Mansfield, L., *The House We Ought to Live In* (London: Duckworth, 1923)

Heath Robinson, W., *Absurdities* (London: Hutchinson, 1934)

Heath Robinson, W., and Browne, K.R.G., *How to Live in a Flat* (London: Hutchinson, 1936)

Heath Robinson, W., and Browne, K.R.G., *How to be a Perfect Husband* (London: Hutchinson, 1937)

Howard, E., *Garden Cities of Tomorrow* (London: Faber and Faber, 1946)

Lake, F. (ed.), *Daily Mail Ideal Home Book, 1952–3* (London: Associated Newspapers, 1952)

Lancaster, O., *A Cartoon History of Architecture* (London: John Murray, 1958)

Lancaster, O., *Homes Sweet Homes* (rev. edn, London: John Murray, 1953 [1939])

Lancaster, O., *Pillar to Post: English Architecture without Tears* (London: John Murray, 1956 [1938])

Leavis, F.R., *Mass Civilization and Minority Culture* (Cambridge: Minority, 1930)

Mass Observation, *An Inquiry into People's Homes* (London: Murray, 1943)

Miles, E. [Hallie Killick],*The Ideal Home and Its Problems* (London: Methuen, 1911)

Mitchinson, N., *The Home and a Changing Civilization* (London: John Lane, The Bodley Head, 1934)

Orwell, G., *The English People* (London: Collins, 1947)

Orwell, G., *The Road to Wigan Pier* (Harmondsworth: Penguin, 1989 [1937])

Peel, C.S. [C.D.E.], *The Labour Saving House* (London: John Lane, The Bodley Head, 1917)

Pember Reeves, M., *Round About a Pound a Week* (London: Virago, 1979 [1913])

Pevsner, N., *An Enquiry into Industrial Art in England* (Cambridge: Cambridge University Press, 1937)

Priestley, J.B., *English Journey* (London: Heinemann, 1984 [1934])

Randall Phillips, R., *The Servantless Home* (London: Country Life, 1920)

Read, R., *Art and Industry: The Principles of Industrial Design* (London: Faber and Faber, 1934)

Rowland Pierce, S., and Duncan, R.A., *The House of the Future*, with a foreword by Arnold Bennett (London: Associated Newspapers, 1928)

Spring Rice, M., *Working-Class Wives: Their Health and Conditions* (London: Virago, 1981 [1939])

Taylor, F.W., *The Principles of Scientific Management* (New York: Harper, 1913)

Women and Housing: Labour Saving in the Home. Report of a Conference of Women's Organisations Held at the Daily Mail Ideal Home Exhibition, Olympia, London, on February 10th, 1920 (Garden Cities and Town Planning Association, 1920)

Yorke, F.R.S., *The Modern Flat* (London: Architectural Press, 1934)
Yorke, F.R.S., *The Modern House* (London: Architectural Press, 1934)
Yorke, F.R.S., *The Modern House in England* (London: Architectural Press, 1937)

Autobiographies, published diaries and letters
Campion, S.R., *Sunlight on the Foothills* (London: Rich and Cowan, 1941)
Chamberlain, M., *Growing Up in Lambeth* (London: Virago, 1989)
Fraser, R., *In Search of a Past: The Manor House, Amnersfield, 1933–45* (London: Verso, 1984)
Heath Robinson, W., *My Line of Life* (London: Blackie, 1938)
Holtby, W., *Women and a Changing Civilization* (London: John Lane, 1934)
Peel, C.S. [C.D.E.], *Life's Enchanted Cup: An Autobiography (1872–1933)* (London: John Lane, The Bodley Head, 1933)
Reynolds, C., *Autobiography* (London: The Bodley Head, 1947)
Richards, J.M., *The Castles on the Ground* (London: Architectural Press, 1946)
Russell, G., *Designer's Trade: Autobiography of Gordon Russell* (London: Allen and Unwin, 1968)
Thompson, F., *Lark Rise to Candleford* (Harmondsworth: Penguin, 1973)
Vaughan, P., *Something in Linoleum: A Thirties Education* (London: Sinclair-Stevenson, 1994)
Weir, M., *Shoes Were for Sunday* (London: Penn, 1973)
Wilmott, P., *Growing Up in a London Village: Family Life Between the Wars* (London: Peter Owen, 1979)

Exhibition catalogues
British Empire Exhibition Guide: Official Guide (London: Fleetway Press, 1924)
Council of Industrial Design, *Britain Can Make It* (London: HMSO, 1946)
Daily Mail, '1 January 2000' [special Ideal Home Exhibition edition], February 1928
Daily Mail Ideal Home Exhibition Catalogue (London: Associated Newspapers, 1920–38)
Design and Industries Association, *An Exhibition of Household Things, Whitechapel Gallery* (London: DIA, 1920)
Design and Industries Association, *Exhibitions Held in Department Stores* (London: DIA, 1935)
Grant Cook, M., in collaboration with Fox, F., *The British Empire Exhibition 1924: Official Guide* (London: Fleetway Press, 1924)

Magazines and newspapers
The Architectural Review
Art and Industry
Britannia and Eve
The Builder
Commerce and Industry
Commercial Art
Daily Mail
Design for Today
The Electrical Age
Good Housekeeping
Home and Country
Home Chat
Illustrated London News
Journal of the Royal Society of Arts
Modern Home
The Times
Woman

Novels
Ashton, H., *Bricks and Mortar* (London: Persephone Books, 2004)
Cooper, L., *The New House* (London: Persephone Books, 2004)
Grossmith, G., and Grossmith, W., *The Diary of a Nobody* (Stroud: Alan Sutton, 1991 [1892])
Mackail, D., *Greenery Street* (London: Persephone Books, 2002)
Orwell, G., *A Clergyman's Daughter* (Harmondsworth: Penguin, 1990 [1935])
Orwell, G., *Coming up for Air* (Harmondsworth: Penguin, 2001 [1939])
Orwell, G., *Keep the Aspidistra Flying* (Harmondsworth: Penguin, 1989 [1936])
Waugh, E., *Decline and Fall* (London: Penguin, Kindle Edition (2012–05–31)
Wells, H.G., *The Shape of Things to Come: The Ultimate Revolution* (London: Everyman, 1993 [1933])

Television and films

Metro-Land, written and presented by Sir John Betjeman; produced by Edward Mirzoeff, BBC Enterprises, 1984

Websites and online materials

Airminded – To-day and To-morrow, http://airminded.org/bibliography/to-day-and-to-morrow/ (accessed 15 June 2016)

Grant, P., 'Ernest Trowbridge: Kingsbury's Extraordinary Architect' (London: Brent Archives), http://brent.gov.uk/media/387517/Ernest%20Trobridge%20 –%20Kingsburys%20Extraordinary%20Architect.pdf (accessed 21 June 2016)

Grant, P., 'From Cottages to Castles. A walk around Trobridge's Kingsbury' (London: Brent Archives), www.brent.gov.uk/media/387525/From%20 Cottages%20to%20Castles,%202012%20edition.pdf (accessed 21 June 2016)

photoCLEC, 'Photographs, Colonial Legacy and Museums in Contemporary European Culture', http://photoclec.dmu.ac.uk/content/visual-nostalgia (accessed 17 June 2016)

Reiss, C., *R.L. Reiss – A Memoir*, http://cashewnut.me.uk/WGCbooks/web-WGC-books-1965–1.php (accessed 27 July 2015)

Spokes Symonds, A., 'The Cutteslowe Walls', www.bbc.co.uk/oxford/content/ articles/2009/03/26/cutteslowe_feature.shtml (accessed 31 July 2013)

Secondary sources

Books and articles

Adburgham, A., *Liberty's: A Biography of a Shop* (London: George Allen and Unwin, 1975)

Ainley, R., *2 Ennerdale Drive: An Unauthorised Biography* (London: Zero Books, 2011)

Alexander, J.K., *The Mantra of Efficiency: From Waterwheel to Social Control* (Baltimore, MD: Johns Hopkins University Press, 2008)

Alexander, S., *Becoming a Woman and Other Essays in 19th and 20th Century Feminist History* (London: Virago, 1994)

Anderson, G., *The White-Blouse Revolution: Female Office Workers Since 1870* (Manchester: Manchester University Press, 1988)

Andrews, M., *The Acceptable Face of Feminism: The Women's Institute as a Social Movement* (London: Lawrence and Wishart, 1997)

Anscombe, I., *A Woman's Touch: Women in Design from 1860 to the Present Day* (Harmondsworth: Penguin, 1985)

Arber, K., *Thirtiestyle: Home Decoration and Furnishings from the 1930s* (London: Middlesex University Press, 2015)

Atkinson, H., *The Festival of Britain: A Land and Its People* (London: I.B. Tauris, 2012)

Attfield, J., *Bringing Modernity Home: Writings on Popular Design and Material Culture* (Manchester: Manchester University Press, 2007)

Attfield, J., *Wild Things: The Material Culture of Everyday Life* (Oxford: Berg, 2000)

Attfield, J., and Kirkham, P. (eds), *A View from the Interior: Feminism, Women and Design History* (London: Women's Press, 1989)

Ballantyne, A., and Law, A., *Tudoresque: In Pursuit of the Ideal Home* (London: Reaktion, 2011)

Barrett, H., and Phillips, J., *Suburban Style: The British Home, 1840–1960* (London: Little Brown, 1993)

Battersby, M., *The Decorative Thirties* (London: Studio Vista, 1976)

Bayliss, D., 'Revisiting the cottage council estates: England, 1919–39', *Planning Perspectives*, 16 (2001), 169–200

Beauman, N., *A Very Great Profession: The Woman's Novel 1914–39* (London: Virago, 1983)

Beddoe, D., *Back to Home and Duty: Women Between the Wars, 1918–1939* (London: Pandora, 1989)

Beevers, R., *The Garden City Utopia: A Critical Biography of Ebenezer Howard* (London: Macmillan, 1988)

Benton, C. (ed.), *Documents: A Collection of Source Material on the Modern Movement* (Milton Keynes: Open University, 1975)

Benton, C., Benton, T., and Wood, G. (eds), *Art Deco 1910–1939* (London: V&A Publications, 2003)

Benton, T., Benton, C., and Scharf, A., *Design 1920s* (Milton Keynes: Open University, 1975)

Berman, M., *All That is Solid Melts into Air: The Experience of Modernity* (London: Verso, 1983)

Bourdieu, P., *Distinction: A Social Critique of the Judgement of Taste* (London: Routledge and Kegan Paul, 1984)

Bowden, S., and Offer, A., 'The technological revolution that never was: gender, class, and the diffusion of household appliances in interwar England', in V. de Grazia and E. Furlough (eds), *The Sex of Things: Gender and Consumption in Historical Perspective* (London: University of California Press, 1996), 244–74

Boym, S., *The Future of Nostalgia* (New York: Basic Books, 2001)

Branson, N., *Britain in the Nineteen Twenties* (London: Weidenfeld and Nicolson, 1975)

Branson, N., and Heinemann, M., *Britain in the Nineteen Thirties* (St Albans: Panther, 1973)

Braybon, G., and Summerfield, P., *Out of the Cage: Women's Experiences in Two World Wars* (London: Pandora, 1987)

Bruegemann, R., *Sprawl: A Compact History* (Chicago: University of Chicago Press, 2006)

Burnett, J., *A History of the Cost of Living* (Harmondsworth: Penguin, 1969)

Burnett, J., *A Social History of Housing, 1815–1985* (2nd edn, London: Routledge, 1986)

Burnett, J., *Useful Toil: Autobiographies of Working People from the 1820s to the 1920s* (London: Allen Lane, 1974)

Busch, A., *Geography of Home: Writings on Where We Live* (New York: Princeton Architectural Press, 1999)

Cantacuzino, S., *Wells Coates: A Monograph* (London: Gordon Fraser, 1978)

Cardiff, D., and Scannel, P., *The Social History of Broadcasting*, vol. 1 (Oxford, Basil Blackwell, 1991)

Carey, J., *The Intellectuals and the Masses: Pride and Prejudice among the Literary Intelligentsia, 1880–1939* (London: Faber and Faber, 1992)

Carrington, N., *Industrial Design in Britain* (London: Allen and Unwin, 1976)

Chapman, D., *The Home and Social Status* (London: Routledge and Kegan Paul, 1955)

Cieraad, I., '"Out of my kitchen!" Architecture, gender and domestic efficiency', *The Journal of Architecture*, 7.3 (2002), 263–79

Clendenning, A., *Demons of Domesticity: Women and the English Gas Industry, 1889–1939* (Aldershot: Ashgate, 2004)

Cohen, D., *Household Gods: The British and their Possessions* (New Haven, CT: Yale University Press, 2009)

Colls, R., and Dodd, P. (eds), *Englishness: Politics and Culture, 1880–1920* (London: Croom Helm, 1986)

Constantine, S., '"Bringing the Empire Alive": The Empire Marketing Board and imperial propaganda, 1926–33', in J.M. MacKenzie (ed.), *Imperialism and Popular Culture* (Manchester: Manchester University Press, 1986), 192–231

Constantine, S. (ed.), *Emigrants and Empire* (Manchester: Manchester University Press, 1990)

Craig, P., 'The house that Jerry built: building societies, the state and the politics of owner-occupation', *Housing Studies*, 1 (1986), 87–108

Crossick, J. (ed.), *The Lower Middle-Class in Britain, 1870–1914* (London: Croom Helm, 1977)

Csikszentmihalyi, M., and Rochberg-Halton, E., *The Meaning of Things: Domestic Symbols and the Self* (Cambridge: Cambridge University Press, 1981)

Daniels, S., *Fields of Vision: Landscape Imagery and National Identity in England and the United States* (London: Polity, 1994)

Darling, E., 'Finella, Mansfield Forbes, Raymond McGrath, and modernist architecture in Britain', *Journal of British Studies*, 50.1 (2011), 125–55

Darling, E., *Re-forming Britain: Narratives of Modernity before Reconstruction* (London: Routledge, 2007)

Davidoff, L., L'Esperence, J., and Newby, H., 'Landscape with figures: home and community in English society', in J. Mitchell and A. Oakley (eds), *The Rights and Wrongs of Women* (Harmondsworth: Penguin, 1976), 139–75

Davidoff, L., and Hall, C., *Family Fortunes: Men and Women of the English Middle Class, 1780–1850* (London: Routledge, 1992)

Davidoff, L., and Westover, B. (eds), *Our Lives, Our Words: Women's History and Women's Work* (London: Macmillan, 1986)

Davidson, C., *A Woman's Work is Never Done: A History of Housework in the British Isles, 1650–1950* (London: Chatto and Windus, 1982)

De Stasio, C., 'Arnold Bennett and the late Victorian "woman"', *Victorian Periodicals Review*, 28.1 (1995), 40–53

Dean, D., *The Thirties: Recalling the English Architectural Scene* (London: Trefoil Books, 1983)

Delap, L., *Knowing their Place, Domestic Service in Twentieth Century Britain* (Oxford: Oxford University Press, 2011)

Douglas, M., and Isherwood, B., *The World of Goods: Towards an Anthropology of Consumption* (London: Allen Lane, 1979)

Dover, H., *Home Front Furniture: British Utility Design, 1941–1951* (Aldershot: Scolar, 1991)

Edwards, A.M., *The Design of Suburbia: A Critical Study of Environmental History* (London: Pembridge Press, 1981)

Edwards, C., 'The context and conservation of patent metamorphic furniture 1780–1920', in *The Object in Context: Crossing National Boundaries* (Munich: International Institute for Conservation of Historic and Artistic Works, 2006), 275–89, https://dspace.lboro.ac.uk/dspace-jspui/handle/2134/9472 (accessed 7 September 2017)

Edwards, C., '*Multum in parvo*: "a place for everything and everything in its place". modernism, space-saving bedroom furniture and the Compactom wardrobe', *Journal of Design History*, 27.1 (2014), 17–37

Edwards, C., *Turning Houses into Homes: A History of the Retailing and Consumption of Domestic Furnishings* (Aldershot: Ashgate, 2005)

Edwards, C., *Twentieth Century Furniture* (Manchester: Manchester University Press, 1994)

Ehrenreich, B., and English, D., *For Her Own Good: 150 Years of Experts' Advice to Women* (London: Pluto Press, 1979)

Elliott, B., 'Art Deco worlds in a tomb: reanimating Egypt in modern(ist) visual culture', *South Central Review*, 25.1 (2008), 114–35

Elliott, B., 'Modern, moderne, modernistic: Le Corbusier, Thomas Wallis and the problem of Art Deco', in P.L. Caughie (ed.), *Disciplining Modernism* (Basingstoke: Palgrave Macmillan, 2009), 128–46

Fallan, K., 'One must offer "something for everyone": designing crockery for consumer consent in 1950s' Norway', *Journal of Design History*, 22.2 (2009), 133–49

Faulkner, W., and Arnold, E. (eds), *Smothered by Invention: Technology in Women's Lives* (London: Pluto Press, 1985)

Felski, R., *The Gender of Modernity* (Cambridge, MA: Harvard University Press, 1995)

Ferguson, M., *Forever Feminine: Women's Magazines and the Cult of Femininity* (London: Heinemann, 1983)

Forster, M., *My Life in Houses* (London: Chatto and Windus, 2014)

Forty, A., *Objects of Desire: Design and Society 1750–1980* (London: Thames and Hudson, 1986)

Fraser, W.H., *The Coming of the Mass Market, 1850–1914* (London: Macmillan, 1981)

Freeman, J., *The Making of the Modern Kitchen: A Cultural History* (Oxford: Berg, 2004)

Gale, A., 'Form becomes functional', *Art & Antiques* (26 March 2003), 120–5

Gardner, J., *Britain's Forgotten Decade. The Thirties: An Intimate History* (London: Harper, 2010)

Gardner, J., *Houses of the Art Deco Years* (Felixstowe: Braiswick, 2004)

Geffrye Museum, *Utility Furniture and Fashion 1941–1951* (London: ILEA, 1974)

Giedion, S., *Mechanisation Takes Command: A Contribution to Anonymous History* (New York: W.W. Norton, 1969 [1948])

Gilbert, D., 'The Edwardian Olympics: suburban modernity and the White City games', in M. O'Neill and M. Hatt (eds), *The Edwardian Sense: Art, Design and Performance in Britain, 1901–1910* (New Haven, CT: Yale University Press for The Yale Center for British Art and The Paul Mellon Centre for Studies in British Art, 2010), 73–97

Gilbert, D., and Preston, R., '"Stop being so English": suburban modernity and national identity in the twentieth century', in D. Gilbert, D. Matless and B. Short (eds), *Geographies of British Modernity* (Oxford: Blackwell, 2003), 187–203

Giles, J., *The Parlour and the Suburb: Domestic Identities, Class, Femininity and Modernity* (Oxford: Berg, 2004)

Giles, J., *Women, Identity and Private Life in Britain, 1900–50* (Basingstoke: Macmillan, 1995)

Giles, J., and Middleton, T., *Writing Englishness: An Introductory Sourcebook* (London: Routledge, 1995)

Gilroy, P., *The Black Atlantic: Modernity and Double Consciousness* (London: Verso, 1993)

Girouard, M., *Sweetness and Light: The Queen Anne Movement, 1860–1900* (New Haven, CT: Yale University Press, 1984)

Gittins, D., *Fair Sex: Family Size and Structure in England, 1900–1939* (London: Hutchinson, 1982)

Gloag, J., *The Englishman's Castle: A History of Houses, Large and Small, in Town and Country, from AD 100 to the Present* Day (London: Eyre and Spottiswoode, 1944)

Gloversmith, F. (ed.), *Class, Culture and Social Change: A New View of the 1930s* (Brighton: Harvester, 1980)

Glucksmann, M., *Women Assemble: Women Workers and the New Industries in Inter-War Britain* (London: Routledge, 1990)

Gold, J.R., and Gold, M.M., '"Outrage" and righteous indignation: ideology and the imagery of suburbia', in F.W. Boal and D.N. Livingstone (eds), *The Behaviourial Environment: Essays in Reflection, Application and Criticism* (London: Croom Helm, 1988), 163–81

Gold, J.R., and Gold, M.M., '"A place of delightful prospects": promotional Imagery and the selling of suburbia', in L. Zonn (ed.), *Place Images in Media: Portrayal, Experience and Meaning* (Savage, MD: Rowman and Littlefield, 1990), 159–82

Gould, J., 'Gazetteer of modern houses in the United Kingdom and the Republic of Ireland', *The Modern House Revisited – Twentieth Century Architecture 2, The Journal of the Twentieth Century Society*, 2 (1996), 112–26

Graves, R., and Hodge, A., *The Long Weekend: A Social History of Great Britain, 1918–1939* (London: Cardinal, 1991)

Greenhalgh, P., 'The English compromise: modern design and national consciousness, 1879–1940', in W. Kaplan (ed.), *Designing Modernity: The Arts of Reform and Persuasion 1885–1945* (London: Thames and Hudson, 1995), 111–42

Greenhalgh, P., *Ephemeral Vistas: The Expositions Universelles, Great Exhibitions and World's Fairs 1851–1939* (Manchester: Manchester University Press, 1988)

Greenhalgh, P. (ed.), *Modernism in Design* (London: Reaktion, 1990)

Guffey, E.E., *Retro: The Culture of Revival* (London: Reaktion, 2006)

Guillery, P. (ed.), *Built from Below: British Architecture and the Vernacular* (London: Routledge, 2011)

Hackney, F., '"Use your hands for happiness": home craft and make-do-and-mend in British women's magazines in the 1920s and 1930s', *Journal of Design History*, 19.1 (2006), 23–38

Hamilton, N. (ed.), *Design and Industry: The Effects of Industrialisation and Technological Change on Design* (London: Design Council, 1980)

Hamilton, N. (ed.), *From Spitfire to Microchip: Studies in the History of Design from 1945* (London: Design Council, 1985)

Hannah, L., *Electricity before Nationalization: A Study of the Development of the Electricity Supply Industry in Britain to 1948* (London: Macmillan, 1979)

Hardy, D., *Utopian England: Community Experiments 1900–1945* (London: Routledge, 2000)

Hardy, D., and Ward, C., *Arcadia for All: the Legacy of a Makeshift Landscape* (London: Five Leaves Publications, 2003)

Hardyment, C., *From Mangle to Microwave: The Mechanisation of Household Work* (Cambridge: Polity, 1988)

Harris, J., *Private Lives, Public Spirit: A Social History of Britain 1870–1914* (Oxford: Oxford University Press, 1993)

Hayden, D., *The Grand Domestic Revolution: A History of Feminist Designs for American Homes, Neighborhoods, and Cities* (Cambridge, MA: MIT Press, 1981)

Heathcote, E., *The Meaning of Home* (London: Frances Lincoln, 2012)

Hebdige, D., *Hiding in the Light: On Images and Things* (London: Routledge, 1988)

Heffernan, M., and Gruffudd, P. (eds), *A Land fit for Heroes: Essays in the Geography of Inter-War Britain* (Loughborough: Loughborough University Department of Geography Occasional Paper no. 14, 1988)

Heskett, J., *Industrial Design* (London: Thames and Hudson, 1984)

Higgott, A., and Jeffrey, I., *Frank Yerbury: Itinerant Cameraman* (London: Architectural Association, 1987)

Higgott, A., *Travels in Modern Architecture, 1925–1930* (London: Architectural Association, 1989)

Highmore, B., *The Great Indoors: At Home in the Modern British House* (London: Profile Books, 2014)

Hillier, B., and Escritt, S., *Art Deco Style* (London: Phaidon, 2003)

Hiller, N.R., *The Hoosier Cabinet in Kitchen History* (Bloomington, IN: Indiana University Press, 2009)

Hobsbawm, E., and Ranger, T. (eds), *The Invention of Tradition* (Cambridge: Cambridge University Press, 1984)

Hoggart, R., *The Uses of Literacy: Aspects of Working-Class Life, With Special Reference to Publications and Entertainments* (London: Chatto and Windus, 1957)

Holder, J., '"Design in everyday things": promoting modernism in Britain, 1912–1944', in P. Greenhalgh (ed.), *Modernism in Design* (London: Reaktion, 1990), 123–43

Hollow, M., 'Suburban ideals on England's interwar council estates', *Journal of the Garden History Society*, 39.2 (2011), 203–17

Hollows, J., *Domestic Cultures* (Maidenhead: Open University Press, 2008)

Hollows, J., 'Science and spells: cooking, lifestyle and domestic femininities in British *Good Housekeeping* in the inter-war period', in S. Bell and J. Hollows (eds), *Historicizing Lifestyle* (Aldershot: Ashgate), 21–40

Hooper, G., 'English Modern: John Gloag and the challenge of design', *Journal of Design History*, 28.4 (2015), 368–84, doi:10.1093/jdh/epvo18

Horwood, C., *Keeping Up Appearances: Fashion and Class Between the Wars* (Stroud: Sutton Publishing, 2005)

Hoskins, J., *Biographical Objects: How Things Tell the Stories of People's Lives* (London: Routledge, 1998)

Humble, N., *The Feminine Middlebrow Novel, 1920s to 1950s: Class, Domesticity and Bohemianism* (Oxford: Oxford University Press, 2001)

Hurdley, R., *Home, Materiality, Memory and Belonging: Keeping Culture* (Basingstoke: Palgrave Macmillan, 2013)

Huyssen, A., *After the Great Divide: Modernism, Mass Culture and Postmodernism* (Basingstoke: Macmillan, 1988)

Huyssen, A., 'Mass culture as woman: Modernism's other', in T. Modleski (ed.), *Studies in Entertainment: Critical Approaches to Mass Culture* (Bloomington, IN: Indiana University Press, 1986), 44–62

Jackson, A.A., *The Middle Classes, 1900–1945* (Nairn: David St John Thomas, 1991)

Jackson, A.A., *Semi-Detached London: Suburban Development, Life and Transport, 1900–39* (Didcot: Wild Swan, 1991)

Jensen, F., *The English Semi-Detached House: How and Why the Semi Became Britain's Most Popular House-Type* (Huntingdon: Ovolo, 2007)

Jensen, F., *Modernist Semis and Terraces in England* (Aldershot: Ashgate, 2012)

Jeremiah, D., *Architecture and Design for the Family in Britain, 1900–1970* (Manchester: Manchester University Press, 2000)

Johnson, A., *Understanding the Edwardian and Inter-War House* (London: Crowood Press, 2006)

Johnson, P., *The Freedoms of Suburbia* (London: Frances Lincoln, 2009)

Kelly, J., *Women, History and Theory* (Chicago: University of Chicago Press, 1984)

King, A.D., *The Bungalow: The Production of a Global Culture* (London: Routledge and Kegan Paul, 1984)

Kirkham, P. (ed.), *The Gendered Object* (Manchester: Manchester University Press, 1996)

Kuchta, T., *Semi-Detached Empire: Suburbia and the Colonization of Britain, 1880 to the Present* (Charlottesville, VA: University of Virginia Press, 2010)

Lanchester, J., *Making Time: Lillian Moller Gilbreth – A Life Beyond "Cheaper by the Dozen"* (Boston, MA: Northeastern University Press, 2004)

Langan, M., and Schwarz, B. (eds), *Crises in the British State, 1880–1930* (London: Hutchinson, 1985)

Langdon, R. (ed.), *Design and Society* (London: Design Council, 1984)

Langhamer, C., 'The meanings of home in postwar Britain', *Journal of Contemporary History*, 40.2 (2005), 341–62

Latour, B., *Reassembling the Social: An Introduction to Actor-Network-Theory* (Oxford: Oxford University Press, 2005)

Law, M., *The Experience of Suburban Modernity: How Private Transport Changed Interwar London* (Manchester: Manchester University Press, 2014)

Lees-Maffei, G., 'Studying advice: historiography, methodology, commentary, bibliography', *The Journal of Design History*, 16.1 (2003), 1–14

Le Mahieu, D.L., *A Culture for Democracy: Mass Communication and the Cultivated Mind in Britain Between the Wars* (Oxford: Clarendon Press, 1988)

Lewis, J., *Women in England, 1870–1950: Sexual Divisions and Social Change* (Brighton: Wheatsheaf, 1984)

Lewis, J. (ed.), *Labour and Love: Women's Experience of Home and Family, 1850–1940* (Oxford: Basil Blackwell, 1986)

Lewis, P., *Everyman's Castle: The Story of our Cottages, Country Houses, Terraces, Flats, Semis and Bungalows* (London: Frances Lincoln, 2014)

Light, A., *Forever England: Femininity, Literature and Conservatism Between the Wars* (London: Routledge, 1991)

Light, A., *Mrs Woolf and the Servants: The Hidden Heart of Domestic Service* (Harmondsworth: Penguin, 2007)

Loch Mowat, C., *Britain Between the Wars, 1918–1940* (London: Methuen, 1955)

Logan, T., *The Victorian Parlour: A Cultural Study* (Cambridge: Cambridge University Press, 2001)

Long, H.C., *The Edwardian House: The Middle-Class Home in Britain 1880–1914* (Manchester: Manchester University Press, 1993)

Lowe, G.S., *Women in the Administrative Revolution: The Feminisation of Clerical Work* (Cambridge: Polity, 1987)

McCracken, G., *Culture and Consumption: New Approaches to the Symbolic Character of Consumer Goods and Activities* (Bloomington, IN: Indiana University Press, 1988)

McCrindle, J., and Rowbotham, S. (eds), *Dutiful Daughters: Women Talk About Their Lives* (Harmondsworth: Penguin, 1979)

MacFarlane, B., 'Homes fit for heroines: housing in the twenties', in Matrix (ed.),

Making Space: Women and the Man-Made Environment (London: Pluto Press, 1984), 26–36

MacKenzie, D., and Wajaman, J., *The Social Shaping of Technology* (London: Open University, 1985)

MacKenzie, J.M., *Propaganda and Empire: The Manipulation of British Public Opinion, 1880–1960* (Manchester: Manchester University Press, 1985)

MacKenzie, J.M. (ed.), *Imperialism and Popular Culture* (Manchester: Manchester University Press, 1986)

MacCarthy, F., *A History of British Design 1830–1970* (London: George Allen and Unwin, 1979)

Malos, E. (ed.), *The Politics of Housework* (London: Allison and Busby, 1980)

Mandler, P., *The Fall and Rise of the Stately Home* (New Haven, CT: Yale University Press, 1997)

Matless, D., 'Ages of English design: preservation, modernism and tales of their history, 1926–1939', *Journal of Design History*, 3.4 (1990), 203–12

Matless, D., *Landscape and Englishness* (London: Reaktion, 1998)

McCarthy, F., *A History of British Design 1830–1970* (London: George Allen and Unwin, 1979)

McCracken, G., *Culture and Consumption* (Bloomington, IN: Indiana University Press, 1990)

Melman, B., *The Culture of History: English Uses of the Past, 1800–1953* (Oxford: Oxford University Press, 2006)

Melman, B., *Women and the Popular Imagination in the Twenties: Flappers and Nymphs* (London: Macmillan, 1988)

Merrett, S., *State Housing in Britain* (London: Routledge and Kegan Paul, 1979)

MoDA, *Little Palaces: House and Home in the Inter-war Suburbs* (London: Middlesex University Press, 2003)

Miller, D., *The Comfort of Things* (London: Polity, 2009)

Miller, D., *Material Culture and Mass Consumption* (Oxford: Basil Blackwell, 1987)

Miller, D., 'Modernism and suburbia as material ideology', in D. Miller and C. Tilley (eds), *Ideology, Power and Prehistory* (Cambridge: Cambridge University Press, 1984), 37–49

Miller, D. (ed.), *Home Possessions: Material Culture Behind Closed Doors* (Oxford: Berg, 2001)

Miller, R., 'The Hoover in the garden: middle class women and suburbanization', *Environment and Planning D, Society and Space*, 1.1 (1983), 73–87

Montgomery, J., *The Twenties* (London: George Allen and Unwin, 1970 [1957])

Morris, J., *Heaven's Command: An Imperial Progress* (Harmondsworth: Penguin, 1979 [1973])

Muthesius, S., *The English Terraced House* (New Haven, CT: Yale University Press, 1990)

Myerson, J., *Home: The Story of Everyone Who Ever Lived in Our House* (London: Harper Perennial, 2005)

Nava, M., and O'Shea, A. (eds), *Modern Times: Reflections on a Century of English Modernity* (London: Routledge, 1995)

Navemore, J., and Brantlinger, P., *Modernity and Mass Culture* (Bloomington, IN: Indiana University Press, 1991)

Newton, J., Ryan, M., and Walkowitz, J. (eds), *Sex and Class in Women's History* (London: Routledge and Kegan Paul, 1983)

Oakley, A., *Housewife* (Harmondsworth: Penguin, 1976)

Oakley, A., *The Sociology of Housework* (Bath: Martin Robertson, 1974)

Oldfield, S. (ed.), *The Working-Day World: Women's Lives and Culture(s) in Britain, 1914–1945* (London: Taylor and Francis, 1994)

Oliver, P., Davis, I., and Bentley, I., *Dunroamin: The Suburban Semi and Its Enemies* (London: Pimlico, 1994 [1981])

Pawley, M., *Home Ownership* (London: Architectural Press, 1978)

Peel, C.S. [C.D.E.], *A Hundred Wonderful Years: Social and Domestic Life of a Century, 1820–1920* (London: John Lane, The Bodley Head, 1926)

Porter, G., 'Putting your house in order: representations of women and domestic life', in R. Lumley (ed.), *The Museum Time-Machine: Putting Culture on Display* (London: Routledge, 1988), 102–7.

Pounds, N.J.G., *Hearth and Home: A History of Material Culture* (Bloomington, IN: Indiana University Press, 1989)

Penner, B., *Bathroom* (London: Reaktion, 2014)

Powers, A., *Britain* (London: Reaktion, 2007)

Powers, A., *Modern: The Modern Movement in Britain* (London and New York: Merrell, 2005)

Powers, A., 'Was there a George VI style?', *Apollo*, 160.10 (2004), 72–7

Pugh, M., *'We Danced All Night': A Social History of Britain Between the Wars* (London: The Bodley Head, 2008)

Pumphrey, M., 'The flapper, the housewife and the making of modernity', *Cultural Studies*, 1.1 (1987), 179–94

Putnam, T., and Newton, C. (eds), *Household Choices* (London: Futures, 1990)

Quennell, M., and Quennell, C.H.B., *A History of Everyday Things in England* (London: Batsford, 1959)

Rappaport, E.D., *Shopping for Pleasure: Women in the Making of London's West End* (Princeton, NJ: Princeton University Press, 2000)

Ravetz, A., 'Housework and domestic technologies', in Maureen McNeil (ed.), *Gender and Expertise* (London: Free Association, 1987), 198–208

Ravetz, A., with Rurkington, R., *The Place of Home: English Domestic Environments, 1914–2000* (London: Taylor and Francis, 2011 [1995])

Readman, P., 'The place of the past in English culture c.1890–1914', *Past and Present* 186.1 (2005), 147–200

Reed, C., *Bloomsbury Rooms: Modernism, Subculture, and Domesticity* (New Haven, CT: Yale University Press, 2004)

Reyner Banham, P., *Theory and Design in the First Machine Age* (London: Architectural Press, 1960)

Rice, B., and Evans, T., *The English Sunrise* (London: Matthews Miller Dunbar, 1977)

Richards, J.M., *A Miniature History of the English House* (London: Architectural Press, 1938)

Richards, J.M., *An Introduction to Modern Architecture* (Harmondsworth: Penguin, 1940)

Rijk, T. de, 'Pioneers and barbarians: the design and marketing of electrical household goods as Dutch Americana, 1930–45', *Journal of Design History*, 22.2 (2009), 115–32, doi: 10.1093/jdh/epp012

Riley, D., *Am I That Name? Feminism and the Category of 'Women' in History* (London; Macmillan, 1988)

Rivers, T., Cruickshank, D., Darley, G., and Pawley, M., *The Name of the Room: A History of the British House and Home* (London: BBC Books, 1992)

Roberts, E., *A Woman's Place: An Oral History of Working Class Women, 1890–1940* (Oxford: Basil Blackwell, 1984)

Roberts, J., 'The gardens of Dunroamin: history and cultural values with specific reference to the gardens of the inter-war semi', *International Journal of Heritage Studies*, 1.4 (1996), 229–37

Roberts, M., *Living in a Man-Made World: Gender Assumptions in Modern Housing Design* (London: Routledge, 1991)

Roberts, R., *The Classic Slum: Salford Life in the First Quarter of the Century* (Harmondsworth: Penguin, 1979)

Rock, I.A., *The 1930s House Manual: Care and Repair for All Popular House Types* (Yeovil: Haynes Publishing, 2005)

Rothschild, J., *Machina Ex Dea: Feminist Perspectives on Technology* (Oxford: Pergamon, 1983)

Rutherford, J.W., *Selling Mrs Consumer, Christine Frederick and the Rise of Household Efficiency* (Athens, GA: University of Georgia Press, 2003)

Ryan, D.S., '"All the world and her husband": the Daily Mail Ideal Home Exhibition, 1908–39', in M. Andrews and M.M. Talbot (eds), *All the World and Her Husband: Women in Twentieth-Century Consumer Culture* (London: Cassell, 2000), 10–22

Ryan, D.S., *The Ideal Home through the 20th Century* (London: Hazar, 1997)

Saler, M.T., *The Avant-Garde in Interwar England: Medieval Modernism and the London Underground* (Oxford: Oxford University Press, 1999)

Rybczynski, W., *Home: A Short History of an Idea* (London: Heinemann, 1988)

Samuel, R., 'Middle class between the wars: part one', *New Socialist*, January/February 1983

Samuel, R., 'The middle class between the wars: part two', *New Socialist*, March/April 1983

Samuel, R., 'North and south: a year in a mining village', *London Review of Books*, 17.12 (22 June 1995), 3–6

Samuel, R., 'The suburbs under siege: the middle-class between the wars: part III', *New Socialist*, May/June 1983

Samuel, R., *Theatres of Memory: Past and Present in Contemporary Culture, vol. 1* (London: Verso, 1994)

Schwarz, B., 'Englishness and the paradox of modernity', *New Formations*, 1.1 (1987), 147–55

Schwartz Cowan, R., *More Work for Mother: The Ironies of Household Technology From the Open Hearth to the Microwave* (London: Free Association, 1989)

Scott, P., 'Did owner-occupation lead to smaller families for interwar working-class households', *Economic History Review*, 61.1 (2008), 99–124

Scott, P., *The Making of the Modern British Home: The Suburban Semi and Family Life Between the Wars* (Oxford: Oxford University Press, 2013)

Scott, P., 'Mr Drage, Mr Everyman, and the creation of a mass market for domestic furniture in interwar Britain', *Economic History Review*, 62.4 (2009), 802–27

Scott, P., 'Selling owner-occupation to the working-classes in 1930s Britain', discussion paper, University of Reading Business School, 2004

Scott, P., 'The twilight world of interwar British hire purchase', *Past and Present*, 177.1 (2002), 195–225

Scott, P., 'Visible and invisible walls: suburbanization and the social filtering of working-class communities in interwar Britain', discussion paper, University of Reading Business School, 2004

Sharp, D., *The Rationalists: Theory and Design in the Modern Movement* (London: Architectural Press, 1978)

Sharp, T., *English Panorama* (London: Dent, 1936)

Sharp, T., *Town and Countryside* (Oxford: Oxford University Press, 1932)

Silverstone, R. (ed.), *Visions of Suburbia* (London: Routledge, 1995)

Simpson, D., 'Beautiful Tudor', *History of Taste*, no. 3, *Architectural Review*, clxii.695 (July 1977), 29–36

Smiles, S. (ed.), *Going Modern and Being British: Art, Architecture and Design in Devon, c.1910–60* (Exeter: Intellect Books, 1998)

Sparke, P., *As Long as it's Pink: The Sexual Politics of Taste* (London: Pandora, 1995)

Sparke, P., *Consultant Design: The History and Practice of the Designer in Industry* (London: Pembridge Press, 1983)

Sparke, P., *An Introduction to Design and Culture in the Twentieth Century* (London: Routledge, 1989)

Sparke, P. (ed.), *Did Britain Make It? British Design in Context, 1946–86* (London: Design Council, 1986)

Spender, H., *Worktown: Photographs of Bolton and Blackpool, Taken for Mass Observation 1937/38* (Brighton: Gardner Centre Gallery, 1977)

Speight, G., 'Who bought the inter-war semi? The socio-economic characteristics of new-house buyers in the 1930s', *University of Oxford Discussion Papers in Economic and Social History*, 38 (December 2000)

Stamp, G., 'Neo-Tudor and its enemies', *Architectural History*, 39 (2006), 1–33

Steedman, C., *Landscape for a Good Woman: A Story of Two Lives* (London: Virago, 1986)

Stevenson, G., *The 1930s Home* (Oxford: Shire Publications, 2009)

Stevenson, J., *British Society, 1914–45* (Harmondsworth: Penguin, 1984)

Stevenson, J., and Cook, C., *The Slump: Society and Politics during the Depression* (London: Jonathan Cape, 1977)

Stewart, R., *Design and British Industry* (London: John Murray, 1987)

Stott, M., *Women Talking: An Anthology from the Guardian Women's Page, 1922–35, 1957–71* (London: Virago, 1987)

Sugg, D., 'Dream home', *Design Review*, May 1993, 32–9

Sugg, D., 'The Edwardian house: the middle class home in Britain 1880–1914', *Journal of Design History*, 7.2 (1994), 141–4

Sugg, D., 'Redefining modernism: "ideal homes" at London's Design Museum', *Journal of Museum Education*, 18.3 (1993), 11–14

Sugg Ryan, D., 'Living in a "half-baked pageant": the Tudorbethan semi and suburban modernity in Britain, 1918–39', *Home Cultures*, 8.3 (2011), 217–44

Sugg Ryan, D., '"Pageantitis": visualising Frank Lascelles' 1907 Oxford Historical Pageant', *Visual Culture in Britain*, 8.2 (2007), 63–82

Sugg Ryan, D., 'Reynolds, Nancie Clifton [*real name* Agnes Margaret Warden Hardie; *married name* Reynolds] (1903–1931), domestic advice writer and broadcaster', *Oxford Dictionary of National Biography* (Oxford: Oxford University Press, Sept 2015), www.oxforddnb.com/view/article/105938 (accessed 4 September 2016)

Sugg Ryan, D., 'Spectacle, the public and the crowd: pageants and exhibitions in 1908', in M. O'Neill and M. Hatt (eds), *The Edwardian Sense: Art, Design and Spectacle in Britain, 1901–1910* (New Haven, CT: Yale University Press, 2010), 43–71

Sullivan, M., and Blanch, S., 'Introduction: the middlebrow – within or without modernism', *Modernist Cultures*, 6.1 (2011), 1–17

Swenarton, M., *Building the New Jerusalem: Architecture, Housing and Politics 1900–1930* (Watford: IHS BRE Press, 2008)

Swenarton, M., *Homes Fit for Heroes: The Politics and Architecture of Early State Housing in Britain* (London: Heinemann Educational Books, 1981)

Swenarton, M., 'Tudor Walters and Tudorbethan: reassessing Britain's inter-war suburbs', *Planning Perspectives*, 17.3 (2002), 267–86

Swenarton, M., and Taylor, S., 'The scale and nature of the growth of owner-occupation in Britain between the wars', *Economic History Review*, 38.3 (1985), 373–92

Taylor, J., *A Dream of England: Landscape, Photography and the Tourist's Imagination* (Manchester: Manchester University Press, 1994)

Taylor, N., *The Village in the City* (London: Temple Smith, 1973)

Thackara, J., *Design after Modernism: Beyond the Object* (London: Thames and Hudson, 1988)

Thirties: British Art and Design Before the War (London: Arts Council, 1979)

Thompson, F.M.L., *The Rise of Suburbia* (Leicester: Leicester University Press, 1981)

Thompson, P., *The Edwardians: The Remaking of British Society* (London: Routledge, 1992 [1975])

Thorns, D.C., *Suburbia* (London: MacGibbon and Kee, 1972)

Tillyard, S.K., *The Impact of Modernism, 1900–1920: Early Modernism and the Arts and Crafts Movement in Edwardian England* (London: Routledge, 1988)

Tilson, B., 'Plan furniture 1932–1938: the German connection', *Journal of Design History*, 3.2–3 (1990), 145–55

Todd, S., 'Domestic service and class relations in Britain 1900–1950', *Past and Present*, 203 (2009), 181–204

Todd, S., *The People: The Rise and Fall of the Working Class, 1910–2010* (London: Hodder and Stoughton Kindle Edition, 2014–04–10)

Veblen, T., *The Theory of the Leisure Class* (London: George Allen and Unwin, 1970 [1912])

Vickery, A., 'Shaking the separate spheres', *Times Literary Supplement* (12 March 1993), 6–7

Walker, J.A., *Design History and the History of Design* (London: Pluto Press, 1989)

Walkerdine, V., *Schoolgirl Fictions* (London: Verso, 1990)

Ward, C., *Cotters and Squatters: Housing's Hidden History* (London: Five Leaves Publications, 2002)

Ward, M., and Ward, N., *Home in the Twenties and Thirties* (London: Ian Allan, 1978)

Weightman, G., and Humphries, S., *The Making of Modern London* (London: Sedgwick and Jackson, 1984)

Weiner, M.J., *English Culture and the Decline of the Industrial Spirit, 1850–1980* (Harmondsworth: Penguin, 1985)

Werkerle, G.R., Peterson, R., and Morley, D. (eds), *New Space for Women* (Boulder, CO: Westview, 1980)

White, C., *Women's Magazines, 1693–1968* (London: Michael Joseph, 1970)

White, J., *The Worst Street in North London: Campbell, Bunk, Islington, Between the Wars* (London: Routledge and Kegan Paul, 1986)

Whitehand, J.W.R., and Carr, C.M.H., 'England's interwar suburban landscapes: myth and reality', *Journal of Historical Geography*, 25.4 (1999), 483–501

Wilk, C., *Modernism: Designing A New World, 1914–1939* (London: V&A Publications, 2006)

Williams, R., *The Country and the City* (London: Chatto and Windus, 1972)

Williams, R., *The Long Revolution* (Harmondsworth: Penguin, 1961)

Williams, R., *The Politics of Modernism* (London: Verso, 1989)

Wilson, E., *The Sphinx in the City: Urban Life, the Control of Disorder, and Women* (London: Virago, 1991)

Wilson, K., *Livable Modernism: Interior Decorating and Design During the Great Depression* (New Haven CT: Yale University Press in association with Yale University Art Gallery, 2004)

Wolff, J., 'The invisible flâneuse: women and the literature of modernity', *Theory, Culture and Society*, 2.3 (1985), 37–48

Woodham, J.M., 'Design and Empire: British design in the 1920s', *Art History*, 3.2 (1980), 229–40

Woodham, J.M., *The Industrial Designer and the Public* (London: Pembridge Press, 1983)

Woodham, J.M., 'Managing British design reform I: fresh perspectives on the early years of the Council of Industrial Design', *Journal of Design History*, 9.1 (1996), 55–8

Woodham, J.M., 'Twentieth-century Tudor design in Britain: an ideological battleground', in T.C. String and M.G. Bull (eds), *Tudorism: Historical Imagination and the Appropriation of the Sixteenth Century* (Oxford: Oxford University Press, 2011), 129–53

Woodham, J.M., and Maguire, P. (eds), *Design and Cultural Politics in Postwar*

Britain: The "Britain Can Make It" Exhibition of 1946 (Leicester: Leicester University Press, 1998)

Worden, S., 'A voice for whose choice? Advice for consumers in the late 1930s', in *Design History: Fad or Function?* (London: Design Council, 1978), 41–8

Wright, L., *Home Fires Burning: The History of Domestic Heating and Cooking* (London: Routledge and Kegan Paul, 1964)

Wright, P., *On Living in an Old Country: The National Past in Contemporary Britain* (Oxford: Oxford University Press, 2009 [1985])

Wylie, D., *Elephant* (London: Reaktion, 2008)

Yarwood, D., *Five Hundred Years of Technology in the Home* (London: Batsford, 1983)

Yerbury, F.R., *Georgian Details of Domestic Architecture* (London: Ernest Benn, 1926)

Yerbury, F.R., Slothouwer, D.F., and Jarrett, E.R., *Old Domestic Architecture of Holland* (London: Architectural Press, 1924)

Yorke, T., *Art Deco House Styles* (Newbury: Countryside Books, 2011)

Yorke, T., *The 1930s House Explained* (Newbury: Countryside Books, 2006)

Young, K., and Garside, P., *Metropolitan London: Politics and Urban Change, 1937–1981* (London: Edward Arnold, 1982)

Young, M., and Wilmott, P., *Family and Kinship in East London* (Harmondsworth: Penguin, 1962)

Zmroczek, C., 'The weekly wash', in S. Oldfield (ed.), *The Working-Day World: Women's Lives and Culture(s) in Britain 1914–1945* (London: Taylor and Francis, 1994), 6–17

Unpublished works

Attfield, J., 'The role of design in the relationship between furniture manufacture and its retailing 1939–1965 with initial reference to the furniture firm of J. Clarke', PhD dissertation, University of Brighton, 1992

Darling, E.A., 'Elizabeth Denby, housing consultant: social reform and cultural politics in the inter-war period', PhD dissertation, University College London, 1999

Hackney, F., '"They opened up a whole new world": feminine modernity, the feminine imagination and women's magazines, 1919–1939', PhD dissertation, Goldsmith's College, University of London, 2010

Hogan, K., 'A woman's place; from conception to consumption: design and ideology in the all-electric kitchen in Britain, 1880–1938', MA dissertation, V&A/ Royal College of Art, 1987

North, D.L., 'Middle-class suburban lifestyles and culture in England, 1919–1939', PhD dissertation, University of Oxford, 1988

Preston, R., 'Our chief hobby: the design and culture of English suburban gardens, 1920–1940', MA dissertation, V&A/Royal College of Art, 1994

Ryan, D.S., 'The Daily Mail Ideal Home Exhibition and suburban modernity, 1908–51', PhD dissertation, University of East London, 1995

Speight, G., 'Building society behaviour and the mortgage lending market in the interwar period: risk-taking by mutual institutions and the interwar house-building boom', DPhil dissertation, University of Oxford, 2000

Taylor, C., 'The Regency period library metamorphic chair', MA dissertation, University of Central Lancashire, 2009

Welbourne, J., 'Design theory and exhibition practice in Britain, 1924–38: the articulation and representation of modernist design theory between the Empire Exhibitions', PhD dissertation, University of Essex, 1986

Whitworth, L., 'Men, women, shops and "little shiny homes": the consuming of Coventry, 1930–1939', PhD dissertation, University of Warwick, 1997

Willey, S., '"Housework made Easiwork": Easiwork Limited: the ideal modern kitchen 1919–1939, BA (Hons) History of Art dissertation, Edinburgh University, 1989

Worden, S.A., 'Furniture for the living room: an investigation into the interaction between society, industry and design in Britain from 1919 to 1939', PhD dissertation, Brighton Polytechnic, 1980

Index

Page numbers in *italic* refer to figures.
Note: publications, illustrations, artworks and buildings can be found under authors', artists' and designers' names.